Transatlantic Translations: *Dialogues in Latin American Literature*

Transatlantic Translations
Dialogues in Latin American Literature

Julio Ortega

Translated by Philip Derbyshire

REAKTION BOOKS

Published by Reaktion Books Ltd
33 Great Sutton Street
London EC1V ODX, UK

www.reaktionbooks.co.uk

First published 2006

Printed and bound in Great Britain
by CPI/Bath Press, Bath

British Library Cataloguing in Publication Data
Ortega, Julio, 1942–
    Transatlantic translations : dialogues in Latin American literature
    1. Latin American literature - History and criticism
    I. Title
    860.9'98

    ISBN-13: 978 186189 287 4
    ISBN-10: 1 86189 287 X

Contents

Introduction:

The Subject of Abundance

Although 'New World' was a metaphor that implied a pristine newness, the geography that opened up to the discoverers' gaze and to their exploration and exploitation had not been sought out as a blank space in which to begin again, but was rather a continuation of the search for what was already well-known: spices, precious metals, labour. The reconstruction of the genealogy of this 'invention of America' has long occupied Latin American historians and intellectuals. It is as if the history of the Spanish Conquest were fantastic and outrageous and as if the search for El Dorado, the Fountain of Youth, the Amazons and the Lost City demonstrated the epic excess of Spain's imperial destiny, whose self-definition as a Catholic monarchy was formed through the expulsion of Islam and the Jews and culminated in the monologue of the Counter-Reformation. Bartolomé de las Casas sought to demonstrate that the colonial enterprise was directed against a people of Christian origin, citing Church authorities to prove this, and constructing an alternative history that showed how the Indians were neophytes, favoured children of God and sheep waiting to be brought into the fold.[1] An equally imaginative proposal was that the aboriginal peoples were descendants of one of the lost tribes of Israel mentioned in the first books of the Bible. Their wandering was a sort of pilgrimage. *En route* they had lost their religion and their language and had fallen back into idolatry, but providence had chosen them to return to the Truth. The construction of such genealogies were just part of the greater debate involved in the attempts to organize and manage the colonies. Power always had to be legitimated in Christian terms. Slowly but surely it also had to become imperial. Most of the time, however, power took the form of exploitation, tribute, forced trade and systematic violence.[2]

What the Indians demonstrated, perhaps, was that Spain, especially in the middle of the seventeenth century was neither a Christian empire, nor a modern state. The authority of the Church and the Inquisition, religious intolerance, concern with purity of blood and the hierarchy of Spanish were all evident in the Iberian peninsula. They were equally prevalent in Europe in general, in large part no less authoritarian, and similarly plagued by hunger and poverty. In the Indies, the regime became even more rigid by means of exclusion, censorship and the imposition of the *encomienda*. There were also the violent attempts to eliminate idolatry and the practice of a remorseless colonization, which took an extended period to establish itself, only achieving its full extent in the eighteenth century, and which constantly renewed its cycles of exploitation. Ironically, however, given the enormous diversity of languages and nations, the varied economic geographies and different natural histories, these overseas regions gradually acquired the paradoxical character of an advanced modernity. Nature there was understood to be in a process of development, and despite their colonial status, the Indies were seen as nature's most fertile terrain, where the fruits of Spain flourished even better than on the peninsula itself. Father Acosta attributed this to the diversity of favourable climates. Garcilaso Inca de la Vega thought that the Indies was the superior realization of Spain.

The Caribbean was the best example of this excess of variety. This was due to its rapid repopulation, the experiments in production carried out there and the long contention over this laboratory of the modern by the European powers. As Antonio Benítez Rojo has observed, the Caribbean 'meta-archipelago' becomes the setting for Chaos, and the islands repeat this history in a decentred way.[3] Europe experimented with the first forms of the modern in this Caribbean setting, but their reiteration was a consequence of colonialism, a disruptive system, lacking in continuity, where exploitation was intensified. Colonialism divided the already divided and accelerated the extension of the cheaper mode of production. From then on the colonial experience would be one of disarticulation, hence the drama of the colonial subject and the dispute of its reconsolidation. The nomadism of work would mark a rootless *economos* of precarious production and transient settlements.

The purpose of this book is not to reconstruct the lineage of the American marvellous, and even less to dispute it. Today this is a rather insubstantial intellectual project, which says more about the writer who wants to tell America's wonders one more time than it does about the much over-read object. Nor is it to produce a history of native and postcolonial resistance, a project inherited from the spirit of the sixties in which ethnology privileged autarchic visions, which had their basis in the ethnic consciousness. This sort of enlightened culturalist militancy conceived the native as heroic or especially endowed with wisdom, and presented him or her as a victimized 'minority' in need of compensation. It would be more interesting to examine how the new was perceived in terms of the already conceived, the different constituted by what was already known, and the unnamed seen through what had been already read. That is, to examine the cultural history of representations which, in our reading, are formalized around forms of categorization and validation, which produce a semantic field of rich textuality. For that reason, we will begin with the construction of representations, but with the intention of identifying the subject that maintains them, produces and retransmits them and acts as their interlocutor or antagonist. By examining a series of texts, histories and 'cases', privileged by their density of information, we will try to understand the formation of these changing and diverse subjects, produced in history and language. But they are also produced out of the political need to respond to the process of colonization, by means of narrative strategies, negotiations, appropriations and trans-codifications, demands and debates which form a new 'geotextuality', a cultural practice of *hybridation* and *mestizaje*. It is here that we find the radical principle of the new: intermixing.

In previous works we have followed the traces of the representation of America through the historical chronicle, where, at the very beginnings of Spanish exploration and conquest of the continent, it finds its elaboration in three different paradigms. The first we have called the discourse of abundance or plenty, which offers a hyperbolic vision of American nature. The second is the discourse of scarcity, which offers a contrary, critical vision of poverty and disillusionment. And lastly there is the utopian discourse, which offers alternative futures and the hope of an end to violence. These paradigms are not merely the archival forms of a hermeneutic predetermined by an interest in persuasion, assertion or judgement, which is based on a primary repertoire of norms (juridical, medical or religious). Rather they are discursive flows or processes, staging narratives of the open experience of the new. As such they are generative fabulations that at times constitute simple commonplace truths, and yet at other times bear a radical, innovative force.

Thus, abundance begins with the chronicle of the marvellous that turns a world that is never 'empty' into discourse, reference and narrative. This New World begins to have a 'natural history' even before objects have unique names. Taino and Spanish nomenclatures are superimposed in the same chronicle, followed immediately by translations and equivalents from English and French. Abundance is also an excess of language, and the value of the object is multiplied in these transatlantic translations, in the movement that is itself part of a fertile exchange, yielding a profit on goods and returns in the shape of welfare. The emblematic miscellany that this language prefers is therefore another mark of its historicity. The repertoire of 'natural history' is a historical form of geographical exploration. Exploration and exploitation are symmetrical with naming and representation, and this symmetry is measured as factual as well as symbolic profit.[4]

In the discursive formation that comprehends the colonization of the New World, which includes other genres in addition to history and the chronicle, we can see the gestation, alternation and contestation of these three modes of representation. They are discursive, but they are also iconic, narrative and even testimonial. They comprise books of travel and at the same time the history of everyday *mentalités*. These modes of representation are reformulated over and over again and will come to define the cultural history of America. They bear a peculiar tension. They begin from the rhetorical formulations of the garden and desert in the traditions that include the *locus amenus* and regions of hell. These belong to popular millenarian culture with its *topoi* of fertility and plague, banquet and famine. They are woven into the historical debate and articulate an attempt to discern the present even as different powers struggle to impose the authority of their own version. The functions of this discursive formation are those of recording and classification. They give an account of the order of perception and produce the system of representation. In this activity, at once cognitive and interpretative, discourse constructs the place of the other, the meaning of the others, the destiny of an otherness that it invariably reads, reorders and assimilates. It is a cultural transaction that naturalizes what are particular processes of cognition and formal reasoning. Naming and comparison, the basic mechanisms of recording, are developed as the power of representation. Description is already interpretation, as in the grand descriptions that Inca Garcilaso de la Vega gives of a marvellous Cuzco, as if it were 'another Rome'. Representation becomes incorporation, as happens when Gonzalo Fernández de Oviedo bases his catalogue of fruits on the physical processes of tasting and eating. It is this valorization of experience, taste and touch, of naming and testimonial, of body and communication that makes the paradigms of abundance and scarcity into the discourse of a subject, the speech of a community, and the system of a culture.[5]

However, even inside this powerful rhetorical apparatus of translation, characteristic of a hegemonic culture in expansion, the specificity and difference of American objects and subjects would slowly displace and then subvert the ordering networks that were assigned for their naming and figuration. The great drama of naming, description and representation, the unleashing of figurative production, began with the object itself, which exceeded the field of the gaze. Then language displayed its uneasiness with the task of accounting for the different, and comparison began its long digressive attempts to approach the object. Then there was the crisis of nominal logic in the face of objects, which were revealed as processual, fluid and proliferating. The translating subject, who turned to metaphor and oxymoron, and then fell back into hyperbole and allegory, acted out the drama of contradiction between name and thing. After all, the rationality of such a rhetorical apparatus was made up from various tensions and ambivalences within early modernity, which included the margins where the new realities of the Indies would give rise to their own versions, translations and appropriations. Even if hegemonic ideology brought together Cross and Sword, native rationality knew that in order to pass from defeat and colonization to resistance and negotiation it was necessary to distinguish between the two. As Guamán Poma de Ayala's protest makes clear, it was necessary to reappropriate the promise of the Cross, as well as the memory that writing reproduced.

When Columbus in his 'Letter to the King' (from his third voyage) appealed to the authority of religious discourse in order to assert that

Paradise was in fact to be found in the Indies, he had already transformed the topos of the *locus amenus* into the new American topos of
abundance. Paradise is a land that has all the trees that yield fruit and
timber. It never gets too hot or cold, and enjoys eternal spring.
Columbus fulfilled the promise of Isidore of Seville's emblematic paradise but with a decisive shift. The topos ceased to be non-utilitarian.
Abundance was marvellous and new, but above all it was useful. This
usefulness, extolled by the dominant code of trade, was nevertheless
based on a justifying religious code. Nobody could come to Paradise,
Columbus assures us, 'save by Divine Will'. In order to represent the
object, mercantile perception was supported by (universal) ideology.
For Las Casas, 'the great gentleness, comfort and health of the land'
meant that death was almost a stranger to the natives. For the colonial
enterprise from Columbus onwards, however, these same natives would
acquire a use value, which would make them foreigners in their own
land. In his 'remedies' Las Casas demanded that the Indians be allowed
to live on their lands so that these latter could be 'converted into the best
and richest land in the world'. 'Shall we not know what the fruits of our
master's lands taste of?' Inca Garcilaso has two Indians ask each other,
with ironic naivety, whilst they carry the melons that they themselves
have cultivated on land which is no longer theirs, and where they are
forbidden to know the taste of the new. This double ignorance (of
knowledge and taste) is punished by the power of the letter, although
the Inca will wisely suture the wounds with his own writing. Thus the
new American culture begins as a (discursive) humanization of violence. Gómara is astonished at an island which 'has pearls bigger than a
man's eye, taken from oysters the size of hats'; Sor Juana Inés de la Cruz
says that she was born 'in abundant America', and is therefore 'a coun-
trywoman to gold / a fellow citizen of metals', which, she implies, means
that the land is outstanding in its maternal nature ('where the common
sustenance / is found for almost no effort / nowhere else / so displays the
motherland'). But already using a metaphor of scarcity, she finishes her
response by reassigning responsibility to her political mother: 'Europe
. . . / since it has so insatiably / from her abundant veins / bled minerals'.[6]

Abundance for some might well mean scarcity for others. Inca
Garcilaso de la Vega himself developed the discourse of abundance
(which had become a commonplace in the chroniclers' representation
of the Indies) and turned it into a true cultural paradigm of the combinations, amalgams and new creations that were produced by American
difference. Nevertheless, he also refers to the opposing paradigm, that of

scarcity. He writes, contrasting both representations, 'And though the land is so rich and abundant in gold, silver and precious stones, yet as everyone knows, the native inhabitants thereof are the poorest and most deprived people in the world'.7 From Columbus to Guamán Poma, from the earliest *relaciones* to the chronicles of Mexico and Chile, abundance and scarcity mutually interpolate each other, contrasting with each other, as two ways of seeing and interpreting, of translating and evaluating. For Inca Garcilaso it is clear that loss of meaning, that horizon of lack where native reality is dissolved, must be confronted by its reconstruction. This takes place within the horizon in which America gives the possibility of creating a superior realization of Spain. This is not merely by some providentialism, but because in the difference of the one from the other (homogenizing unity against heterogenizing plurality) writing opens the margins of an American subject – produced by restitution, American in origin, Spanish by right, and *mestizo* in its future. He goes on to say, that in order that his people's memories of their homeland 'are not lost altogether, I set down to the immense work that has been mine so far and which remains for me to do, that of writing about the ancient republic until it is complete' (viii, 7). Writing as preservation presupposes the passage from visions of the vanquished to versions of resistance and mixture. These latter are built on a memory, which has been saved by means of writing. This is a task that would occupy Garcilaso all his life, and which would give it a greater meaning: translating America, in European and modern terms, reading a republic that had been realized. Writing here is the flow of desire, that immense task that he has to 'complete', to finish. It is the story of the past, and thus equivalent to history itself, which it thus replaces. The language that reconstructs historical memory is the force that survives history. Referring to excessiveness is not a vain trope: the work of writing 'is excessive for me' and 'remains for me to do' says Inca Garcilaso. This abundance of the letter is a 'has been', the memory of the subject of writing, and a 'yet to be', the promise of the identity of the subject in the act of writing. The subject of writing is the offspring of the republic of abundance.

So, if the conquistadors 'threw that great majesty to the ground . . . bringing it down with such speed that I could only preserve from it these few relics that I have spoken', this means that the present is an abyss. Between abundance and scarcity the present shrinks: 'in whose time the Spaniards came and smashed and brought down everything that was here until today' (7). It makes sense then to suggest abundance

as example and exemplar, and scarcity as warning. Garcilaso elaborates
a political argument on the cultural future of the New World with great
subtlety and with the persuasive force of his Italian models of composition, and does it with the melancholy voice of the memory 'of all that
has been lost'. Cervantes read the Neoplatonic treatise that Garcilaso had
translated. Had he gone on to read the *Royal Commentaries*, as well he
might, he could not have failed to be interested in the notable paradox
of an account that turns a supposedly barbarous world into a political
model of Neoplatonic philosophy. (The opening of *Persiles* suggests
something like this.) He might have found that tension ironic, another
eloquent moment of disillusionment. The fissure between the rhetoric
of Christian providentialism and the rapid reduction in the native population, between the codes of the heroic, chivalric or courtly subject and
the dusty, hungry reality of the seventeenth century Spaniard is already
inherent in the discourse of a modernity composed of fissures, dispari-
ties and exclusions. If the density of the real turned out to be unscathed
and irrecoverable, if discourse could offset all evidence to the contrary,
then the melancholic gaze came to recognize the violence of the real as
fatal and the intolerance of domination as inherent to power.[8] The most
modern writing, for the same reason, is the most plural, inclusive, paradoxical and tolerant. As were, of course, the writings of Inca Garcilaso
de la Vega and Miguel de Cervantes.

Garcilaso's work received a quite different reception. Some considered it little more than an interesting fiction, whilst others held it to be
nothing short of subversive. The colonial authorities banned it during
the great rebellion of Tupac Amaru II. The liberating armies of the South
wanted to have it printed as patriotic propaganda for their campaign in
1820. The Great Chronicler of the Indies, Antonio de Solís, in his *History
of the Conquest of Mexico* (1684), during a discussion of generally recognized histories of America, counsels that 'the history of Peru is contained in the two volumes that Inca Garcilaso wrote, so sharp in their
news and so smooth and pleasurable in their style (following the elegance of the times) that we should blame as ambitious anyone who tried
to improve on him, but we would praise whosoever knew how to imitate him and so follow in his footsteps'.[9] From the perspective of
Baroque historiography, Solís found Garcilaso's Italianate style slightly
anachronistic, in its smooth, rather sweet, even novelesque and deliberately pleasing periods. At the same time Solís criticized Bernal del
Castillo's True *History of the Conquest of New Spain* (1632) for

passing itself off as a true history, with the help of a slovenliness and lack of decoration in his style which thus gave it the appearance of truth and so seemed to demonstrate the sincerity of the writer. Even though he was present and saw what he was writing about, it is known that his own work does not display a vision devoid of passion, so that his pen was well-governed; he showed himself to be as satisfied with his wit as he was petulant and complaining about his fortune.[10]

These two models are clearly contrasted at the level of style, one elaborate, the other rough, both equally full of the events they recount. Although Garcilaso's could be improved with regard to the events it reported, the soldier's might also be improved on from the point of view of dispassionate truth. Solís marks the end of the fascination with adventures, exploits, natural wonders and cultural differences. Even the eulogies that Bernal Díaz dedicated to the Indian painters seem to Solís more emphasis than truth, since the Indian painters 'had little time to linger to acquire details or the exquisite elements of imitation' (II. ii. 72).

The central paradigm had come to dominate colonial representations, and on one side were imposed the virtues of the hero-conquistador Hernán Cortés and on the other the cognate truths of imitation. However, history does not remain literary, that is an evocative reconstruction of the imperial epoch, fuelled by the sumptuous and episodic wealth of the legendary trans-Atlantic adventure. With Solís America becomes part of the museum of Spanish history, that is, it no longer troubles or questions the intellectual setting of the latter part of the seventeenth century. Garcilaso is more modern than Solís, more American but at the same time more European.[11]

The discourse of restitution and possibility appears in Inca Garcilaso's intelligent submissions as a call to dialogue. The letter calls out for reading, the subject calls to *mestizos*. American difference calls for a potential plurality. The Inca Tawantinsuyu is an Arcadia (a nostalgia for a communal past) that functions as a Utopia (a political project of a chivalric patriarchy), but also as something more inclusive. The Neoplatonic rationality of humanism is projected on to the harmonious and tolerant state model of the Inca polity. In a lesson proper to the analogical antitheses of Baroque unfolding, Garcilaso erects out of the scattered ruins of the Inca polity a purely discursive American community that is at the same time historical and mythic, Neoplatonic and native. That polity has certainly been reduced to a condition of lack and scarcity, but its Arcadian abundance recovers it for a future communality.[12]

According to St Ambrose, abundance is the mother of lechery, and he condemns it as a form of excess. One of his readers, Fray Luis de Granada, lists the goods of the natural world to show that sensory knowledge of the world is another demonstration of God's providence. The Creator, who showers his love on men, is for Luis de Granada a God of abundance. In the chapter entitled 'Of the Fertility of Plants and the Fruits of the Earth' in his *Introducción del Símbolo de la Fe* (1583) he mentions two American plants, *lignum vitae* and the *mejoacán* (although the various names refer to the same plant) whose medicinal properties he celebrates. In these aggregations that Divine Providence multiplies, the historian of divinity turns abundance into a natural paradigm of conservation: God has foreseen a 'plenteous . . . remedy' so as to conserve the species of plants, but much more 'plentiful' is what He provided to 'repair and hallow the species of men'.[13] It seems quite likely that Inca Garcilaso, who had read Fray Luis de Granada, was responding to these arguments. His argument would begin with the American experience of scarcity, pass through heteroclite abundance (exemplified in the paradigm of the graft) and finally open out on to cultural possibility (carried forward through writing, in its turn rich in difference and remedial power). If Fray Luis can read the universal harmony of the divine order within American nature, Garcilaso finds that the same nature is abundant thanks to intermixing. We can therefore read in it the development of the new, the open and the incomplete, which becomes a political paradigm, reordering the possible aggregations and combinations of the future.

Another figure who read Luis de Granada was the Dominican Gregorio García (1575–1625), who wrote a somewhat difficult if fascinating and erudite treatise, the *Origin of the Indians of the New World* (1607), in order to prove that Peru had once been the biblical land of Ophir.[14] His detailed biblical and patristic erudition, as well as his tenacious attempts to show how American languages derived from other languages – European, Oriental and Semitic – run parallel to Antonio de León Pinelo's monumental *The Paradise of the New World: An Apologetic Commentary, Natural History and Pilgrimage through the Western Indies, Islands and Mainland of the Ocean Sea* (1650). This almost unreadable text, also inspired by a hyperbolic philology, had been written to prove that Paradise had been situated in the Andean Region, close to a particular *mestizo* village. These rich translations of Christianity's most important discursive nuclei (the biblical origin of American Man, the history of his Fall and American redemption) constituted a long and erudite attempt to give the Indian a legitimate place in the map of the chosen peoples. However, their proposals also confirmed colonial hierarchies, since they sought to erase differences in the name of a universal manifestation of divine truth. In this case America was legitimated through the use of founding mythologies such as Paradise or Ophir. These savants were not moved by an incipient national or Creole consciousness, however, as some have ingenuously and mistakenly claimed. Rather they were engaged in a dispute over the place of discourse (a precarious one in the American social compact) which in order to acquire authority or symbolic power had to follow the road all the way back to its beginning and superimpose Chachapoyas on Eden. Father José de Acosta, with his authoritative logic – even if this was no less conjectural that that of his victims in debate – had repeated many times that the Indians could not have biblical origins, or, even less probably, could their language have derived from Hebrew, since they had no knowledge of writing, and therefore could not be children of the Book. According to Marcel Bataillon, it was Acosta who decided the fate of the Andalusian heretic Francisco de la Cruz, who had preached that the Indians were the original biblical tribe whilst the Spaniards were the thirteenth lost tribe of Israel. Acosta testified at the Inquisition's tribunal and demonstrated that the Indians could not derive from Sacred Scripture because they ignored writing. The poor heretic paid for this demonstration with his life.[15] Gregorio García took up the task of refuting Acosta, citing as evidence the fact that various Hebrew terms were indeed to be found in Quechua or in the Mexican languages. Mexico's own name is in fact Hebrew, he argued, deriving from *Mesi*, meaning 'authorities'. In Mexico, *Mesi* designated captain or chief. These associations, linked to the myth of a primordial language, led García to use the experience of the New World in the construction of a hierarchy of truth. Acosta had disqualified those arguments as 'lightweight conjectures', but

> whoever reads them, as I have, will find that they have some gravity and weight. Furthermore, those who wish to find out and discern within this Opinion the Origin of the Indians, will realize that there have to be proper and obviously true principles that will in this manner generate true knowledge, not that they are probable, or that they have the appearance of truth, or they are

> judged to be true, even though they are not . . . a doctrine that
> no one can deny [122–3].

He had warned in his Introduction that the opinions he records are many and various and often contradictory, depending on the authors, but he records and sums them all up, and adds his own, so that the reader could encounter 'one that squares with his own understanding'. This argumentation is revealing: it takes the logic of demonstrative examples, that is, the rhetorical practice of Doctrine, which presupposes that truth has a discursive route.[16] Fray Gregorio García belonged to the Order of Preachers and must have been tempted by the demon of grandiloquence, since one of the sonnets devoted to him brands him 'Profound Geographer' and concludes: 'To America you gave them different roads / For which (like the Indus and its shores) / Your greedy breast ransacks Heaven'. This hyperbole gives a good idea of these scholarly chroniclers' intentions: they take themselves to be the mediators between the road of imperial truth and the various truths to be found on the many routes through America. In a moment of acuity, freed from having to justify his knowledge, the philologist is overtaken by the interpreter with his own experience of America, which allows him to compare and contrast. He warns us that harsh and uncultivated life incites war: abundance, on the other hand 'creates Peace' (279). The opposite of Solís, García americanizes European history with an emblem of wisdom and tolerance. In his treatise, the New World is an example for the Old.

And this is probably the response of the chroniclers and Americanist scholars who sought to dispute notions that were dominant in Spain. Acosta conceived of the Indies as a site for Christian mission: a state of idolatry that evangelization must convert to Christianity. His powerful vision had a detailed rigour. The native world was provisional and transitory: a superior truth now made its truths relative, supplemented and superseded it.[17] Abundance here was not the extravagance of the other, a manifestation of difference, but was seen as something innately discordant, almost monstrous. In the first place, Acosta says, the diversity of plants that are found in the New World is greater than in Spain, but 'in roots and edible plants from under the earth it seems to me that there is greater abundance there'. Turnips, for example, 'are found there in such abundance that they have spread everywhere, so that they tell me that as they try to sow wheat in the lands there, they cannot overcome the strength of the turnips that have spread so wide. Radishes thicker than a man's arm and more tender, and excellent tasting: we have seen them countless times' (IV. xviii. 174). Acosta observes that things brought from Europe turn out better in America than things carried from America to Europe. But in the case of transplanted turnips and radishes, their abundance turns into excess. Wheat and americanized turnips fight over the new-found lands, and seemingly the furious fertility of these americanized turnips wins out. Then Acosta writes: 'the marrows of the Indies are another monstrosity with their size and the eagerness with which they grow ... There are a thousand varieties of this genus of squash and many of them are deformed through their size, so that if they are left to dry they can be cut in half and turned into baskets' (176). The subject of abundance exerts control over the outcome through the deployment of usefulness and utility, but abundance is naturally avid, and this vice unfolds as deformity, as loss of form. With Acosta's doctrinaire rationalism, the heroic period of the discourse on the Indies comes to a close, leaving behind the times in which Las Casas and Vasco de Quiroga could proclaim a primitive, indigenous Christianity that did not reject the natives' own memory and culture. Acosta, who sees the native world as an error, which can only be redeemed through doctrine, contradicts Quiroga's idea that God permitted the discovery of the New World in order to renew a Christianity that had fallen into decadence. For Quiroga the Indies lived in a Golden Age whilst Europe suffered the Iron Age. Maravall has observed that 'to such a virtuous predisposition towards the true faith in humanity corresponds an excellent and beautiful conception of nature'. He sees the origin of this correspondence in Columbus and its apogee in Pedro Mártir, who 'presented the American world as fertile, exuberant and sensuous and describes its inhabitants as living in the golden age'.[18] Looked at closely, these are two different evangelizing practices: one believes that the Christians in the Indies are like the apostles and that it is necessary to 'organize their goodness'; the other believes that Christians there will have a tough encounter with the devil. Goodness cannot be organized, but the fight against the devil can be. Colonization can therefore be seen as another chapter of Christianity, the redemption of Man in this world, but also his conversion from barbarism and ignorance to Christian civilization. Even if colonial practice had a superior legitimacy in this discourse, and even though we now know that the result was a *mestizo* religious sensibility, a Christianity turned native, it is nevertheless true that the European invasion sought its meaning in the grand design of evangelization and the cautioning of the new Christians, the subjected Indians, in so many ways similar to early Christians. Or so matters were understood by Las Casas, who was the Indians' most eloquent defender, and the first to warn that if colonization took place in any other way, it would not only be meaningless but would be a contradiction in terms. Walter Benjamin famously saw every document of civilization as one of barbarism, defining modernity as self-contradictory. Las Casas was the first to warn that Europe could well have achieved its own condemnation in the New World, negating itself in causing the imminent demise of the native population, which he feared was on the point of disappearance. As Fletcher indicates in his *The Barbarian Conversion*, the resort to coercive force during the conversions in Europe in the thirteenth and fourteenth centuries provided the models for the spiritual conquest of Mexico and Peru in the seventeenth and eighteenth centuries.[19] There is an often repeated story of the Caribbean chieftain sentenced to be burnt at the stake, who, when offered the possibility of being baptized asks whether the Spaniards will be in heaven or hell, and chooses damnation rather than have to meet them again. Without a real choice, the colonial subject chooses irony.

This paradigmatic discourse of abundance in which America is represented as a fertile space and American Man as a subject of intermixing and translation, finds its expression over and over again. We find it in the eighteenth century American faith in the nomenclature of the proper and in the debates around 'intellectual independence' in the nineteenth century. But it also suffuses the vision of the agrarian countryside that is seen as a properly American agency in the face of the modernizing city, in writers from Bello to Martí. It inheres in the promise of civilization that inspired Sarmiento, whose axis is the modernizing city, as well as in the vision of America as the 'granary of the West' disseminated by the *fin-de-siècle* account of New World riches. Critical representations of abundance reappeared in Regionalism and Creolism, which promote a romantic anti-capitalism, condemning cities as places of decadence and foreign influence and offering the consolation of local colour. Lately, visions of abundance and scarcity converge in Magical Realism, which dismantles socialization and attempts to go beyond the production of the social by deploying popular mythology, carnival and exception.

But we can also see the emergence of a discourse of Latin American promise, a theatre of perpetual trial and experiment, a discourse where alternatives contend and horizons of dialogue open up, giving new inspiration to the Latin American belief in *réculer pour mieux sauter*. This process is visible in the vast critical interplay found in the following historical examples: humanist utopianism, the nationalism generated by modernization and its promises, democratic anti-oligarchic movements, the explorations of identity that seek to create consensus and ties of community, the attempts to reform authoritarian and excluding institutions, the disciplines that reveal and document the plural life of the nation, and the movements that set out to recover ethnic memory, minority energies and the promise of dialogue.

Abundance, scarcity and possibility presuppose choices of interpretative configuration, and for the same reason, act as paradigms of an American narrative, in which American experience changes sign in order to remake its meaning.[20] The grand *mythemes* of the American narrative (foundation, regional organization, rebellion against the state, political repression, army massacres, Apocalypse, migration) are tantamount to a pilgrimage through social discourse and cyclical memory. The symbolic cost of constructing the possible community works, as expiation or redemption, forging cultural memory, and creating an apparatus that will generate an interpretative reading of history and the future. Each of these paradigms orients particular texts, shapes them, and often enables the move from one to another. It may also exceed and go beyond the text. Garcilaso converts the testimony of abundance into a practice that transplants materials from Spain to the Indies. The hyperbolization of the New World (in reality the cultural mechanism of exchange) is transformed into a natural paradigm of cultural representation. He thus offers us a native tree that has regained its fertility by means of Spanish grafts (not in nature but in discourse). Martí will come to represent this novel Latin American culture with the same emblem; in 'Mother America' he writes: 'The off-shoots of world culture are grafted onto our republics, but the trunk of the tree must necessarily be formed from our own republics.' The notion of abundance is present in his work as the possibility, which refutes the scarcities imposed by colonial domination.

For his part, Guamán Poma bears witness to native abundance, which is located in the political rationality and management of the Andean ecosystem prior to the Incas and subsequently. He contrasts this form of knowledge with the violence and subtractions of colonization. Originally a Quechua speaker, he appropriates the Spanish language. His culture expands through writing (which he recommends to the Indians), incorporating new elements, and allows him to preserve the contents of his detailed memory. Writing allows him to deliver his denunciations and to articulate his demands that colonial discourse and actions be consonant with the Christian compact. Like Garcilaso, Guamán fights over the future with a politics rooted in culture. The paradigm of possibility orients his writing and gives it a powerful utopian conviction. But again, like Garcilaso, he is more than a utopian: he proposes to re-establish a universal cosmic order whose parts will live out plurality and difference. This order is the world put right after the world has been turned upside down by invasion and colonization. Garcilaso, in a gesture characteristic of a writer between different languages, traditions and media, presented himself as Quechua, interpreter, man of letters, translator, historian, native of Cuzco, Spanish noble and man of the future, and in each role generated a dialogue composed of many voices. Guamán Poma turned the dialogical system of communication into the very material of his history – chronicle, letter, memorial, iconography, encyclopaedia and submission. Every modulation of genre is a rhetorical act: it produces a speaker, invokes an interlocutor, modulates a message and proposes a common plan of action. Guamán describes himself as a prince when he is addressing the authorities and pursuing political reform. He calls himself an author when he is talking to historians and men of letters in his bilingual autobiography, in which he offers a novel account of familiar events. And he calls himself lord and native wise man when he addresses his own people, creating an encyclopaedia of the Andean world to sustain memory and to manage the crisis that follows the Conquest. But he is also a translator, a draftsman, a clerk or secretary, a *lucanas*, that is someone from a powerful and important ethnic group, which differentiates him from the Incas. The country and its nations all speak in the *New Chronicle and Good Government*. In the first place this constitutes a Letter or Report to the King, which Guamán handed in to the Viceroy's palace in Lima, the product of someone who has completed their travels through the realm, but it consists of complaints, protests, summons, proposals, accounts of weakness and conviction. All of these are assembled to demonstrate one thing: the world is upside down, scarcity is prevalent but the common task must be to press on, summon up resolution and agree on what can be done. It is a question of an intellectual practice that transcends the present and, as is also the case with Garcilaso, owes its existence to the synergy of *mestizaje*. What's more, Guáman's manuscript did not come to light until 1911 and it was first published in 1936. When we read such a text which is marginal to official history yet finds support in contemporary ethnology, we are forced to reconsider the history of the colonization of the Andean world, this time from the point of view of a lettered native who was able to take cognizance all points of view, and thus speak to us in an inclusive way, even whilst remaining attached to the Spanish language, and to the farther shore of the future.[21]

A more contemporary metaphor for the world turned upside down, albeit one no less archaic in that it continues to address the fate of the American subject caught between the promise of Paradise and damnation with no right of appeal, is Juan Rulfo's novel *Pedro Páramo* (1955). This has to be the most radical text to deal with Spanish-American scarcity: its characters are dead, victims of the violence and illegitimacy of power, and the world itself has undergone a radical de-representation, that is, it has lost its quality of reference and become a phantasmatic space. Nevertheless, even here abundance (derived from maternal speech) provides a tacit point of comparison. The son who returns to the patriarchal paradise seeks to acknowledge it using his mother's language, but the world has been disturbed and rearranged by the father's power so that it has now turned into a region of hell, a wasteland of guilt and poverty, covered with the ideological residue of a penitent Christianity. This extreme figure of disillusionment displays all the mechanical fatality of a drama by Calderón de la Barca as it turns the authoritarian state into a force of dispossession, which erases nature and turns life into a tale of death. Thus, scarcity is produced by the violence of the political system, but is reproduced within the system of ideology, in the helplessness of the Christian without Christianity.

In José Lezama Lima, on the other hand, the subject possesses all the powers of religious language. He gives the name 'supernature' to the abundance of the poetic image, which articulates a semantic field of mediating figures. The subject sees its environment as a forest of symbols to be read by means of a key that is at once Baroque and Christian. Lezama's novel *Paraíso* (*Paradise*) (1966) is a 'novel of art' where Lezama transcends Cuban history, re-writing it as theodicy and the young boy from Havana, José Cemí, who already displays his allegiance to the Tainos in his name, which is that the fertility idols 'cemís' made by the Caribbean peoples, embodies the journey of poetic apprenticeship. Lezama Lima's reinauguration of the subject is produced at the confluence of Creole nationality, worldly wisdom, family history and republican patience. Abundance is now a Baroque source of poetic restitution.

José María Arguedas returns us, like Rulfo, to the torn spaces where the native and peasant can observe abundance in their communication with the natural world. This abundance provides the subaltern subject with a creative potentiality, even though in the national society communication proves that one man can no longer speak freely to another. With notable acuity, Arguedas sees the post-colonial human map as one of conflictual communication in a profoundly anti-democratic society.

The negation of the other produces a self-dissolution of the Subject. The fragmentation of the national narrative subtracts the 'I' from the 'You', which now become antagonistic and therefore uncertain. Subjectivity, for the same reason, is the territory of an excessive, meticulous and impassioned mutual violence. When the people of the countryside are displaced by internal migration to the city, this latest ratchet of modernization puts the very existence of the native world into question. The native world moves to the margins and undergoes the distortions of a wild capitalism. In *The Fox from Above and the Fox from Below* (1971) Arguedas creates a powerful vision of industrial exploitation close to Rulfo's vision, where scarcity becomes a form of hell and modernity Apocalypse. Amidst this enormous destruction, Arguedas assembles a fractured religious discourse, derived from the Book of Jeremiah and the Epistles of St Paul. Its violence of address nevertheless attempts to recover a space of agreement, the space of a primitive Christianity, which its helpless characters finally come to incarnate. The narrative exceeds the usual conventions and takes on a contemporary relevance, connecting with then current debates, and often coinciding with the critical thought of Liberation Theology. (One of the latter's most persuasive theologians, Father Gustavo Gutiérrez, wrote on Las Casas, and would later write about Arguedas.) The novel was left unfinished when Arguedas committed suicide, but he succeeded in bearing witness to his final agony in diary fragments interpolated into the account. This parallelism perhaps also demonstrates that the ultimate truth of Arguedas's world lies in the extremity of this writing, which constantly makes and unmakes itself. The postulate that the poor man is the subject of Christianity can be understood as a religious conclusion but also as a moral and practical choice. The genealogy of this proposal goes all the way back to the first period of colonization, which finds its repetition in this latest version of globalized modernization.

In *One Hundred Years of Solitude* (1967), Gabriel García Márquez passes from abundance (the period of foundation) to scarcity (the deterioration that history imposes). In the process, he suggests that there might be other possibilities: the novel exercises the art of memory recovering the past so as not to repeat it. The novel is a chronicle of a particular region and the story of a family. It is suffused with Rabelaisian humour and the breath of carnival, and thus comes close to popular culture. In this fertile and celebratory abundance, the novel's different temporalities (legend, myth, history) are organized by the collective pleasures of telling. In *No one Writes to the Colonel* (1958), on the other hand, Márquez produces an allegory of lack, which begins with the novel's first image. The old colonel scrapes about in a tin for the very last grounds of coffee. This emptiness is reinforced by the colonel's poverty, by the letter that never arrives, by the illegitimacy of the state, and by the miserable future. García Márquez's paradoxical heroes are anti-canonical. They are both historical subjects deprived of history and culture heroes engaged in struggle. They are subjects with heroic echoes, but are predominantly parodic or fantasmatic, comic figures or grotesques. This is shown very well in the story 'The Most Beautiful Hanged Man in the World', in which the culture hero is a dead giant turned by a village lost in the landscapes of scarcity into a new founding figure, who could transform everyday life and return the village to the carnival of abundance. In *The General in his Labyrinth* (1989), the last days of Simón Bolívar are told in parallel with the story of Latin American political independence, now seen as incomplete, its revolutionary promise waylaid and its political destiny no longer its own. And in *Love and Other Demons* (1994), eighteenth-century Colombia is the setting for a tale where different interpretations make any agreement on the facts impossible. A young girl, whose declining parents have abandoned her, is adopted into African slave culture. A supposedly rabid dog bites her and every book-based authority then interprets her behaviour in a completely different way. Finally, the supreme religious authorities judge her to be possessed by demons and subject her to exorcism with fatal consequences. The young girl is a victim of authoritarian institutions and lacks any other social destiny. Yet she is fiercely independent, almost wild. She becomes emblematic of the very subject of lack, in that she has no discursive status. She becomes a scapegoat, sacrificed in order to prove the rationality of others. Not even the man who loves her, a true Petrarchian swain, can save her from prison. There she perishes at the hands of the dominant truth, that of a Church whose only mission is Power.

In the novels of Carlos Fuentes, abundance unfolds as a protean and Baroque form that explores the depths and mirages of crisis. In this interaction of *fiesta* and catastrophe a new Latin American cultural citizenry emerges in the very act of reading. *Terra Nostra* (1975) is a re-reading of the hyperbolic figures of power and history that tie together Old and New Worlds, in their labyrinth of passion, adventure, intrigue and *mestizaje*. In *The Buried Mirror* Fuentes gives a rich cultural history of the Encounter between Old and New Worlds, in which he offers a set of theses on *mestizaje*, and the cultural and ethnic amalgams of

America. This leads him to conceive of Latin America as continuous, despite interruptions, with Spain, and through Spain with the coalesced cultures of Europe – Greco-Roman, Judaeo-Islamic and Indo-African. Later, in *The Orange Tree* (1993) he proposes to rewrite the Conquest from a vantage point on the Western side of the ocean: this time the Maya invade Spain. In the monologues of Cortés's two sons we have the drama of political identity caught between absolute authority and centre-less disaggregation. Fuentes has given his work as a whole the title 'The Age of Time' and has assigned different temporalities to particular sub-groupings, showing how the very process of his writing is novelesque. The 'age of time' suggests a cyclical organization. Narrative time is not only linear but, being an age, returns to its origin only to advance again towards the future, in a spiral of stories that seek to capture time and embody it. In this way, the work reflects the abundance of what is Latin American, which becomes an inexhaustible presence. As with the encyclopaedists of the seventeenth century, Fuentes's Latin America is prodigal, offering proposition and refutation at one and the same time couched in a strategy of rhetorical nobility and efficient empathy. Fuentes's narrative work is produced in vast complicity with the reader. It indicates the periods, transitions and changes of Mexican life as if it were a metaphor for memory itself, that is, the source of durable fruits of the imagination.

In Rosario Ferré's *Maldito amor* (1988) the name of Puerto Rico already takes on the appearance of an oxymoron. 'Rico' (rich) is imposed by the discourse of abundance manipulated by the self-account of a nationalist patriarchy that is in fact the agent of neo-colonial capitalism. 'Puerto' (port) corresponds to the discourse of lack, to the poverty of a dispossessed and exploited people. Women's subversion, the counter-discursive force of the feminine, is here the potential (re)founding act. The heroine sets fire to representation in order to reject history and to start afresh. Right from its beginnings, Puerto Rico has been the crossroads between different interpretations of the colonial experience. It lies between the claims of nationality and those of the metropolis, between the United States and Latin America, between the project of annexation and that of independence, between a neo-colonial status or one of integration as a state of the Union, between Spanish and English ... In spite of everything, Spanish has become the instrument of identity, the definition of common nationality. The island is thus the privileged space of trans-Atlantic interactions and the intermediate term between the practices of pluralizing difference and the forces of homogenization.

During the years of General Pinochet's vicious dictatorship and afterwards, the Chilean writer Diamela Eltit has tirelessly reflected on the difference that would constitute writing that belonged both to women and to the people. Out of these reflections came a saga that rewrites the epic tradition of the conquest of Chile. In *La Araucana* (1569–78), Alonzo de Ercilla tells of the warrior heroes and their exploits during the Spanish conquest. Eltit, by contrast, in *Por la patria* (*For the Fatherland*) (1986) gives an account of how impoverished women open up a territory within the space occupied by the dictatorship, which is constructed from the displaced margins and threshholds of resistance. But the dictatorship has also occupied language, and the women have to recover popular language as if they were recovering their voice. Homeland, family, nation, flag have been turned into authoritarian forms and the novel must re-appropriate them. The story unfolds outside the codes allotted to consumption, in fragmentary narrative syntax and demotic language. Subsequently, in *The Fourth World* (1988), Eltit constructs a project of radical de-socialization, through the reconstruction of the seemingly natural terms that order the nuclear family. On the first – or is it the last – day, a pair of twins explore the city as culture heroes of an un-founding, achieved through helplessness, demonstrating the power of lack, the *tabula rasa* of an anti-utopia. The heroic subjects of Eltit's incisive, passionate stories are always marginal – the parents who have gone astray, the transvestite or transsexual children, a woman on the run, and even lovers in the madhouse. Her characters stage an opera of the poor, which is a setting for a subjectivity concerned with neither power nor the market, but one in which the flows of desire, dream and rebellion circulate. The novels take over deprecatory and insulting names: *sumac*, a racist term used to refer to South American immigrants in Spain; *coy*, a Quechua term used for a native woman; and *matzo*. These subtract the parts that have been reconciled in the discourse of the nation-state and create the additive ensembles of new differences. The work thus confirms the project of reconstruction of the space of potentialities, where the scions of neglect seek to articulate their desire, satisfy their hungers and heal their wounds. The symbolic social body is articulated through the plenitude of this critical and poetic intelligence. It produces a smooth flowing tale, which is the basis for action, even if it offers no programme. In an era when literature as entertainment wallows in the mythology of globalize consumption, Eltit's project, with her marginal heroines and radical heroes, produces a systematic debasement of dominant representations and clichés of consolation.

In the end these modes of representation create the identity that embodies them, acts them out or rejects them. In what follows, we will see that in each case it is not only a question of a hypothetical subject (a theory of the American subject forged by the discourses that construct it), but also an exploratory subject, since each subject allows the message to be situated in a tradition, that is constantly remade by politics and history. Thus we will reconstruct the cultural subject of the New World, a subject whose history begins in its learning how to speak (in the fable of Caliban), and then continues in its learning how to read (other fables illustrating the power of the letter). Then, the subject learns how to write, in a reappropriation of signs that will allow it to better read this new world. The subject then learns to translate and how to draw: natural history supports an iconography of abundance. This process presupposes that at the same time the subject is named, read, written, translated, drawn . . . It is obvious, that this is the very subject of the West, which has a second chance to remake itself in the New World. As Europe expands, during the course of modernity, this 'logocentric subject' evolves into a new character in the discourses of difference, acting in the name of universal, Christian and humanist values. The subjects of these accounts are more than American individuals: they are topoi, when not types, even if at times they do refer to historical characters. And even if their American difference confers individuality on them, they are inter- preted not in their own terms, but through the puzzlement they pro- duce in the European setting. We will also see, however, that this tension between the American and the European – a dilemma formulated in characteristically European terms – will gradually turn the American subject into a native interlocutor, and into a man of mixed origins, a subject of passage, who is configured between Europe and the Indies, and whose voice speaks from a privileged and provisional 'here and now', in the open-ended process of the different. The cultural history of the New World subject would be a chapter within European Renaissance history. But with its diversity and creative co-existence, its tolerance and will to the future, it would also be the most modern account produced in Spanish after its Italianizing peak.

'There is only one world', Inca Garcilaso wrote in *La Florida*, invok- ing the universal principle of Christian rationality, even if his own case demonstrated rather well that there were many different languages and nations. Even if the sixteenth-century concept of race had not yet acquired its exclusionary force, there would soon appear the elaborate classifications of the many racial blending that would demonstrate the sensitivity of the term. Even Garcilaso himself laments the fact that the term *mestizo* is deprecatory, and in order to affirm it against prevailing opinion, he decides to assume it 'with pride'. In any case, if the chronicles offer their information as evidence, it is nevertheless clear that much is owed to the frameworks of interpretation in which they are set. One part derives from patristic and humanist scholarship; another part derives from the debate about colonization and evangelization, a tension which Las Casas sees as decisive for the meaning of the Spanish enterprise in the Indies. Furthermore, some fables are constructed out of the facts, as exemplary outcomes of historical lessons. So that in the discursive formation of the Chronicle of the Indies, the fluidity of genre frameworks is more important than the mediaeval and Renaissance traditions of the historical account with its various rhetorical formulations. This fluidity means that the gathering of evidence makes use of testimony, quotation, commentary, gloss, and natural, moral and factual histories. Interpretative configuration, however, exceeds these modes of formulation determined by a will to demonstrate. Hence the typologies of the chronicle finish up as guides to an almost unlimited territory, or better, as obsolete with each new reading. Enrique Pupo Walker saw this well, when he analysed the imaginative character of the chronicle, revealing its literary antecedents.[22] Our comparison between the fables which construct the native as Noble Savage, self-taught philosopher, child of Paradise and primitive Christian and the histories of depopulation, mine labour and violence allows us to pursue the following: first, the construction of the figure of the native of American abundance, and second, the testimony of a subject who is the victim of this very abundance now converted into scarcity and lack. The native intellectuals, even when they contrasted the two versions, sought to situate them in a wider political figure, which derived as much from native sources (the repair of disorder) as from European (the need for Christian tolerance, the good government of inclusion and negotiation). In a contemporary perspective, there is a continuing relevance in the fact that the native of abundance whose labour reproduces a regime that condemns him to lack, is, when all is said and done, the poverty stricken human being of a modernity dedicated to multiplying resources and wealth. In Christian evangelization the subject is the Indian (potential convert or idolater depending on the point of view). This subject is already destitute and helpless: represented as tractable, lacking interest in economic values, and diligent in carrying out its subaltern function. Las Casas's preaching leaves no doubt: the native is the new primitive

Christian, and therefore the most authentic Christian. The fact that the Devil fights over him is proof not of the Indian's guilt but of his innocence as he awaits the truths of revelation. Oviedo sees the virtues of poverty but also sees the perversion of customs that come to obsess him as a stigma. Father Acosta, who sees the Indian from the point of view of the institutional Church, prefers to believe that native ingenuousness merely guarantees the divine will for a conversion in the long term. Mass baptism, furthermore, only deals with Divine accounts. Garcilaso de la Vega who sees further, understands that the Indian already knew Christian teaching and merely required spiritual guidance to show him the right path, since there is no conversion without the absorption of doctrine. Guamán Poma de Ayala goes even further: the subject of abundance is also the victim of every form of power, including the ecclesiastical, and therefore the Indians are the 'poor in Christ', that is, they are the poorest people who follow Jesus. In a new age, Jesus himself will have to return to begin the Christian conversion of the Indies again, only this time the Europeans will be included. With all its contradictions, the history of the New World and the configuration of the *mestizo* subject are an integral part of modern Christianity. One of its products is just this poor human being, the subject who has no place in his own world, but is in the charge of every discourse, including the greatest of all, that of Divine Decree.

Two notes of caution are in order. If Garcilaso Inca de la Vega becomes more intelligible when the European dimension of his writing is foregrounded, nevertheless it is a theoretical absurdity to reduce him to the literary codes of the Europe of his times and to dissolve him into historical typology or into the dominant ideology. This book seeks to demonstrate that Latin American texts follow a different route. This is one of heteroclite appropriations which displace codes, make free use of archives, 'nativize' canonical repertoires, widen native registers and instrumental resources, and in the end begin to construct representations of fusion, combination and the site of the subject of a new culture. For the same reason, I do not share the desire to dissolve Felipe Guamán Poma de Ayala into Andean ethnological documentation. Garcilaso and Guamán Poma are textual instances, transatlantic discursive elaborations. In the multiple transitions that they unleash, in the activity of reformulation, their voices express complex critical demands and new creative communication.

one

Speaking:
Caliban

His name is an anagram of the Spanish word *canibal* ('cannibal') and clearly refers to the Caribbean. In Shakespeare's last work, *The Tempest* (1612–13), Caliban becomes a fascinating representation of New World man.[1] The figure derives from a number of different sources in literature and legend, most notably those of Europe's colonial history, in which the exploration of the American colonies gives rise to a sense of wonder and adventure. He corresponds to a notion of 'natural man', where the colonized native is understood as primitive, lacking language and, therefore, morality. From Aristotle onwards, this idea of the savage as wholly dominated by his condition within nature has been used to justify slavery, and to underpin the power of the master's rule.[2] In the Folio edition, which opens with *The Tempest*, the list of characters describes Caliban as 'a savage and deformed slave'. However, his innate wickedness is innocent, lacking self-consciousness and guilt, a fact that reinforces the civilizing function of his master, whose authority guarantees the process by which Caliban will cease to be a monster and become human.

Prospero, Duke of Milan, having been stripped of his power by his own brother, has taken over Caliban's island and, with the aid of his magic has transformed it into an enchanted place. In retirement from the world, with his daughter Miranda, and served by Ariel and Caliban, Prospero devotes his life to his books, that is, to the power of language through which he controls nature. Language is here the form through which conflict will be resolved. It transfigures the natural world, provides the justification for the native's servitude and re-establishes political order. American nature is expressed in its extravagant abundance but only becomes intelligible as a support for the legitimate order of the city of men. In the end, colonization is the staging of the powers of allegorical language, making its magic literal and reading it as political. Colonization constructs an Other to Europe, a clarifying mirror in which Europe's own legitimacy can be recognized. Caliban's island gives the Italian city-state a means for its own restitution. The Caribbean becomes Milan's mirror, as Shakespeare's parable provides the setting for the classical lesson: good government and the best ruler are in harmony with the fertile order of the Cosmos. This island of Renaissance discourse becomes, therefore, the place where the child of nature, Caliban, will be redeemed, so becoming the offspring of language. Learning to speak, he will learn to recognize his own world, and thence to list its contents, and thus take possession of it within discourse.

Shakespeare might have taken this fable from chapter four of Antonio de Eslava's *Las noches de invierno* ('Winter Nights'; 1609), which tells the story of the overthrow of Dardanus, the King of Bulgaria, by Niceforus, the King of Greece. Like Prospero, Dardanus is also a sorcerer, and has a daughter, Serafina, with whom he decides to take leave of the world, seeking refuge in a palace at the bottom of the sea.[3] This history probably has an even earlier Italian source. In any case, the parallels of Shakespeare's play and this Spanish fable about power, where the Orphic magician confronts the Machiavellian politician, underline common conflicts in the political debates of the time. At the beginning of the seventeenth century, those debates were given added importance by the discovery of the natural riches of the New World set against the untold strangeness of its peoples. The debates were also driven by the need to transform the colonies into legitimate estates and plantations, with their consolidations of native labour, so that they could become centres for the production and reproduction of goods, both pragmatic and symbolic, within the new imperial map. Beyond the coincidences of plot, both fable and play display a similar correspondence between the rupture of political order (the usurpation of the legitimate ruler) and the fracture of the natural order (magic as metaphor for the supernatural). Eslava's exemplary fable, the 'winter night', is a tale about the definition and limits of Nature and the power of the man of wisdom, Aristotle's virtuous subject. The magician explains to his daughter that 'everything in this inconstant world exists in a state of perpetual war'. Cosmic and human forces are ruled by contrary movements, where 'adverse elements battle with each other'. Dardanus ends by saying: 'If this is so, then, in insensible and inanimate creatures, how shall it be with the sensible and the rational? And so . . . I swear to you by Eternal Chaos no longer to make my home amongst men' (111). Whilst, at one level merely the reiteration of a literary topos, this oath in the name of the authority of an Eternal Chaos, uttered by a wise and beneficent mage is also the exact reverse of another image, symmetrical and opposed, that of the 'magical palace' below the sea, constructed through art and preserved by enchantment. If nature (the world and human beings) is dominated by the discord of unequal passions and forces, magic is the supernatural art, capable of imitating the superior order of moral philosophy. In the dialogue that follows the tale, Eslava gives an extensive commentary on magic, and offers what could be seen as a first Caliban-like image, full of horror and wonder:

> Teodoro Gaza, a learned man who died not long ago, saw one day that there having been a great storm at sea, its contentions had thrown upon a strand a great quantity of fish, amongst which there was a nereid, who had the form and features of a woman down to the waist, but from there on down her body passed into the form of a thing like an eel, that is the very manner in which sirens and nereids are painted [124].

In this unknown and discordant nature, the storm gives rise to both a disorder of forms and the hybridity of ambiguous subjects, true enigmas in which it is possible to read the inner irrationality of the natural. Nature unleashes strange combinations of forms, and is itself material for the alternative and supplementary order of magic. The disenchantment of the world gives rise to a secret enchantment. Yet human nature comes to impose itself, with its cycle of cosmic regeneration: Serafina demands a companion and her father finds him in the prince who will restore the political order and the legitimacy of a wise power. A cosmic and political theatre thus concludes as a family romance, favouring an order gained at the expense of a nature rich in enigmas and wonder.

By setting *The Tempest* on a Mediterranean island, Shakespeare flees from both history (Bulgaria) and myth (the magical palace beneath the sea), to take up residence on his own terrain, the theatre of the supernatural and the stage of politics. He endeavours to create a work that is more romance than history. The island is raised like an enchanted lure, and by means of his magical powers Prospero will ensure that the storm brings his usurper brother to him, so that political order can be re-established, Prospero himself restored and lineage confirmed. The pleasing chaos of artifice no longer corresponds to the Eternal Chaos of opposites, but to Prospero's strategy for his own restoration. In the play, chaos and magic are principles of staging, instruments in the performance. This unfolding of an artifice that can replace nature, finds its forces of transformation in fertility and mutation. The island is a place of abundance, but it is also the setting for the change that will announce the modern. This double valence (abundance, change) is the sign of the Caribbean. Caliban, son of an incubus and a witch, the product of savage nature's original sin, is in fact the first incarnation, the first mask of the modern colonial subject. That is to say, Caliban is a representation of the Other, primordial and savage, incapable yet of moral responsibility, but capable of learning and responding, of refashioning himself through the humanist discourses that prophesy modernity and promise grace. More than a representation of the aboriginal or the inhabitant of the Caribbean, the figure of Caliban is an attempt to produce an image, albeit an image in crisis. His origin, nature and form are incapable of representation. Not even his description and much less his designation are altogether fixed. He is a character who throws the very possibility of giving an account of his radical difference into crisis.

However, it is not just Caliban's name and the figure of the wicked savage that refer to the New World, but also the wonders found in the play's fantastic geography which derives from the tales of transatlantic voyages. In fact, *The Tempest* is inspired by the popular accounts of a famous shipwreck off the island of Bermuda. In July 1609, the fleet taking the North American colonies their new governor was scattered by a storm, and the governor's ship was sunk in the Bermudas, leaving the crew stranded for nearly a year, supposedly in a state of paradisiacal bliss. The accounts of this journey captivated the English-reading public and undoubtedly Shakespeare read some of them and the letters that also circulated, and

made free use of them. He may have omitted historical details but exploited their exotic resonance, above all the novelty and strangeness of the
New World, those far-distant colonies and unknown islands which filled
Europeans with curiosity. It is the context of this colonial reality that lends
verisimilitude (or at least credibility) to the presence of a native of the
island like Caliban. Even though Eslava's fable is itself archaic with its roots
in Italian romance, the contemporary colonial reality inserts the play into
the unfathomable space of the American adventure.[4]

In any case, for the purposes of our reading there is something more
important than this fusing together of diverse sources. This is the interrogation that the enigma of Caliban poses for the naturalizing gaze itself.
For it soon becomes evident that his status as 'natural man', his unre-
deemed aspect as primordial being, is in tension with the possibility of
his becoming fully human, that aspect of his condition as a 'noble savage'
that can be redeemed. Miranda has taught him how to speak, and his
capacity to learn is also his consciousness of the power of language. His
reply repeats the perennial response of the colonized who becomes a
subject through the language of the Other, even while he is himself the
Other of language. That is to say, Caliban constructs himself and is constructed as an identity that can only be affirmed thanks to language: 'You
taught me language, and my profit on 't / Is I know how to curse.'

Language, in effect, has given him a contradictory subjectivity, not
only because language has taught him how to curse, but because curs-
ing is the 'profit' that he recognizes in having learned how to speak. It is
'my profit' he says, because it is the only part that belongs to him, the
proof of his inner freedom as a knowing subject. Being able to curse
becomes a metaphor for his taking possession of language, an appropriation that is self-conscious and sarcastic and makes him capable of
humiliating others. That is why, recognizing the power of his master,
and the necessity for controlling the scene of speech, Caliban says to
himself in an aside: 'I must obey' – he fears the power of the magician.
The language he has learned allows him to know his own limits, affirm
his body, and represent his own role. But it also allows him to act out the
identity as native that the others have attributed to him, even playing
with his name and his evil reputation. On his first appearance, Miranda
declares her disgust and pity toward him, because the slave has demonstrated his savagery in trying to rape her. She berates him severely and
he is thus affirmed in his contradictory identity. But his attempted
infraction cannot be considered too great because he is a man without
malice, instinctive and animal-like but also grotesque and even farcical.

His reply is at once villainous and playful: Miranda and he could have 'people[d] this isle with Calibans' he says (1. 2).

But Caliban, like his distant relatives the Indians of the Antilles, should not be seen merely as the consequence of archaic representations of 'natural man' or savage. In Shakespeare's hands, his figure bears the mark of another representation, that of the inhabitant of Arcadia, the native of paradise. His hybridity is physical – he is a monster made out of discursive fragments – and therefore theatrical. It is a metaphor for the strangeness of the Caribbean. That is, a European nightmare, whose background reveals both the bad conscience of the colonial enterprise and its rhetorical justification. But this hybridity also reveals the inconsistency and tension between the two models of representing the Other: as savage, and therefore slave, and as the offspring of abundance, and therefore capable of redemption. In the first model, Caliban is excluded from order and therefore condemned to suffer it; in the second, his wickedness is merely that of a brutish child. Prospero pardons his behaviour, and Caliban himself announces at the end of the play that he has learned his lesson: he will be wiser, he says, going forward in search of grace. His new consciousness will convert him into a citizen.

There are other resonances within Caliban's American hybridity. At the beginning of the first act, he announces:

> This island's mine, by Sycorax my mother,
> Which thou tak'est from me. When thou cam'st first,
> Thou strok'st me and made much of me, wouldst give me
> Water with berries in't, and teach me how
> To name the bigger light and how the less,
> That burn by day and night. And then I loved thee.
> And showed thee all the qualities o' th' isle,
> The fresh springs, brune pits, barren place and fertile . . .
> [1. ii. 396–405]

This declaration indicates the centrality of the master–slave relation with the colonial form of power. It also signals something less obvious and more important: the native is torn apart when he is colonized by language, and even more so when he comes to acquire a new faith (he has learned how to name the stars, he tells us in a reference to Genesis 1: 16). His education is at the cost of his inheritance and his belonging. His identity, then, is just this dispossession. This gesture has a powerful resonance in the context of seventeenth-century America and alludes to the discourse of the *mestizos* (those of mixed blood), the first inhabitants of colonial hybridity. Like Caliban the *mestizos* challenge colonial authority, declaring that the land is theirs by double filiation: they inherited it from their mothers and won it through their fathers. Property and conquest, inheritance and profit are combined in them. They are the children of that founding violence, but also the begetters of a new American discourse, one that combines the discords of origin with the possibilities of the future.[5]

Moreover, the play unfolds on a privileged terrain: Caliban's island is the emblem of fertility. Prospero has transformed it into a magical setting, still abundant and fertile, where Ariel and Caliban are his bound slaves. The farcical rebellion that Caliban prepares to mount with his accomplices is made in the name of this self-same emblem: 'I'll show thee every fertile inch o' the island' (ii. ii. 154), and then immediately thereafter: 'I'll show the best springs, I'll pluck thee berries. I'll fish for thee and get thee wood enough' (ii. ii. 166–7). The scene is comical because the conspirators are drunk, but abundance is one of the motives behind this rebellion against Prospero's power, just as it also inspires Caliban's servility before the poor devils that he confuses with lords. Abundance is thus a first cause and even the source of a possible new order. The noble Gonzalo ('an honest old counsellor') confirms its emblematic quality, when, glossing Montaigne, he exclaims:

> I' th' commonwealth I would by contraries
> Execute all things; for no kind of traffic
> Would I admit; no name of magistrate;
> Ketters should not be known; riches, poverty,
> And use of service, none; contract, succession,
> Bourn, bound of land, tilth, vineyard, none;
> No use of metal, corn, or wine, or oil;
> No occupation; all men idle, all
> And women too, but innocent and pure;
> No sovereignty.
> [...]
> All things in common nature should produce
> Without sweat or endeavor; treason, felony,
> Sword, pike, knife, gun, or need of any engine
> Would I not have; but nature should bring forth
> Of its own kind all foison, all abundance,
> To feed my innocent people [ii. ii. 162–80]

At the end of this speech, Gonzalo reiterates Nature's fertility (*foison*, abundance) as a common good, as a source of free sustenance for all. This emblematic scene (where the counsellor Gonzalo deploys a commonplace image of the Golden Age) displays the complementary symbolism that underlies Shakespeare's system of representations. In the native world (that of nature's fertility), the picture of the different ages, deriving from classical sources, is realized as a political model, with features of common wealth, ideal justice and shared property. On a paradisiacal Caribbean stage Shakespeare mounts a scene of abundance converted into a philosophical and social utopia. The colonial contract of master and slave (the ethic of civilizing power proclaimed by Prospero before Ariel and Caliban) is here contrasted with an aesthetic vision of ethical substance (the notion of good and egalitarian government). The contrast is no less powerful for being speculative, and its nostalgic elements cannot disguise its connections to the disquieting newness (Otherness) of the Caribbean islands.

Nor is it coincidental that Gonzalo's utopian proposals should be find support in Montaigne's essay 'On the Cannibals', where we read:

> So we can indeed call those folk barbarians by the rules of reason but not in comparison to ourselves, who surpass them in every kind of barbarism. Their warfare is entirely noble and magnanimous: it has as much justification and beauty as that human malady allows: among them it has no other foundation than a zealous concern for courage. They are not striving to conquer new lands, since without toil or travail they still enjoy that bounteous Nature who furnishes them abundantly with all they need, so that they have no concern to push back their frontiers. They are still in that blessed state of desiring nothing beyond what is ordained by their natural necessities: for them anything further is superfluous. The generic term that they use for men of the same age is 'brother'; younger men they call 'sons'. As for the old men they are the 'fathers' of everyone else . . . [6]

This excessive abundance is both a source of social happiness and an aesthetic vision of a communal ethics. At once philosophical and critical, this scene sketches out the common good, and at the same time questions the ethics of Montaigne's own society, where men are detached from one another. For Montaigne, Americans are 'still . . . close neighbours to their original innocence' (232). That is, they are still unconquered by historical guilt, by interpretations exercised by those with the power to condemn them to servitude. The abundance in which these natives live is for Montaigne the contemporary reality of the Golden Age, but European domination will be its adulteration ('They are still governed by the laws of Nature and are only very slightly bastardized by ours', 232). Montaigne adds drama to his disquisition on the New World with a certain melancholy scepticism. His political vision is no less contrasting: the emblem of an adulterated abundance suggests that the relativism of interpretation belongs to modern critical thought: the fate of representation, though, is in the hands of the powerful.[7]

Stephen J. Greenblatt claims that Shakespeare takes up a condemnatory attitude toward Savage Man, even exaggeratedly so in the figure of Caliban, who, he therefore concludes, is anything but a Noble Savage. Nevertheless, 'natural man' still beats somewhere inside the figure of Caliban and is doubled in the figure of the Innocent Savage. The first image condemns him to contractual subjection by the civilizing master: the second rejects the master's power with a collectivist utopianism.

Greenblatt also asserts that: '*The Tempest* utterly rejects the uniformitarian view of the human race, the view that would later triumph in the Enlightenment and prevail in the West to this day. All men, the play seems to suggest, are *not* alike; strip away the adornments of culture and you will *not* reach a single human essence'.[8] One might argue, however, that this conclusion could only illustrate a moral philosophy that differentiates historical subjects in the face of power and politics. By contrast, the differences between Caliban, the servants, the courtiers, the usurpers and the magician are representative of gradations between primordial nature and legitimate political society. The axis of representation runs between a return to natural sources (the island of abundance and the supernatural) and a return to the city restored to legitimacy and good government. It is thus the process of becoming human that reveals the common quality of humanity. In this way, the good that lies in abundance is reflected in the common good of legitimate government.

Caliban and the Caribbean are at the centre of the debate, which is unresolved in Shakespeare's play. Instead, it is transferred to a dimension of beneficent magic – a humanist metaphor, whose fantasy mediates the immanent wonder of the natural. If nature is prodigal in its gifts, how do we account for its miserliness with human beauty, and the fact that the benevolent material reality of the island is contradicted by the pathetic hybridity of the offspring of incubus and witch (in effect, the American progeny of two negativities on the margins of Europe)?

Perhaps the problem is different: there is a universal human essence but not everyone conforms to it. As Montaigne understood, the human essence is nature in formation, and whilst these Caribbean avatars are perhaps horrible from our representational and epistemological point of view, they are nevertheless free of the deformations that attend the adulterations of meaning, morality and the common good imposed by all forms of power (colonial, ideological and cultural). In the end, the 'human race' is a metaphor for a humanity that is evolving by means of human beings. Culture is the form of its 'essence', its system for staging reflection and action. It is no coincidence then, that in *The Tempest*, Caliban encounters his counterparts in the servants, and that his 'savagery' is less blameworthy than the moral and political violence that is represented by Antonio, Prospero's brother, 'the usurping Duke of Milan'. Disinherited from his island of origin, Caliban inherits the fragments of a discourse that construct and fight over him. It is for this reason that he curses: contradicting these discourses is a first gesture toward establishing control over them. But his innocence has no social destiny: he cannot yet articulate those discourses as an instrument with which to reconstruct his lost island.

To a large extent, Shakespeare finds in Caliban the paradoxical subject, created in innocence, but framed by irony, that could inhabit the delightful paradise envisaged by Montaigne. We know that *The Tempest* makes use of the latter's essay 'On the Cannibals', where we read:

> Those 'savages' are only wild in the sense that we call fruits wild when they are produced by Nature in her ordinary course: whereas it is fruit which we have artificially perverted and misled from the common order which we ought to call savage. It is in the first kind that we find their true, vigorous, living, most natural and most useful properties and virtues, which we have bastardized in the other kind by merely adapting them to our corrupt tastes. Moreover, there is a delicious savour which even our taste finds excellent in a variety of fruits produced in those countries without cultivation: they rival our own. It is not sensible that artifice should be more reverenced than Nature, our great and powerful Mother. We have so overloaded the richness and beauty of her products by our own ingenuity that we have smothered her entirely. Yet wherever her pure light does shine, she wondrously shames our vain and frivolous enterprises [231–2].

Montaigne's reflections thus appear as a source for the figure of Caliban and the theme of abundance, appearing not so much in Shakespeare's theatrical game of mirrors, but in the reflexive play where a certain questioning is set up by way of contrasts. What Montaigne calls 'Nature in her ordinary course' is just what Shakespeare sets in motion in his staging. Shakespeare reveals this 'evolution' in the various masquerades and unmaskings that construct the adventure through which other worlds and other human beings come to be imagined and known. Returning from the islands, with knowledge of the other, the European subject comes to a new knowledge of its own self, its own I: a different subject is projected through disjunction, otherness and combination. Prospero's island refers us to the Mediterranean archive, but it also projects the contemporary reality of America. The abundance in which Nature is expressed means that Caliban's inconsistency can be resolved by seeing him as a hybrid combination, not yet equal to European humanity but in a process of unfolding. On the one hand, Caliban is the sum of legends, models and perceptions derived from different sources and authorities and forged in Europe; but on the other, his hybridity already belongs to the New World. Caliban will cease to be a monster out of legend to become the first man of his island. Finally, he will preside over a language that evolves from being the setting of loss to become a stage for occupation and habitation.

Newer readings of the play have gone beyond the traditional clichés about romance as dominant genre and the now over-determined idea that the play supports the colonial ideology of its time. On the one hand there is a map of its interconnected contexts – the enterprise of colonial domination, maritime exploration, the debate about humanity in the Americas, etc. On the other, there is a series of parallel discourses – on the natural and the supernatural, the artificial and political, slave and master, natural man and noble savage. What these make evident is that every assertion in the play has its counterpoint, and at times its refutation, to such an extent that the work is suffused by a 'radical ambivalence'. The sequence of contrasts includes opposing figures and contrasting languages, confronting natural law and supernatural art, appearance and reality, the given and the constructed, the literal and the hyperbolic. The play is a dynamic configuration, staged with exemplary figures undergoing moral trial. These mediated tensions recall the image of Chaos glossed by Eslava and the pre-Socratic theme of forces in discord. The 'tempest' after all is not just the contrary winds, but also the central metaphor for the play's transformations and potentialities. It is the emblem of newly found objects, newly discovered shores and different voices. In the final analysis, the play of meaning turns these series and allegories into another 'masquerade'. Every attempt to fix language seems to be contradicted by language's own potential to undermine its nominative and normative role. This is why not even Prospero's language represents the work itself but is merely one of the axes. Gonzalo, the intellectual of the play, senses that the new demands articulation and wishes to provide it with an appropriate discourse. But even as he eloquently unfolds his natural philosophy, he is immediately refuted by a farcical sarcasm from those who contrast his echoes of utopia with the brutality of an environment that is more hostile than paradisiacal. All this suggests that ambiguity constantly stands in for a fluid and changing reality. Even if the development of the play is that of a schematic fable, its unfolding as masquerade takes on a baroque quality. Words do not always function as referential or constative, since language unfolds human experience as narrative hyperbole. This celebration of the powers of language, however, is another form of the interrogation of naming. Thus, it is just this disautomatization of the language of naming and restriction, the breaking of the chain between word and thing, that enables the play to exult in exchange, masquerade, and rewriting. Not even Miranda, the play's most literal being, speaks a single language. Rather, she seems on her way to becoming a new subject. She arrives from Europe and in passing through the islands (Enchanted or Diabolic depending on the scene) she is transformed, turning a new page of self, capable now of replacing her father and assuming her own narrative voice, calling where she has come from 'a brave new world'. America has made the Old World New. There is an opening up of abundance within language, as soon as words are no longer limited by things. Montaigne imagines a dialogue that Plato might have written on the Indies, anticipating a conversation that would have begun: 'I would have said to Plato . . .'. However, the nostalgia that he feels also supports another discourse, the language of utopia, which in contrast with nostalgia has an instrumental quality and an openness to the future. If there is an ironic distance revealed in Gonzalo's humanist sermon, then perhaps part of the allegory that he tries to shape as he crosses the Island's fertile forests is derived from More's *Utopia*. Given the multiple contrasts that reinforce this ambivalence of language, there is undoubtedly a further turn of the screw, when the play asks of Gonzalo, 'no more', no More.[9]

As John G. Demaray observes, 'Before the final reconciliations that constitute a metaphoric rebirth, characters in the imperfect world of the play indulge themselves with social "imaginings". The essentially good counselor Gonzalo fancies an "antic" commonwealth of political and personal lassitude fortuitously supplied by a superabundant Nature.'[10]

The motifs of the play are derived from equally rich sources: More and Burton, as well as Ovid and Virgil. On the other hand the play also delivers sarcastic rejoinders to the normativity of certain treatises on how courtiers should behave. This series of oppositions becomes itself the theme of Caliban's library.

Critical readings of neo-colonialism in the 1980s tended to simplify the figure of Caliban, for, as Peter Hulme recalls, even the colonial experience includes different discourses, not just those determined by the schema of domination. Caliban's servitude corresponds to the role that natives played as providers of food in the early chronicle's. This connection and mediation through food, generating a network of communication between explorers and natives, also supported the symbolic interactions of mutual dependence between master and slave. It underlines the growing importance of food and drink as the axes of a certain everyday reality – domestic, economic and practical. This density of connections and language would become the social space – immanent and symbolic – that would play an equal role to that of the taxonomies and catalogues of a fertile and extravagant Nature in constructing the sphere of the everyday. If making lists is the rhetorical resource for colonial appropriation, Caliban reappropriates this resource in order to list the glories of his native soil. He has no peer in his knowledge of names and the places where this extravagance of goods is to be found. Fruits, shellfish, fresh water: only Caliban can provide these for Prospero, just as he provides the necessary menial labour for carrying wood. Prospero recognizes his dependence on these services. But Caliban also expresses the joy of the magical forest. He is the dweller in paradise who reflects the transparency of his world and his intimacy with it:

> Be not afeard. The isle is full of noises,
> Sounds and sweet airs that give delight and hurt not.
> Sometimes a thousand twangling instruments
> Will hum about mine ears; and sometimes voices
> That, if I then had wak'ed after long sleep,
> Will make me sleep again; and then, in dreaming,
> The clouds methought would open and show riches
> Ready to drop upon me, that, when I wak'd,
> I cried to dream again [III. ii. 129–37].

Barbara Baert comments: 'the wild man can complement the human condition, can actually improve it'.[11]

Shakespeare found his historical sources for the play in the chronicles and reports of the voyages to the coast of New England and the islands of the Caribbean, and their subsequent exploration. Study of these accounts reveals that the plants, fruits, birds and animals that the playwright mentions come from both regions, and that Shakespeare has mixed elements from both areas to avoid identifying the island specifically. He has also avoided those typical products which would have identified the island, such as the *palmeto*, the small palm, that would have indicated the Bermudas. The efforts of Edward Everett Hale and Henry Cabot Lodge to show that Cape Cod in New England is closer to the original source of 'Prospero's island' are nevertheless illuminating in this regard.[12]

Equally significant is the fact that today we call it 'Caliban's island'. But it is no longer the same island since it is no longer a question of the same readings of the text. Nor is a question of the same characters. Caliban is designated as a slave, deformed and filthy. He is conceived as a monster and monstrous human being, but he is also dehumanized, put on a par with fish, dogs, lizards, monkeys, turtles . . . His double nature – natural man and noble savage – transforms him into a figure of crisis, that is, into a new American cultural subject, who throws into question the prevailing repertoire of representations, the language of definitions, and its systems of classification. In this, he is like the palm trees that Columbus saw, which emerged from the field of vision demanding a metaphorical language to describe them. Caliban, like his name, is an anagram, an oxymoronic figure, a principle of contradiction. It is revealing that within critical discourse he is no longer a monster, tragic and comic at the same time, but has become increasingly human with each subsequent reading of the play, so that he has eventually come to be the most human of the characters, the most historical and the most truthful.[13]

David Norbrook ably indicates the force field of this signifying process: 'The play is not overtly oppositional or sensationally "subversive"; but it subjects traditional institutions to a systematic, critical questioning. The play does not consider language and power as timeless absolutes; rather in counterposing an unmediated, presocial nature to a deterministically conceived language, it is concerned with language in specific social contexts, with the effect of political structures on linguistic possibilities. All of the play's utopian ideals, not excepting Ariel's,

44

come in for ironic scrutiny in the course of the play, precisely because they tend to an idealism that refuses to recognize the material constrains of existing structures of power and discourse. But that awareness need not imply a pessimistic determinism. A skeptical relativism about claims to an unproblematic "human nature" is played against a searching, universalizing quest for a more general notion of humanity'.[14]

Caliban transforms the offspring of discourse, the heirs of the long European tradition of mimesis and rhetoric: he makes them human. His recently acquired language and his newly found humanity put models of naming and representation into crisis. In his wake language is no longer the same. As in a mirror, he reflects back the features of the one who names him. Caliban emerges out of dialogue, from oppositions and articulations, from differences and conflicts. More than a legible product of discourse, Caliban will be the first child of the new history, a history constructed in interpretations.

Caliban's island, the space of the new American language, is constructed through these interpretations as a place where abundance is extant. Learning to speak the language of colonial power could confirm the order of a new normativity, making the colonized subject a means of reproduction of this power. But the excessive abundance of nature also becomes the matrix of a discourse that exceeds the normative archive that seeks to reproduce control over what it names and classifies. Abundance is the fissure of the world in language, the creative potential of a space as yet without discourse, prefigured in the force of those objects that are the alphabet of the new empirical reality. Colonial power was a continuously extending cartographic enterprise, seeking to map all spaces, even the ones emptied out by its own depredations. The administration of this abundance - actual and potential - required the constant augmentation of bureaucratic power, in much the same way as the imperial project required the growth of the banking institutions of Flanders and Italy. The lengthy, time-consuming inquiries that the Spanish administration continuously sent to the authorities in the Indies included various questions about native plants and the ones introduced from Europe, how they were growing, what the results of interbreeding were and so on.[15] But even the island of Bermuda could be represented as a space of lack, because of its arid and inhospitable land. Or at least this is how it is described in the account of the shipwreck of Sir Thomas Gates, governor turned contented native, by W. Strachey (1610). In the privileged space of interpretation, there is room for contrary representations of the island. According to the chronicle written by Pedro Martir, Bermuda is named after its discoverer, Juan de Bermúdez. But subsequently it is referred to as 'Devil's Isle' by several travelers unfortunate enough to land there. This process of contradictory description eventually produces the enchanted island, with its sweet air full of music, but also its slaves Ariel and Caliban hungry for freedom. *The Tempest* is a masquerade that stages its own plural reading. It could be said to be a long quotation of the Caribbean as transatlantic trope and topos.

It is unsurprising that on two critical occasions in the history of modern Latin America, Prospero and Caliban's island has been represented as the space of a potential future. The first is José Enrique Rodó's essay *Ariel* (1900), which stands at the crossroads between the nineteenth-century idealist tradition and a temptation towards positivism. The essay seems to suggest that Caliban is the symbol of a triumphant materialism represented by the United States, and Ariel the symbol of a threatened spirituality, represented by Latin America. Gordon Brotherston argues that this interpretation of the book owes more to the moment of historical crisis in which it was published than to any deliberate intention of Rodó's, who was much less categorical and systematic.[16] In any case, the essay takes Shakespeare's play and its moral lesson as its starting point, and 'inspired' by Ariel, becomes a call to the future, to the young, and bids them defend and continue with their spiritual and intellectual development in the face of the triumph of the forces of materialism.[17] By contrast, in his much discussed *Caliban: Notes on Culture in Our America* (1973), Roberto Fernández Retamar sees Ariel as the intellectual of the island who is in a position to make an alliance with the rebel Caliban against the powerful and imperial Prospero. In this political re-reading of the colonial scene, Retamar constructs a revolutionary manifesto from within the experience of the Cuban Revolution. It is an oppositional discourse, which intellectuals like Edward Said have seen as 'resistance' and others like Gayatri Spivak have assimilated to post-colonial criticism. Rooted in ideological conviction and motivated by a polemic drive, the manifesto rewrites the scene in which Caliban appropriates language in order to curse. Now Caliban's aim is to *contra*-dict, to speak against. Retamar is just as connected to his historical moment as Rodó, and in his discursive pragmatics, imagines Che Guevara as the figure who resolves the opposition Ariel/Caliban in his evangelical advocacy on behalf of the inclusive subject of the revolution to come.[18]

In his *Caliban* of 1878 Renan had already foreseen the fate of Ariel and Caliban as revolutionaries who replace Prospero only to turn into him. Finally, destroyed by their joint revolution, Ariel laments to Caliban that the people no longer believe in them, in their magical power: 'The people are positivist', he insists. That is to say, the people have changed their discourse and are now owed a new interpretation of the world. Aimé Césaire's version is more powerful and persuasive. In his *Another Tempest* he responds to Shakespeare from an Antillean perspective, and one based on an anti-colonial practice.

We can perhaps conclude by saying that Caliban has learned to do more than curse. In reality, he has learned how to catalogue all that is rich, free and fertile in his island. He recovers his island not through the comic rebellion against Prospero, nor by his assimilation to the colonial system. Rather he achieves his goal in the act of naming the island, in listing its inhabitants and resources, in short, in the act of speech. This act of speech is an act of life, a new history. He has learned the language that judges him and that condemns him to curse (a double curse that ends up being empty profit). But it is thanks to language that he can now take charge of his own mission. Names give him back the island of abundance. He still does not know what to do with this uncertain power, but learning to speak has taught him that the world becomes valuable by virtue of the way it is named. It is in language that the power of naming – the power of transformation and recovery – will be decided.

This first American lacks a language of his own. We do not know if he even spoke one at all. It might be that he learned not only how to speak a particular language, but how to speak *tout court*. In this case he would be the first modern character to be born directly from language. He has no other memory than the alphabet of Nature which he articulates as the language of a world made for the future. Caliban leads us from the abundance of Nature and the absence of freedom to a space of becoming, to that space where he is touched by the grace of European discourse that he has already made his own on the American shores of speech. The language that he has learned is his first profit from becoming human. Caliban becomes the first self-taught philosopher of the Caribbean, the native who will discover things through their names.

America spawned many other similar creations, which took shape at the boundaries of the European imagination. If they had once been fantasies and phantoms haunting the tales of the unknown, at the frontiers of Europe's vision and representations, then they were to become the offspring of knowledge about America, the places where its inhabitants lived, what they ate and what they drank. A new narrative would in its turn give an account of the violence, hunger and misery that corroded native life. But now its critical knowledge possessed the memory of its own previous wealth. The use of language would become a common good, internalized like the very freedom of these beings created by the grammatical license of America. Learning to speak was learning how to speak in two or more languages: those of ethnic memory and that of the colonial future. The language of Europe would become the space of dominant speech, but its cartography would entail a constant transposition, an interweaving of fluent translations. Partly aided by their agglutinative form, the native languages quickly assimilated Spanish, or at the very least contaminated it. Spanish soon came to be understood as a space of negotiation.

Caliban learns to speak not merely to curse, but in order to put words to work as instruments with which to remake his double cultural inheritance. Words will oppose violence and serve the common good. Even if we must watch Caliban fade, diminished by the comedy directed at him, we can see how his figure is the product of the amalgam of European and American in the wonder and extravagance of the New World. Columbus compared the speech of one of the Caribbean islands with the howling of dogs. Other commentators believed that the indigenous languages were full of terrible sounds because they imitated the birds of the jungle. Even the scholars of the eighteenth century still believed that the languages of America had no grammar. But Shakespeare, inspired by Montaigne, shaped a much more complex and ambiguous emblem in Caliban: the offspring of colonial language who begins to speak, as though this language could be the recovery of his own world.[19]

Language is the historical form of the modern American subject, who remakes himself in the conflicts and fusions of a common speech, in this truly new world.

two

Reading:
The Children of the Letter

In recent years critics have constructed an over-simple opposition between Spanish as a Western written culture and an Andean culture that is oral and unwritten. It has been claimed that even illiterate soldiers like the conquistador Francisco Pizarro automatically belong within the rationality of writing merely by the fact of coming from a literate culture. This fact is used to explain the rapid collapse of the Inca Empire, which was powerless in the face of the invasion of the letter. However, given that the Mesoamerican cultures possessed a complex writing system, comprising pictographic signs, hieroglyphs and phonetic elements, orality cannot be simply dismissed as an inferior stage of language. It is clearly a system of representation by signs: it is a form of inscription, that is, a fully functional regime of language. Interestingly, it is Spanish that Quechua appropriates in order to widen its register. Spanish does not replace Quechua or erase it. Rather Spanish translates Quechua, decodes and preserves it, whilst

Quechua, assisted by its agglutinative character, makes use of Spanish writing. Quechua interweaves with Spanish, contaminating it with its own word order, intonations and dislocations. Every Andean writer, from Inca Garcilaso de la Vega and Guamán Poma de Ayala to José María Arguedas, will have to define his use of Spanish within the wider setting of Quechua. Rather than being adjacent languages, Quechua and Spanish become alternative, and at times superimposed, models of vision, representation and description. In other words, they become apparatuses for reading the world as a plurilingual text, constructed in Quechua and Spanish, often disputing with each other, but often hybridizing and producing elaborate fusions of heteroclite elements.

This is the communicative horizon of a bilingual or plurilingual society. More interestingly, the allegedly illiterate Quechuas were perceived as subjects with a part to play in the drama of reading, and were represented as such. This was not simply because of the opposition literate / illiterate, which produced a hierarchy on the basis of the power of writing and the mastery of Imperial Spanish. More crucially, it was because there was an intimate interaction between the 'literacy' inculcated in the Andean subject (through the tales, languages, myths, fables, and interpretations of the various native magico-religious, traditional and community orders) and the 'oralization' (or remaking of literacy) promoted by the priests and humanists. These colonial figures often had utopian aims and their knowledge of the Andean world took the form, revealingly, of translation into Spanish: their knowledge begins as a transcription from Quechua. Quechua thus becomes a language that inhabits the mediating form of Spanish. In one of those paradoxes of the colonial world, it was the very expansion of Spanish that enabled Quechua to develop.

It is a comforting assumption that written Spanish was the unifying instrument of imperial and colonial expansion (as Nebrija famously observed), but that unity might well turn out to be illusory. In fact, Spanish strengthened the native languages, which in turn contributed new vocabulary to Spanish and widened its register. The native languages not only diversified the expressive capacity of Spanish, but also adapted the new phonetic structure of five vowels to their own, three-voweled language. They imposed their own syntax on Spanish and gave the invading language a function within the native language, where it became a mechanism for the mediation and negotiation of events and interactions, movements and transpositions, cultural interweavings and historical traumas. Spanish in Quechua thus acquired the function of processing the violence of the Conquest, channelling and even human-izing it, and so preserving an instrumental memory. It also maintained the native capacity for adaptation and response – a means for permanent negotiation with all its possibilities of dialogue and restorative litigation.

From the beginning, the American natives were understood as beings whose essence was fully given by their language. Resources were allocated to establish networks of communication: an array of transla-tors was involved producing hastily compiled dictionaries and maps with local names. The dramatic element involved in communication does not come from the fact of exchange (which presupposes the indi-vidualization of the subjects involved in the barter) or even from the possibility of misunderstanding (which occurs when codes are trans-posed, and this veritable trans-coding gives rise to an extended 'mis-reading'). In fact, the communicative drama begins with the rules for communication as such. Whose turn is it to speak? How do we judge the rationality and eloquence of speech? How effective is translation? What does writing represent? In the end what is at issue is the permanent transcription of an incessant inscription. Here the different parties sought channels of transmission and legibility, coding and decoding. In this process, the natives who lacked writing were configured as the Subject of reading. They would soon discover that the new, flexible, hybrid language would yield a different writing that would allow this new nature and its different peoples to be read. The wealth of the envi-ronment and the novelty of the other, the native encyclopaedia and the Spanish archive, would all become legible through it.

The world of abundance and, later, native culture become scenes in a writing that spreads its folds over colonial practice as a territory of otherness, intersections, losses and fusions. Without Spanish, native cul-ture would have for the most part disappeared in the face of colonial violence. Without Quechua, Spanish would not have been able to main-tain a new and model civilization, which refracted Hispanic identity through Andean otherness. This different human universe, Hispano-Quechua and Andean-Christian, had a cultural richness that lacked a modern political form, save that of deferral and refusal. It was this Quechua framework that allowed the Andean nations to survive the extended violence of the national state, as they retreated to the margins of the imposed order. Here they formed the ethnically heterogeneous moments of a multinational culture, which came to transcend the inter-nal boundaries of the hegemonic state. Influenced by the ideology of the expanding market, some commentators believe that the Andean peoples have to modernize or disappear. In these circumstances, the cultural memories that derive from colonial times offer an exemplary lesson.

But what does it mean to say that Spanish made the native world literate? Not that Spanish stole the world from Quechua or Aymara, imposing itself instead, but rather that Spanish read that world in all its abundance, as if it were tracing a new map of the structures that native culture had imposed upon the world. The colonial subject took this reading as its own myth of origin. This foundation took place not in history (in itself domination and disaggregation) but in writing, which was articulated sometimes as syncretism, at other times as heterotopia, and often as hybridity. The vanquished civilization was a daughter of writing that supplied the best instrument for the reconfiguration of that civilization. Illiterate, it would be inscribed in a reading that it would then make its own. The abundance of nature and cultural history would become the spaces of reconfiguration, and in them the new American subject would learn to read and represent itself within a plethora of signs and symbols, fables and legends, histories of redemption and myths of consolation.

It was as though writing had found a new beginning in the New World. The world was mobilized as writing and man as reader, and this conjunction would articulate the project of America as a place privileged by the fertility of its signs and the promises that could be read there.

The description of American nature was an intellectual enterprise that profoundly affected the registers of knowledge, and one that had an effect on the very vision of that nature. After all, the forms of knowledge are catalogued according to the taxonomies that are available within the disciplinary archive: each new object becomes part of the series that confirms its place. But as the new objects found in America proliferated and began to exceed their place in the catalogue, they introduced a tension into their nomenclature and threw their sequencing into crisis. These prodigious objects raised a question about nature itself. This interrogation would come to confirm the more general system. A number of writers asserted that the abundance of nature was another aspect of divine grace. Perhaps in these novel fruits of the earth, God had given his favoured creatures a set of exquisite items to play with. The catalogue of the new is therefore suffused with a sense of gratification, wonder and possession.

In the Indies, Nature becomes self-referential: it quotes itself, as if it were a theatrical language full of extravagant touches. Objects resist domestication, however, and they tend towards excess and spectacle.

The European gaze, from Columbus to Hegel, has repeatedly looked upon the objects of America in astonishment and surprise. Time and again, this capacity for surprise reworked the meaning of the catalogues of species: it also reformulated the function of subjects. Order and difference would generate vastly diverse repertoires, and engender a permanent renewal of forms. Each period would construct its own catalogue of American references, figuring both bodies and the landscapes in which they are found. The representation of the American subject is both collective and discordant. It releases and is at the same time anti-canonical, as one can see in the following historical examples: the images of cannibal feasts and the voluptuous Indies; the paintings of colonial markets and the people's fiestas during the early republics; the Andean figures of Indigenism and the Negroid images of Creolism. These representations are underlain by a principle of formal freedom but also by a principle of licence derived from the marginal. When the Surrealists travelled to Mexico and the Caribbean they understood this immediately. Artaud thought that the hallucinations created by peyote gave access to a visionary freedom, alternative and complementary to everyday reality. Rivera replaced the arrangements of heroes characteristic of Renaissance painting with Mexican peasants, who no longer carried crosses and swords but baskets of flowers.

As he contemplated the diversity of nature, the great Fray Luis de Granada came to the conclusion in his *Introduction to the Symbol of Faith* that the Divinity had been lavish with plants and fruits because he wanted 'the teeming valleys to be another star-spangled heaven for us' (240).[1] But even as God took care to provide his creatures with nourishment, He did not forget to provide them with things for their recreation. The 'Sovereign Lord', he tells us, 'took special care to create so many different kinds of things for men's honest recreation, and these so plentifully that none of the bodily senses would lack objects of its own in which to delight' (241). The diversity of providence privileges the Renaissance subject and through the mirror of Nature confirms his place as elect. Natural difference, concludes Fray Luis in a spirit of joy, allows there 'to be an abundance that will sustain men as well as assuage their tedium with a variety of fruits' (242). The Creator takes pleasure in his creature and this latter recreates himself in creation in his turn.

But although Fray Luis de Granada could give an agreeable humanistic gloss to the writings of the Church Fathers, he did not neglect to point out, albeit with great delicacy and tact, that St Ambrose had seen abundance as 'the mother of lechery' (*Exacm*, v, i. 2): natural delights had been created prior to Man as temptations for him. When Fray Luis translated this verdict in his own conciliatory treatise he treated it as an exaggeration and gently corrected it. He says: 'But the Creator did not make this for temptation, but as a gift and provision for men, showing through this that he treated them as his children to be given gifts, so that the smoothness and savour of these foods would lead them to love and praise the Creator, as food and drink bound them' (223).

Maravall observed that Spanish humanist naturalists and authors of 'natural history' passed over the geographical accounts of the travellers to America in favour of the 'fantastic narratives of monsters and unconfirmed marvels that Pliny and other writers of Antiquity produced'.[2] However, contemporary accounts were often hard to verify, and could seem more fantastical than anything found in the European imagination. The accounts purported to give evidence of Paradise and the Fountain of Youth, so making those 'unconfirmed marvels' into reality. They also held that Nature itself was not only the literal trace of the Divinity, His sanctioned, universal writing, but also something in process, open, possibly even incomplete, and perhaps tending toward a resolution that was superior to the natural history that was already known. The differences and extensions to familiar European nature that America produced are not disjunctive but intriguing. Spanish representation of the natural world, which based its interpretations of diversity on the cultural and regional differences of the Peninsula, must have suffered a series of shocks, since it was forced to adjust to a novel reality. The challenges to the discourse of natural representation and its systems of classification provoked by these new discoveries would have had a massively discordant impact. Perhaps this explains why certain perceptions that seem most characteristic of the Middle Ages (such as the notion that all metals 'desire' to become gold, and that they seek each other out underground and intermix so as to turn into gold) emerge during the exploration of the New World: they are archaisms and anachronisms in an age of intense exploitation.

Fray Luis found a place within his catalogue of marvels for certain objects that had come from the Indies. He saw them as the profit that a benevolent abundance extended. His humanist system could process and incorporate every phenomenon as yet one more demonstration of Natural Good. He mentions the *bezoar* stone, a sort of antidote to poison, which comes from America, and is itself the symbol for cure. Fray Luis articulates this medical perspective as if the educative and reparative value of certain medicinal herbs were the most important thing about the Indies. He goes on to refer to the *mejoacán* that was used as a purgative, and the famous *lignum vitae* used against venereal disease. He writes: 'The provision and abundance of things that the earth gives there is so great that it declares the providence that Our Lord, like the father of a family, displays in his house, in his support, cure and provision for his children' (240). Revealingly, the notion of 'cure' comes from the discussion of America, and is no less significant for the brevity of its mention. Christian domestic economy converts the Indies into part of its panoply of contemplative enjoyment.

The providential model of abundance with its symbolic economy makes the family home into the privileged centre of the natural order. It develops as a sensual dialogue between the Renaissance Subject and the Magnanimous Creator. This model, with its reasoned yet pleasing fullness, must have had a powerfully persuasive impact on Inca Garcilaso de la Vega, an attentive reader of Fray Luis and someone whose self-appointed task was to interpret the differences and wonders of the Indies. In his readings of Pedro Mexía and Luis de Granada, Garcilaso must have concluded that the objects of the Indies acquired their function within the narrative model and discourse that classified them and gave them meaning. If the documentary truth of history could be disputed, even arbitrarily rejected (for example, in the history of his own father, who was dismissed from royal favour because of a distorted version of his role in a rebellion) then the order and interpretation of facts and things depend on their nomenclature, cataloguing and representation. In consequence, his *Royal Commentaries of the Incas* takes over the narrative model of history (which entails a contest to determine warranted truth), but the catalogue of facts and objects that he produces has a more elaborate and, in the final analysis, a more political interpretative perspective: the catalogue will introduce an American principle of difference. His narrative account will produce a history with claims on truth and credibility because it includes the certainty of testimony 'from the inside'. Garcilaso stakes a claim to the sources of knowledge. He says that he has 'suckled' on the Quechua accounts, on the tales of his Inca relatives, just as much as he has on the truth of qualified witnesses. He will produce a history that sets down the facts and then struggles over their meaning.

His 'natural history' of the fate of Spain's fruits in the Indies thus turns into a 'cultural history' of an opposite sign. The seeds of these Spanish fruits, as they grow to gigantic size in the American earth, show that the abundance created by transplantation (geographical, but also metaphorical) is further proof of historical providentialism. But at the same time it is also proof that nature is not just a current wonder, but is also something in the process of growth. Therefore the extraordinary abundance that is engendered in the Indies is the product of intermixing. New plants are created by a process of grafting, but then so are human beings, and so, finally, are cultures. If the Indies thus turn out to be the realization of Spain's potential, then natural intermixing turns out to be the model for cultural hybridization.[3] Since *mestizaje* lacks social value, Garcilaso has to undertake a laborious discursive strategy in *Royal Commentaries* in order to legitimize it: *mestizaje* is hymned as a synthesis of past history, present abundance and the space of futurity.

As well as being amalgams of past and future, Garcilaso's *Royal Commentaries* (1609) are also a compendium of humanist virtues.[4] The imperial narrative model is that of evangelization and the Conquest is given a providentialist interpretation. Garcilaso, by contrast, shows not only that the Word of Christ was already awaited in the Indies, but also that the providential could be turned back on itself: the Discovery and the Conquest make the Indies into a mirror of Spain. The things that are found in America are not substantially foreign even though they may be different. They cannot be foreign or else they could not form the rational basis for combination and amalgam: but they must be different because, as Garcilaso says, in the New World *everything* is different. In a certain sense, abundance presupposes a new birth, a second creation or re-creation, for everything begins anew, as a root or a fruit, and with increased fertility. By the same token, Garcilaso's catalogue is a history of origins, even if it is at times an apocryphal one, a version composed of other versions. Once more it is the model that narrates, and in this case the model makes America the origin of the things of Spain, building bridges across the ocean and making both parts of the empire equally necessary. The one gives greater meaning to the other. Evidence is now adduced to support stock judgements. Oviedo, Gómara, Cieza and Acosta are called as witnesses to the richness of the American soil, which permits two or three harvests per year. They also attest to the size of the novel fruits and plants that grow there, and to the extraordinary fertility that Spanish seeds display when planted in American soil. Garcilaso now adds an account of intermixing and amalgamation, which he presents as exemplary. The origin becomes a lesson for the future, and fable is seen as the beginning of history. He reorders the evidence found in compilations of legends so that *mestizaje* now becomes a model. It is harmonious, fertile, full and joyful.

At the end of chapter xxix of book ix of the *Commentaries*, Garcilaso discusses one of these founding legends that will function as a fable of history. Its purpose is both aesthetic – to make the catalogue 'On Vegetables and Herbs, and their Greatness' more pleasing – and ethical – to offer an example. This chapter on taxonomy gives us a good illustration of Garcilaso's rhetorical strategy. He begins by listing the Spanish plants that are not to be found in the Indies, arranging them by category: vegetable, seed or flower. This long list of absences demonstrates in negative fashion the miraculous presence of those very plants in America after their transplantation and acclimatization. He says:

> Of all these flowers that I have named, and those others that I cannot bring back to memory, there is such an abundance that many of them are already very dangerous, such as turnips, mustard, yerbabuena and camomile, which have spread so widely in some valleys that they have defeated the efforts and attentions that men have made to uproot them, and have prevailed to such an extent that they have scored out the ancient names of the valleys, forcing them to be called by a new name, such as the Valle de Yerbabuena on the coast which was once called Rucma, and others likewise . . . the monstrousness of size and abundance of some of the vegetables and grains they harvested was incredible [261].

This excess of presence suggests that their fertility transcends existing forms of classification, changing the map of the region and imposing another nomenclature. In this map of abundance, excess turns certain plants into ones that are 'very dangerous': their fertility has become monstrous. It is odd that Garcilaso's listing of plants does not include trees but only bushes and shrubs. Here the catalogue loses its formal quality and expands to become a rewriting of an eccentric nature. At the end of the previous chapter, Garcilaso has recommended that the olive tree be grafted on to another similar native plant, although this latter, he adds, 'does not bear fruit', unlike the grafts of Spanish fruit-trees on to those of Peru. Garcilaso's wooded valleys seem to announce a new terrain, a paradigmatic space where Nature begins forcefully anew, an object of choice as well as wonder. This humanist garden has its tacit subject. It is not the subject of the senses satisfied by the pleasures of diverse phenomena, which Fray Luis extolled, but the absent subject (the American subject) that can manage excess and give form to abundance.

Inca Garcilaso has thus far used discourse to support his account of exceptional fertility. Now he draws on testimony and 'witness statements', but here the testimony is his own and provides another chapter in his American autobiography. History becomes an eloquent recitation of examples, which will document the origins of the present world. In the fable that he will tell us, the origin of things lies in their being eaten. Garcilaso tells us that on his journey to Spain he passed through a Peruvian town where a former servant of his father's received him. At dinner the servant gave him some bread to try ('Take this bread and eat of it'). The loaf had been baked in the very heart of abundance, where an extraordinarily fertile wheat could produce innumerable loaves (261). Garcilaso immediately turns this event into a story: 'On my telling this self-same tale to Gonzalo Silvestre . . . he said that this was nothing' (261). This allows Garcilaso to tell another tale, that of the famous radish 'of such extraordinary size that five horses could be tethered in the shadow of its leaves' (262), and which was cut down and carried to an inn 'where many people made a meal of it'. And in Córdoba, Garcilaso continues, the gentleman Don Martín de Contreras told him: 'I am an eye witness to the size of the radish . . . and afterwards I ate the radish along with the rest'. And as if to intensify the exceptional quality of nature, this 'noble gentleman' adds: 'And in the Valley of Yúcay, I ate a piece from a lettuce that weighed seven and a half pounds' (262).

Subsequently, it becomes necessary to pass from an oral history of origins to written authorities that warrant his belief in abundance. The writings of Father Acosta provide guarantees that there were places where vegetables 'much exceeded the fertility of those here'. Garcilaso emphasizes the logic of his argument: 'It is Father Acosta whose authority so reinforces my spirit that I can speak without fear of the great fertility that those lands showed in the beginning when they were planted with the fruits from Spain, with such incredible and frightening results' (263).

A historian might have finished his chapter with this endorsement of his catalogue, but Garcilaso needs to finish the chapter with a fable, an example that converts the origin of the present into an exemplary account. The beginning did not consist merely of the freely grown edible fruit: it also contained the prohibition on tasting and knowledge that writing represents. From the spoken story to the written law, the fable of the melons with which he concludes the chapter suggests that the regime that governed the cultivation of fruits presupposed the regime of property and servitude, the order of punishment.

In the work of Acosta that Garcilaso cites, the priest had mentioned 'the melons that are found in the Ica Valley in Peru: of such sort that their roots produce a stock and last for years, and each one yields melons, and they are pruned just like trees, something that happens in no part of Spain to my knowledge'. Fray Luis de Granada, in the chapter of his *Introduction to the Symbol of the Faith* entitled 'On the fertility, plants and fruits of the earth', comments on the 'marvellous virtue' of the seeds which is reparative, such that 'from a melon seed there grows a melon vine, and in each melon there is such an abundance of seeds with which to restore and conserve the species' (253). Gonzalo Fernández de Oviedo in his chapter 'On plants and herbs' (232–47) had pointed out that 'There are so many melons that bestrew the Indies and they are so large that commonly they can weigh half an arroba, or one, or even more; some are so large, that an Indian has a job carrying one on his back'.[5] Further on he says: 'in the lands of Veragua and on the Corobaco Islands, there are tall fig-trees and they have leaves which are longer and wider than the fig-trees of Spain and bear figs as large as small melons'.

Garcilaso's fable takes up far more space than the arguments earlier in the chapter, and is seemingly well known:

> And because the first melons that were found in the region of Los Reyes gave rise to an amusing tale, it would be well if we mention it here, so that we might see the simplicity of the Indians of olden times. The story goes that a neighbour of that city, one of the first conquistadors, called Antonio Solar, a noble man, had some property that he had inherited in Pachacámac, four leagues from Los Reyes, which had a Spanish overseer who looked after his hacienda, and who sent his master ten melons, which took two Indians to carry them on their backs, according to their custom. They also took with them a letter. As they left, the overseer told them: 'Do not eat any of these melons, because if you do, the letter will tell of it'. They went on their way, and after half a day they laid their burden down to take a rest. One of them, moved by temptation said to the other, 'Should we not know what our master's fruit tastes of?' The other said, 'No, because if we eat any of them, the letter will say so, so the overseer said.' The other replied, 'There's a remedy for that: let us throw the letter behind that wall, and that way it will not see us eating, and so will not be able to say anything.' His companion was happy with the advice, which he quickly followed and then they ate one of the melons.

We know very well what happens next. One of the Indians suggests that in order to avoid suspicions they should equalize the loads that they are carrying, so they eat another melon. They arrive with eight melons, but the letter says there should be ten, and the master wants the missing ones back. The Indians lie and say that they were only given eight, but the master replies, letter in hand, 'this letter says that you were given ten, and that you have eaten the other two'. Garcilaso concludes: 'Gómara refers to another story, which happened in Cuba just as the island was being won. Is it not marvellous that such ignorance should be common in such different regions and amongst such different nations, since the simplicity of the Indians of the New World was all of a kind?' (263). The conclusion is revealing: the fable is repeated in other places, but in every case it is true. Garcilaso does not wonder about the veracity of the tale. He does not appear to suspect that if the story is told about figs and melons it is unlikely to be historical truth but rather fable. He seems to believe that the Indians would have done the same thing in different places: they would have eaten the novel fruit and every time the letter (the writing of the law) would have found them out.

But for Garcilaso what is decisive is not whether the tale is true or not but its deeper moral, its subtle lesson. First, Pachacámac was a ceremonial place, the most important religious centre on the Peruvian coast. There is a new property regime in which Antonio Solar (the surname [Solar: of the sun] seems to be emblematic, as is that of Pedro [rock] Serrano [man of the mountains], the castaway of another famous fable within the book) is one of the 'first conquistadors' but at the same time is the owner of 'inherited property'. He has inherited the ancient sacred space on to which 'his hacienda', the new form of property now opens. Perhaps this location is not a matter of chance: melons are associated with Ica, to the south of Lima, as Father Acosta had already pointed out in Garcilaso's quotation from him.[6] Second, there is the pleasure of the story, which Garcilaso narrates with great gusto and touches of irony, but also with a didactic subtlety, mindful of his responsibility as narrator. But what is also notable is his discretion, as he sidesteps the issue of punishment, which is foregrounded in other versions of the story. The Indians' innocence blithely leads them into lying, and the lesson they learn is sufficient. The truth convinces and the Law will find out any secret. But there is thirdly a hidden, paradoxical allusion. The question about knowledge (and taste) of the unknown fruit is a question that might be said to disturb the self-referential system that Fray Luis de Granada has set up. It offers the possibility that a subject of

Christian humanism might not have tasted fruit forbidden by the law of property. Knowledge through taste, this audacious gesture made by guiltless Indians, is, moreover, organized around another polarity: the fruit comes from our master's land, but it also comes from our land. It comes from over there, from Spain, but at the same time it also comes from here, it is a fruit grown in Pachacámac, with the labour of these self-same Indians, who are no longer the owners of the product of their labour: they must taste (and know) in secret what cannot be claimed as their own in public. Writing, the word of the law, which sees everything and recounts everything, has come to occupy the subjectivity of the native subject. It is this self that the exemplary fable (*exempla*) recovers as an innocent subject: an innocent man, an apprentice at letters but already a student of law, and the fable achieves this by its deployment of an inclusive catalogue of humanist features.

This fable of origins has itself no origin: it appears and reappears in different places in America (from the Caribbean to Brazil) and in most cases it is figs rather than melons that are eaten. In *El Nuevo Mundo descubierto por Cristóbal Colón* (*The New World Discovered by Christopher Columbus*), probably written between 1598 and 1603 and published in 1614, Lope de Vega uses one of the most widespread versions of the fable, in which the native eats the fruit on two occasions, and the second time tries in vain to hide the letter. Lope prefers to have oranges as the first temptation, and olives as the second.

Hugo Herman, by contrast, in his *De prima scribendi origine et universa rei literariae antiquitate* (1617) gives another version:

> What I have to tell could seem rather funny, but in truth it was told by a religious man who had returned from Brazil in 1574. Our Ludovicus Richeome writes in a book entitled *L'Adie de l'Ame* that a Peruvian slave, the property of a European noble, who then lived in Brazil, was ordered to take a letter and a basket of figs to a member of his master's family – also a European noble. Whilst he was on the road, the slave, attracted by the aroma and freshness of the fruits, ate a good part of them, even though he had been explicitly warned by his master not to do so, and kept the letter well hidden throughout. On receiving and reading the letter, the noble's kinsman immediately knew what had happened and reproached the slave for having eaten the fruit. The slave was surprised that the noble could know what had happened and denied it. In his turn, the noble brought the letter as witness, to which the

slave asserted that the paper lied and that writing could not bear witness. The slave was sent back with another letter which gave an account of what had happened. His master ignored the matter and a few days later again sent the servant off with another basket of figs and a letter in which their number was specified. Having pondered the question a while, the slave made sure that he was far enough away from the house and, hiding the letter under the stone he was sitting on, said to himself: 'Now neither the letter, nor Argos with the hundred eyes, nor even those with the eyes of Luince can see me enjoying this fruit.' Having said this he emptied the basket and prepared to enjoy the figs, after which only a few remained. With the few that were left, he took the letter to the noble and the latter discovered how many had been sent, even though barely half that number remained in the basket. Again he remonstrated with the slave and scrutinized his hands and pockets. The slave tried to defend himself, showing his empty jacket and cast doubt on the veracity of the letter: for it could not even for a second have seen him or spied on him from under the stone where it had been hidden. In the face of the slave's ignorance, there was no way of convincing him that the letter, written with his master's own pen, gave the exact number of figs.[7]

Father Hugo's long-winded style repeats the slave's protestations as he stubbornly defends his version of events, making the slave's ignorance into a form of bad faith. The story becomes more domestic than exemplary and has lost its subtle irony as the slave has gained in individuality. For this very reason, writing now has nothing to teach. And if writing comes out unscathed, then the slave is altogether excluded from its system: his greater ignorance lies in the fact that he does not recognize that he is ignorant. Therefore, since there has been no lesson, there can be no fable, and since there is no example, there can be no emblem. All that remains is a cruder and more exclusionary story of social division into castes and classes.

Perhaps the writers who produced these glosses on the fable of the first fruits grown in the Indies did not read each other and were limited to collecting oral versions of the fable or to quoting secondhand versions. Each writer, in his turn, gave another interpretation of the fable of the Indian(s) secretly eating their master's fruit under the unanswerable gaze of the letter. Thus the referent of the origin is not oral fabulation ('fables of record') that Garcilaso had seen at the beginning of his own Cuzco genealogy, but writing as truthful documentation, which explains both the origin and the incorporation of the new into the systems of writing.

Nevertheless, writing can only be the referent of its own interpretation, of the catalogue that it feeds and that reorders it. Thus amongst all the versions, the fable that Garcilaso quotes is not only the most elegant, in the symmetry of its internal revelations and pleasing complicities, but also the version that turns back on itself through writing. In the end, this version gives the word – the taste of the fruit and the knowledge of writing – back to the Indians who are innocent of their own simplicity, but nevertheless capable of questioning and learning.

The writing of the fable thus restores them as subjects of voice and letter. It is as if writing were in the final analysis the real forbidden fruit that Garcilaso offers to his distant compatriots in the republic of the fable, where the reparations made by the humanist who holds history in his hands are always a reordering in the name of a poetic justice. If the future culture of hybridity has a place, it is because fruits are different but man, being a sum and amalgam of knowledge is the same. He is a universal creature inclined to the knowledge of memory and the taste of the present and the different. Another virtue of the *Royal Commentaries*, in their sweet melancholy and call to the future, is that the poetry of history becomes at once both a proverbial lesson of Nature and a call to Rational Community.

The perspective of a new American cultural history allows us to re-read these fables of memory as the history of the acquisition of literacy and we discover that abundance of description (the wealth of the Indies) is found in the acquisition of writing (the making literate not merely of the native but of the new land of America). America is a sort of writing in need of reading, and despite their differences, the historians and chroniclers agree in making the native into the subject who is unlettered yet at the same time is already part of the drama of letters. Even those who cannot read are in the end read within a writing that legislates against them, explains them, sanctions and punishes them: in short, gives them their destiny. Their lack is unfolded on to nature's writing of abundance: the Indians, as in Garcilaso's fable, are already immanently prepared to read having been touched by the grace of writing. These new readers will, then, not only discover the renewed goods of the Old World but the full evidence of their own New World. This 'novelty' makes them doubly 'new born', as if they were pupils and disciples of the humanism that reads the world as a common good, and writing as shared memory.

If Caliban learned to speak in order to recognize the names of the abundance that surrounded him, then Garcilaso's naive Indians learn that writing is knowledge of a new taste. They recognize that they are already read by this writing that implicates them and which they must come to possess. For that reason, learning to read will be the characteristic fable of the New World. The colonial subject reappropriates writing so that instead of being the object of natural history he becomes the agent of a cultural history. The New World becomes a new form of memory. Every history, every chronicle will dispute the facts and will be produced in a Spanish that must discover a new beginning as a language. This must happen not merely in the name of a testimonial truth, but by virtue of the other, the Man of America, and the certainty of his testimony. As a new subject of reading, American Man discovers in the powers of writing that his coded fate can be fought over. The struggles over interpretation will mark the dramas of the colonial history of the subject of writing, of his ethnic memory and cultural difference.

In the end, the emblem of Caliban, native accounts of writing, the story of Atahualpa and the book, Garcilaso's discussion of translation, Guaman Poma's admonitions to *mestizo* scribes, and finally, the history of reading and writing in America, that extraordinary exercise in inscribing a world as the renewed origin of a Paradisiacal nature, both archaic Arcadia and millenarian utopia, are, looked at properly, the exemplary history of language remaking its humanizing functions (speaking, reading, writing) and its communal operations (translation, exchange, classification, conversation, prayer). It is as if language were reinvented at every juncture of the discovery and exploration of America, and that these functions and operations construct a fertile space (a mythical scene of writing) and a potential subject (offspring of humanist discourse, made out of its promises). The reading / writing of the American world is therefore an enterprise of enormous register. It exceeds the genres of documentation and unfolds and is displaced as another language. It is put to the test by the lushness and novelty of America, but is also capable of responding to that novelty and abundance as its disquieting representation (control, but also excess, dominion but also difference). Newer than the New World, this language diversifies its powers to become adequate to its world. It is fought over by interpretations and accounts, by ascriptive definition and demarcating inscription. In the cultural history of Spanish in the Indies, the subjects of speech and the characters of interlocution demonstrate that a transitional writing, a dialogical reading, belongs to America.

In what follows we will see how the American hero of the letter that gives him his existence, even if he cannot read it yet becomes capable of a series of strategies of recording and translation forms that will grant legitimacy (*oratio*) to his place in the New World (*ratio*) that is to his own writing. Constructed by language, this American subject will appropriate the power of this writing to give an account of his long heritage and his wider future.

three

Writing:
The Alphabet of Abundance

The *New Chronicle and Good Government* (1612–16) by Felipe Guamán Poma de Ayala is an encyclopedia of the Andean world, an account of the different forms of knowledge that exist in this multiethnic and plurilingual space. He constructs this in two contrasting ways. In the first, parallel yet conflicting information systems (Andean and Spanish) are brought together and combined. The second proves to be a means of systematically preserving the information of the native cultures that had undergone the violence of colonization. The logic of this process of combination reaffirms the Andean models and practices of reproduction, exchange and consumption. The irrational violence of the Conquest in its despoliation of those practices had threatened the very existence of Andean culture and its communal knowledge. One of Guamán Poma's most characteristic and systematic discursive strategies is to rest ideas of the common good on cultural representations of abundance and to show how collective discontent leads to political representations of scarcity. I will discuss both discourses in relation to one of the central metaphors of the book: food.[1]

The categorization and classification of foodstuffs form a language in itself. The process that runs from sowing the plants to harvesting and preparing them preserves the memory of this language, not merely as an archive but as a contemporary reality that has been augmented by Spanish with its array of new plants, fruits and foods. Guamán Poma is one of the very few native intellectuals whose testimony has been preserved. As a *letrado*, he lived through the colonial experience in a number of ways. First, he was in the service of the colonizers, as translator to Cristóbal de Albornoz, whose mission was to root out idolatry. Secondly, he was the critic of colonization, denouncing the degradation of native life in his monumental chronicle, which takes the traditional form of a Letter to the King, protesting against the endemic violence of the colonial process. Last, he was a cultural agent. In this final role he wrote a treatise on the future of America, which is a systematic discussion of remedial projects that would turn the remembered pre-Conquest world into the basis of a harmonious future.[2] Foodstuffs form an aspect of the language of the world. The new technology of writing, acquired from the Spanish, recognizes, articulates and fixes this language, providing a catalogue of the riches of Peru, a lesson on survival and a course in native wisdom. Even though writing is the instrument of the law and punishment and even though its intermediaries – scribes (*escribanos*), priests and administrators – abuse the Indians with the letter of the law in their hands, Guamán Poma recommends that his kinsmen, the Andean Indians, learn Spanish and learn how to write, so that written Spanish might become an instrument of service, criticism and denunciation. This consistent and determined appropriation of writing and the Spanish language allows Guamán Poma to preserve Quechua itself. His book deliberately includes several Andean languages, including his own first language, that is, Spanish as written under the influence of Quechua orality, a hybrid of the two. Thus, language is itself the first demonstration of the unequal fusion of the two worlds, but with the demonstration carried out in the other language, Spanish.[3] Learning to write, then, leads to a superior knowledge of the new world produced by intermixing and amalgamation. Guamán Poma understands that writing is the most powerful weapon in the hands of his people. His fertile appropriation of the natural world makes it part of the human universe: food will be one of the axes of this translation and conversion. As we will see, recording the natural world is an active form of control: both a rationality of use and consumption and a means to preserve names, treatments, knowledge and learning. But the technology is not merely a means of recording, it is also a form of politics: Guamán Poma turns the language of food and foodstuffs into a form of social education, into a means of controlling and preventing misery and degradation. In demonstrating the possibility of abundance, he constructs a vision of a commensal utopia. He imagines the decrees that would put an end to poverty, a project that would take the form of a collective feast in a community created in the squares of the townships, where food would be shared in a communal repast. He seems to suggest that whilst the vocabulary of food gives us back the products themselves, collective repast is a discourse that feeds us on the future, that allows us communally to eat tomorrow.[4]

The word *comida* (food) appears in Spanish in 1490. In the *Journal* of his voyage, Columbus talks incessantly about 'eating' as one of the formal moments of exchange, and he continued to stress the lengthy periods of time that a chief and his people would spend at table (26 December). In Guamán's *Chronicle* 'food' acquires a complex set of values and becomes a term whose semantic field is remarkably wide. John Murra (1980) has observed that in the Andes the natives acquired land at birth and conceived of it as a source of food. The Quechua term *sapsi* ('something shared in common with everyone') denotes land, flocks and textiles. Guamán is, in effect, repeating this term, as if it had no translation, to refer to the collective reserves of common wealth. When he has to confront the paradigm of abundance with the counter-paradigm of scarcity, *sapsi* becomes the latent source of a knowledge that is inexhaustible, which redistributes goods and sustains communal life.[5]

In Guamán Poma's account, abundance is explained by the cosmic order itself. He says: 'Inday is of a higher rank than Castile and Rome and Turkey. So it was called the land of the day, Inday, land of the wealth of gold and silver' (35). And he adds: 'in the world that God has created there is no place of greater wealth, because this place is at the sun's highest degree.' The mythical cosmology that orders the universe above and below is explained by the Divine Will, and in turn explains why the King of Spain is 'very rich'. However, this definition of wealth belongs to the logic of the dominant values: what flows from God to the king and thence to the Indies is gold and silver. What flows in the opposite direction, from Andean origins to the present-day Indian, becomes consubstantial with food. In this 'fourth age of the Indians' Guamán speaks of 'the abundance of food and wide number of livestock and great number of Indians, since God has permitted the Indians to have [the age]' (58). There are thus two parallel logics of wealth: that of metals and that of fertility. He also says that the Indians of this age 'had sufficient food and gifts' (55) and 'There was no pestilence nor hunger nor loss of life nor drought because there was much rain' (58). Fertility is the horizon of the natural, and is sustained by land and water, the common sources of food.

Lack and scarcity also belong to the cosmic plan, but only in the form of a disruption of order. Thus we read, 'pestilence, God's punishment, struck the maize and the potatoes, and hailstones fell on the food' (74). The opposition warm–cold (sun–frost) underlies the opposition abundance–scarcity and forms one of a series of structuring oppositions that writing rehearses and seeks to resolve. In the quotation, the hailstone falling on the food-crops is an image that suggests how wide Guamán's use of the term 'food' is as he applies it to the sown fields themselves. Later, he will even say that 'food' was sown.

In the 'Laws and Statutes of the Incas', Guamán Poma takes on the voice of the communal law: 'We hereby order that throughout the Kingdom there be an abundance of food.' Whilst the Spanish king can preside over riches in gold, the native king will govern food. Juridical discourse, the superior code of the political order, is reappropriated by a restitutive rationality, that seeks not only to resist but also to repair and heal. This rationality will denounce but will also seek to negotiate the new networks of rearticulation. There then follows the order:

> Let much maize and potato be sown, likewise okra, and let there be caui, caya, chuño, tamos [various root crops], chochoca [ground up dry maize], quinua, ulluco, masua and every food even including herbs so that they can be dried and eaten all year round and let there be sown as commons and sapsi maize, potatoes, chili, magno, cotton . . . And every year let them be accounted for [165].

The list is thus a compendium of agrarian knowledge clearly derived from agricultural practice, and it is equally obvious that the novel Spanish produce has simply been brought under Andean principles for the ecological management of available land within its economics of conservation. Guamán's lists are not mere accumulations, but a complete explanation in themselves: they include seeds, tubers, fruits, maritime herbs and produce from various climatic zones. Conservation is always fundamental to Andean rationality: the mode of production is always a mode of preservation. The discourse on food is structured around the following oppositions. There is a first pair, sowing and harvesting, which are practices that imply the use of irrigation and fertilizers. These are organized around the categories of ripe and unripe (the degree of ripeness of fruit has to be recognized by the tenderness of its flesh). Then there is a second pair: the produce and its transformation into preserves, a category beyond that of ripeness, with implications of storage and durability. This is a process that is ultimately defined by the order of distribution. To be able to eat all year round requires that crops be sown by the community as a whole. The process begins with this cultural and political definition of labour and this in turn sets in place a critique of disorder, scarcity and hunger.

The social character of food can be discerned in one of Guamán's statutes (*ordenanzas*), which enjoins that the people 'should eat in the public square' (166). This concept is repeated as the most civilized, that is the most political form of contribution to the common weal as well as to the alleviation of generalized misery, since the poor and the hungry form part of the collective banquet. Bakhtin's work has alerted us to the centrality of the 'public square' in popular culture, but in Guamán Poma's work this 'public space' has an allegorical form, paradoxically synthesizing Andean knowledge and a proposal for political reform, as it combines the square's traditional functions (ritual, compensation for inequality and affirmation of the group) with its modern aspects (popular, operative and Christian). On the one hand it invokes the Andean model: the public square is the place where abundance is shared, and the place, therefore, of collective reparative social control. On the other hand, Guamán witnesses the loss of the public square, whose communal logic is replaced by that of the dispersal imposed by the logic of exploitation.[6] Behind the economic opposition lie the different models of social life: the practice of reciprocal redistribution and the violence of unequal exchange. But politics here is not just criticism but also a demonstration of how change might come about. Time and again, Guamán Poma asserts that the role of the public square needs to be recovered, in the name of Christian values themselves, and as their best exemplification. This is one of Guamán's favourite representations of abundance: food shared by 'the princes, the well-born and the lowly'. In these combinations of reparative meaning, Guamán Poma also combines times, and instead of speaking about the Inca past, he talks about the Christian present as a recovery of the Andean past. An Inca statute says: 'Let all eat out of charity and since it has been use and custom ever since the first people and law and good work and compassion of God in this land.' If use and

custom imply a cultural definition that has become the norm, the combination of the Inca and the Christian God is confirmed by the alliance
of Topa Ynga Yupanqui (who was the source of the statutes) and the
viceroy Francisco de Toledo, who 'informed himself of these ancient
laws and statutes, and revived the best of them' (167). These were then
ratified by Philip II himself, who ordered that 'all should eat in the public square and should feast there'. Thus, the gods and the kings might
change but the public square remains the same: it occupies the present
but is at the same time eternal. This articulation of authorities, institutions and resolutions is the culmination of Guamán's post-colonial
strategy, which unfolds at the very centre of the colonial order. It seeks
to surpass the degradation and violence imposed by the controlling
powers from the site of those very powers, making them responsible for
carrying out the laws and practices that will make the Administration
work for the survival and expansion of native culture.[7]

In the section devoted to 'inspections' (*visitas*), Guamán establishes
another opposition, that between the sown fields and the hospital. The
first comes from the discourse of abundance, the second from the discourse of lack. Guamán says that in the time of the Incas, 'they did not
think to have a hospital, since their fields would benefit [the needy] and
thus there was no need to have a hospital for the poor, the old, the blind,
the crippled, those in need of alms' (175). 'There was no need of hospital nor alms in the sacred and policed order of that kingdom, like no
other kingdom that Christendom nor the Infidels had, nor could have
no matter how Christian' (177). The series of combinations and oppositions lead writing to make abundance hyperbolic by presenting the
senselessness of lack: hospital and alms are the palliatives of disorder,
whilst seed crops and inheritance are the virtues of order. European
ideas, like 'the policed and sacred order', 'Christendom and Infidels'
serve to reinforce native difference, which demonstrates its greater value
by its articulation within Occidental discourse. This demonstration is a
political interpretation.[8]

As he reviews the months, Guamán defines them as seasons of
foods. February is the 'time of waters', he says, because it rains heavily
and there is 'an abundance of *yuyos* (weeds) but a great dearth of food'
(213). This suggests that the *yuyo*, a maritime plant is not quite a food
plant, or only a lesser one. People get sick from eating *yuyos* and from
'eating things when they are unripe and too much green fruit and from
being hungry'. Food is only ripe in March, and sacrifices 'of gold and
silver' are made invoking 'abundance'. March is called *Pacha pucui Quilla*

(the month of the ripening of the earth). '*Pacha Puccuy* means, *pacha*, world, *pucoy*, "much" because in this month of March it rains in buckets and the land of the kingdom is awash with water' (213). This surfeit is equivalent to a famine. In May, on the other hand, things change: 'This is the month of abundance: all the stores are filled up as are the houses of the poor' (219). Once more, an image of past practices of redistribution is invoked and introduced into the present. In June, there is an inspection made to see that 'there is an abundance throughout the kingdom, so that each and everyone has enough to eat, rich and poor alike. And the orphans did not perish for lack of food because they have their seed-crops and sow their *ayllus* from their part' (221). Even if the tenses of Guamán's Spanish are unclear, and the Quechua substrate of his language reorganizes grammatical temporality, it seems clear that the past still exists in the present, as its greatest lesson. It is not in history but culture that contemporary reality has a debt to knowledge. The coming together of rich and poor, for example, is an event in the present, a resolution through traditional order. Memory is an instrument, which can realize itself by resolving conflict in the present. It insists on invoking and displaying the signs of abundance, although in the first place it documents the evidence of hunger. It is not enough merely to denounce hunger: it is necessary to show that abundance is the natural order of things, a conception that had been privileged by European chroniclers and scholars, both as a good conceded by divine will and as an economic good intrinsic to the Indies. Guamán Poma takes over the wide semantic field of the concept in order to reveal it as a natural good *and* as a social good produced by native rationality. The calendar of abundance, which is also an alphabet of the world, occupies all of time, making it material and legible.[9] When he talks about July, Guamán adds another meaning to his use of 'food': 'It is in this month that they first begin to sow food in the Andes' (223).

In October, man is defined as 'he who eats' in this praise of Runa Camac: 'Creator of Man, maker of those who eat / Please send your waters and rain to your peoples' (229). But it is not only the living who eat, since in November, 'they take out the dead from their wrappings . . . and they give them something to eat' (231). The cycle of crops and foods thus presupposes the beginning and the end, but is never interrupted and includes both terms in its permanent ceremony. In his *Journal* Columbus evaluates plants according to their utility, but Guamán operates a radically other rationality, where plants are the very source of life, the language of the world. Life is not separated from the world but is its privileged product. Food requires the cosmic order, but it also needs human labour: it is the fruit of collaboration between earth and man. Thus we can see in the descriptions of the stores (308 ff) that preservation is the superior state of food. In the *collca* the following are kept before being shared out among the people: *chuno, muraya* and *caya*, which are different forms of the same type of fruit which have been treated and conserved. Likewise *charcay*, salted meat, is stored here. Guamán Poma thus presents the knowledge of food as an account of the common sources of reparation and healing. The management of the land and its produce contains the memory of the culture, the store of a discourse that nourishes survival and resistance, systematic reappropriation and complementary, inclusive negotiation. It can be seen as a project of augmented cultural difference. In the chaos that follows great natural disasters, or plagues, or divine punishment, food goes rotten. This loss is as unnatural as the violence that decimated the native population. Because of this, the *suyuyoc*, the administrators, were obliged to oversee 'the seed-stores of every type, foods and fruits and clothes and livestock and mines and whatever belonged to the community and *sapci*', and their work was 'to increase them and not let them be taken away nor to let there be lawsuits, so that there be justice' (321). In the end, justice is the practice of distribution, which supports all the combinations of abundance. It is, in other words, the rationality of the community. By contrast, the other rationality, that of gold and power, meant that, as the chronicler explains, the conquerors of Peru 'At times did not eat for thinking about gold and silver' (347). Once more, abundance as an economic logic takes a different direction to abundance as natural philosophy.

It is no coincidence then that when Guamán comes to pass judgement on the disorder imposed by local government (poverty, lack, moral destitution, chaos) he makes food the image of violence and pillage. Time and again he tells us that the *corregidor* (local official) and his people want 'to eat at the cost of the poor Indians of this realm' (474). 'Each and every one of them demands his *mitayo* [Indian forced to labour] and to eat without cost' (476 and 480). The principle of disorder that the *corregidor* introduces tears apart the social and cultural network: everyone seeks to work for him by 'eating' the Indian, robbing and exploiting him. Instead of multiplying, livestock and croplands 'have been done away with' (495). This collapse is a powerful vision of the violence and irrationality of colonial practice, which destroyed knowledge and created and reproduced scarcity. The steward practised the same abuse: 'if he loses ten sheep, then he makes them pay twenty sheep and takes away all their daily wages and gives them nothing to eat' (496). The same happened in the *tambos* (local inns) where abuse was rife. Spanish beggars, he says, 'eat and rob and help themselves without paying . . . they steal from the people and from the poor Indians' (523). Guamán's mythic Andean thought is the internal thread within the network that unifies his denunciations, making them into powerful protests and demands on the authorities. His capacity for criticism allows him to develop a more complex strategy of novel conjunctions and openings, a properly intellectual work that creates a space for creative affirmation within the degradation and crisis of his times.

In his representation of scarcity, Guamán not only protests about and illustrates the destruction of knowledge, but also shows how the dominant groups do not even follow their own economic rationality (buying, selling, exchange) and operate as a destructive, mechanical force. This is a representation of scarcity as reductive, sustained by violence. Guamán demands restitution (530), following his own historical logic, and interpreting the Christian discourse of colonization to the letter.

In this context, the famous drawing *Indian Poverty* (655) says that there are 'six animals that eat and that poor Indians are afraid of' and they are: snake, *corregidor*; tiger, Spaniards in the *tambos*; lion, estate owner; fox, priest; cat, scribe; mouse, head chief. 'These animals strip the poor Indians bare and there is no remedy against them', Guamán protests. In his reappropriation of the iconic model of virtues and vices, lack and scarcity are represented as an unnatural world, as a world turned upside down. The subjects of domination are animals that eat the bodies of the poor. This is a powerful denunciation of the Spanish, but it also demonstrates the lack of meaning within the colonial experience, which has inverted all roles and robbed life itself of its sense. In another drawing (737), this economy of an upturned world is illustrated by the prince who gives presents to the *corregidor* who asks for more. Communal preservation has been replaced by individual accumulation.

The priests also steal, as do the inspectors and even the head chiefs, in this ferocious despoliation that is opposed to the earth and subjugates the body. The body is the true centre of the colonial experience and its usurpation by power is illustrated in meticulous detail. As is well known, however, Guamán Poma neither surrendered nor remained silent. Against all evidence, omens and fears, he returns to his own: he provides answers, brings together different aspects of knowledge and recommends reforms. His *Chronicle* thus functions as a true *collca*, as a storehouse of the

preserved learning and resistance that can be made out of the combinations of Andean cultural plurality. The fact that this storehouse is built
out of the language of domination only goes to show the direction
which Guamán Poma, like Andean culture itself, must take in order to
resist and to open up its own space. This would be one of a systematic
reappropriation, organizing inherited learning and allowing growth
through the incorporation of new knowledge. This practice, then,
would be based on a structure of parallel combinations and tolerated
differences. Here lies the explanation for the enduring native capacity
for control and wisdom.[10]

It is clear that Guamán's attempts to re-establish order could be
made only within the ruling colonial system, even as he redefined matters in Andean terms: these were articulated within imperial power but
produced their own ethnic resolutions. This was his project, even if it
was daily denied by empirical reality with its degradation and meaning-
lessness. On the other hand, Guamán is firmly rooted in the empirical,
and when he has to make recommendations for reform he does so at the
most basic level, that of the domestic. Thus, he recommends that the
corregidores leave 'the province clean', without '[unnecessary] actions
and expenditure', and suggests that 'eating a hen will suffice, and a chick-
en for supper' (471). And when he recommends that such food ought to
be enough, it is because 'Indians when they eat or are hungry do not
prey on their people' (806). He thinks that the salary of Indian mayors
should consist of a chicken from every house that they inspect (739),
and that Indian aldermen should receive a rabbit every six months from
the houses they visit as their salary. These calculations look to a restorative economic balance in the midst of bitter violence. Perhaps Jesus
Christ himself would have to come back, he says at one point: 'There is
no one to come back for the poor in Christ, so He will have to come
back again Himself, come back to the world for his poor creatures' (453).
And Guamán himself will practise what he preaches: when he comes
across a Spanish beggar, he states: 'out of the little that I in my poverty
possess, I will give you something to eat' (501).

Guamán subtly confronts the colonial authorities with figures of
Andean authority, and even though those same native chiefs and leaders
are corrupted by egotism, Guamán proceeds to outline how a parallel
ethnic order might function, thus eloquently revealing the contradictions of the present. In this sense, his satire becomes sharper with regard
to the clergy, as in his mockery of Father Alvadán (578–9), whom he
compares unfavourably with a Franciscan, who is a true father since he

behaves charitably towards the Indians. In the drawing on page 597, food becomes the substance of a moral example: 'Take this bread and eat of it, my poor man', he says. The emblem of this contradictory knowledge is the Indian astrologer Juan Yunpa, whom Guamán sketches on page 829, describing him as 'the poet astrologer who knows the rounds of the sun and the moon, and the times of eclipses and stars and comets, Sunday and month and year and the four winds of the world so that we can sow food as of old'. He also tells us that this wise man, some 150 years old, 'eats more heartily than a boy'. The sequential list of heavenly bodies and astronomical phenomena aligns the forces of good (sun and moon) with those of evil (eclipses, comets), and also aligns the calendar with the traditional four-part symbolic organization of the world (upper and lower, and these moieties then divided in half). The heavens are read in terms of the earth, since the stellar family regulates the fertility of the earth. These wise men, Guamán goes on, employ their knowledge to 'sow and harvest each year's food' (830). They also 'distinguish between the foods and meats and fruits that can be eaten and those that cannot because of the sicknesses of the month'. These seasonal illnesses which affect sowing echo throughout the *Chronicle* as latent possibility, the underside of the norm, and correspond to a mythical background where productive rationality yields its place to subversive forces, forces of uncertainty, which may yet be regenerative and purifying. In these instances, the *Chronicle* reveals a rich subjectivity, which unties and interrupts series and correspondences at their margins and boundaries. If colonial practice represses and takes sanctions against difference, the latter resumes its course outside what has been mapped, as an excess that emerges from crisis.[11]

But as always in Guamán's work, everything comes back to the most durable meaning, to the strength of the community. Throughout his argument Guamán denounces abuses and violence at the same time as he makes the paradigm of abundance real, and recommends a reordering of affairs through preservation, distribution and charity, which will re-establish community. For that very reason, lack and scarcity can be explained only as absence. The Indians are poor, he says, because they 'cannot enjoy what belongs to their communities' (840). Guamán adds the native produce to the imported Spanish crops and livestock, and lists the fields according to their social function. This exhibition of abundance no longer distinguishes produce by their origin but by their incorporation into the order of culture, where they support the new social order. He will go on to say that this is where difference is glaringly revealed. It has no social place but is sustained in ethnic memory, in the discourse of reappropriation. In the book it is mapped as the need to resolve things from the point of view of difference. Thus the empirical becomes theoretical, customary practice becomes paradigmatic and the past underlies the ruins of the present. And in a final intellectual move, this differentiation of the communal from the anti-communal becomes a political fable within the discourse of a vanquished but nevertheless resistant humanity, which can make its knowledge universal, and make the world Andean through its lessons of good government. Guamán Poma concludes with a new hyperbolic claim, of clearly utopian character. The Indians, he says, 'have had up to this time the law of mercy, which no generation of Spanish Christians, Moors, Turks, Frenchmen, Jews, Englishmen, Indians of Mexico and of China, Paraguay, Tucumán [had] who never ate in the public square nor had feasts therein like the Indians of this realm' (843). The model is derived from the native world. The proposal for a commensal subject is born from the alphabet of abundance, from a native writing dictated by Christian charity and promise, by Andean ecological management and by the celebration of a recovered world, and is probably based on Guamán's reading of Christian authors concerned with the poor.

Guamán Poma describes various cities of the Spanish Empire by means of an Andean cartography of the public weal. He distinguishes them by the virtues of their foodstuffs. Panama: 'abundance of food . . . plenty of silver'. Lima: 'a land of great amounts of food'. Ica: 'abundance of fruit of all kinds and of large amounts of bread and corn'. Nazca: 'it has all manner of wine, food and bread in abundance, little water and a great deal of meat'. In contrast, Cuzco is 'a very cold land, and there food suffers from the frosts'. He goes on to discuss the months of the year, and begins with a prayer that combines different elements: 'God and his Majesty are served with food. And we adore God with it. Without food, man could not exist, nor could his strength' (1,027). This religious moment is also a social demand, a search for equilibrium in a world that has become inexorably riven with conflict. At the same time, it invokes a paradigm of complementarity as the matrix of social rationality, cultural articulation and mythical recomposition of the fragments of the world. January is 'the month when there is a great shortage of food in the realm' (1,028). It is also the month when young produce is eaten, but with care since it can provoke illness. February, by contrast, is synonymous with ripeness: 'from this month on one can eat vegetables without harm because they are ripe' (1,031). March is the month for keeping watch over the corn, 'since all the food has ripened by now'. The Inca has his inspectors keeping watch over the fields in order to guard the crops, 'because there are some who will eat all the food up in a hurry and then soon die of hunger' (1,034). This image of 'soon' corresponds to 'green and unripe'. In April, 'the corn and the potatoes are ripe as are the other foods and fruits' (1,037). In May, we find another symmetry between men and plants: 'the boys and girls who are born then are well-off, fortunate to arrive during that time when food is plentiful' (1,040). June is the time to 'reap the wheat' and store the harvest' (1,047). July is more domestic: 'in this month there is cheap food to buy and they raise laying hens and have many chickens and fatten their pigs' (1,046). This is an image of rural abundance, a scene of Arcadian well-being repeated throughout the book. August is the time for sowing. In September, 'there is little food left throughout the realm' (1,052). In October, Guamán recommends: 'that they all eat in the public squares. And if it rains they should eat in the townhall or set up a lean-to . . . they should all come together and celebrate so that the poor might enjoy it too, which is a holy act of mercy' (1055). This is a version of primitive Christianity, where public space is occupied socially in the name of a communal feast. The seasonal cycle of fruits and crops is a joyful calendrical round and suggests an abundance of time, both pleasant and fertile. November is the month in which the fields are irrigated, although water is scarce and has to be shared out. December is the month in which 'seasonal' produce is sown, that is, crops that will grow during the rainy season. It is no coincidence that this section becomes an emblem of time itself, which is double: verbal and graphic, Spanish and native (799). Although time is double, it is represented on the page as parallel and combined, in a register of information, which is doubly organized.

The Quechua equivalent of 'eat', *micuy*, occurs three times in the *Chronicle* (according to Urioste's index, Guamán Poma, 1980). *Micuy rurac* (193) is 'cook'. *Micuy pachasuc ora* (867) means 'meal time'. *Micuy llullo* (1,141) is to eat young plants. It is clear that the Spanish term for food, *comida*, is more embracing and more important for Guamán. He uses it with the various meanings that we have noted, but most significantly as a figure of the discourse of abundance, in which he inscribes the cultural presence of the Subject of the Andean myth of earth as maternal and collective. In this inscription it is a demand on contemporary social reality.[12] Guamán lists the appropriate seasons for the return of certain crops as if it were a matter of foodstuffs' own discourse. The chronicler of the common good announces that in

December 'The melons start to grow, the *lucmas*, the avocados, the early figs and plentiful peaches throughout the realm' (1,061). In this way, at the end of the year the fruits from both worlds are added together: their combined abundance promises greater sustenance.

The alphabet of the world is in the last analysis a book made from the combined languages of the New World. But this book already belongs to a new order. It is a manual for reading, but also an instrument that acts on the world. It makes legible the place of the new subject that is both Andean and Spanish, aboriginal and modern. It may have its sources in many places, in the Bible and in the Laws of the Indies, but it is reborn out of the knowledge of its gardens, in their sowing and harvesting.

Two other threads are apparent through the course of this extended, contestatory exposition of the advantages of Andean cultivation and the ills precipitated by the social crisis imposed by colonial violence. First, the authority and conviction that inspire this account are rooted in the systematic case for the natives offered by Las Casas (1484–1566), whose powerful *Treatises*, responding to the call for recommendations that the king had made in 1542, defended the natives and proposed 'remedies' for the abuses of the Conquest. The proposals made the assumption that infidels also belonged to Christ's flock, a Christian tenet that Guamán was to appropriate as his own. Secondly, there is the native conviction that human beings are to be distinguished by the food that they cultivate. The communal subject deploys its rationality with regard to nature, so that the latter might give it sustenance and confirmation. Such a rationality has a cosmic articulation, a principle of correspondence with everything that is alive. But it also has a pressing context, dictated by the crisis of famine and degradation that makes the relationship between man and environment, subject and community, unnatural. So in the face of the disorder that is hunger, the chronicler uses the evidence of abundance in an instrumental fashion to change the world. He rewrites the broken discourse of the colony through the language of the native. Las Casas's Christian justice and native wisdom combine to redeem the poverty-stricken Indian as a subject of a humanity 'comprised of an infinity of natural inhabitants'.[13]

The writers who attempted to offer solutions for the terrible waves of famine that decimated parts of Europe and especially Spain during the sixteenth and seventeenth centuries were united in their belief that salvation lay in religious and institutional changes of a different order:

they appealed to Christian charity, and called for the organization of houses and hospitals where the poor would be lodged in a disciplinary manner. The Catalan writer Miguel de Giginta produced a treatise on Houses of Mercy that anticipated the panoptical social re-education that Foucault saw as the model for disciplinary society. Felix Santolaria Sierra, editor of Giginta's *Treatise on the Relief of the Poor* (1579), pointed out the following:

> The gathering together and confinement of the poor, as a social response to poverty and marginalization, were closely tied to the politics of reform of charitable institutions that the European cities experienced from 1520 onwards . . . In the continuous deterioration of economic conditions during the second half of the 16th century, which reached a climax at the end of that century and the beginning of the next (1590–1620), there was an almost perfect correspondence between economic crisis and the deployment of new methods of social control and re-education.

Giganta's treatise is notably systematic and rational. It is preoccupied with the problem of how to feed the confined and organized poor. They would get their food by begging, but in an orderly fashion. In a sort of pilgrimage, the poor would go in twos through the streets towards the city gates, asking for food. This planned itinerary would prevent false beggars from taking over the route of true beggars. The writer, seriously dedicated to the importance of his mission, can only appeal to the rich and to charitable institutions, and offers, in return, the socially rational *quid pro quo* of rehabilitated beggars.[14]

There has been substantial research into the cultural history of food in Europe. This has examined its social rituals, their organization and class stratification, but also the history of cultural and agricultural borrowings, which gave different names and different reputations to the different plants (corn and the potato, for example). Most borrowings were regarded as 'poor people's food' and only a few became valuable, usually in times of hunger. Montanari has devoted various studies to the history of European food, and has discussed the correlations between population growth in the sixteenth century and the crisis of farming in terms of the imposition of 'an ideology of food' that between the fourteenth and sixteenth centuries 'acquired a hitherto unknown rigidity'. He concluded that the ruling classes closed in on themselves and society and culture became profoundly aristocratic. The exclusion of the poor from the more refined pleasures of the table, which had a powerful symbolic charge (thought ideologically rather than pursued in reality) was a means for power to celebrate itself, to represent itself to itself in a moment when social discrimination was at its most concrete and tangible.[15]

Hunger was experienced in Europe over a long period of time and reverberated within literary representations from *comedia bufa* to the picaresque novel, and in the sixteenth and seventeenth centuries traced critical parallels within the transatlantic experience of the modern, between Europe and America. 'We shall soon have relief', Guamán Poma announces as he makes the pilgrimage between the seasons of hunger proclaiming the calendrical round of crops and food. The relief and remedies that nourish and heal come from the fertile fields of memory, whose contemporary reality works upon discourse in the name of its future fruits.

four

Translating:
The Transatlantic Subject

When the last Inca emperor Atahualpa and the Spanish conquistador Fernando Pizarro met at Cajamarca on 16 November 1532, they were worlds apart yet had one thing in common: neither could read. Both popular Andean culture and historical analysis continue to see these two figure as the main actors in this drama of misencounter, in which the most powerful man in Tawantinsuyu, the Inca Empire that extends from Ecuador to Northern Argentina, confronts the Spanish adventurer, who is looking to make a rapid fortune and realizes that this is his best and last chance to do so. The Incas had no form of writing, other than the system of coloured knots known as *quipus* that were used to count population and to reckon and record transactions. Pizarro came from a poor family and appears to have been a swineherd in his youth. Nevertheless, despite his illiteracy, it has been repeatedly claimed that Pizarro belonged to the culture of the sign, whereas Atahualpa, despite his power, was doomed because he belonged to an oral culture. There is a legend, however, that during his captivity, Atahualpa out of curiosity learned how to write a few words, and wrote the word 'GOD' on his thumbnail. He showed this to Pizarro, asking him what it meant, and so discovered that Pizarro could not read it either (Garcilaso, *Historica*, 98, 1, 33).

Thus possibly the first reappropriation of Spanish takes place in the very setting where punishment was inflicted, in the prison cell of the condemned man. The removal of a Spanish word from its context within religious faith and its use in a duel with the conqueror is truly emblematic, with all its echoes of legendary deeds. But it also situates the struggle between the two worlds in language itself. It is unlikely that we can ever separate legend from history in this encounter, but both readings are stagings of interpretation. In the same way, the question of words and reading can be seen as a metaphor for a more complex interrogation of the problem of translation.

Translation implies the possibility of constructing an intermediate setting, which would frame interpretations as dialogical. By the same token, translation is the first cultural act that throws both languages – both subjects – into crisis: speakers have to redefine themselves and there are extended struggles over protocols and interpretations. A new space of agreement and disagreement emerges. The meeting of Atahualpa and Pizarro becomes a memory and yet is permanently reactivated: it becomes a re-encounter where time and again there is a renewed attempt to produce historical meaning. There are only a few eyewitness accounts and some second-hand reports to attest to the events themselves. These have been enough, however, to give rise to a series of historical clichés about the steps that led to this fateful encounter, all of which correspond to the logic of the Conquest. However, there are other, less official accounts, which come from native or *mestizo* historians, as well as from popular oral tradition, which have pointed up the ambiguity of the events. These indicated how the events might be read according to another narrative logic and other cultural strategies. Ironically, the deaths of the last two native emperors, Moctezuma and Atahualpa, have not produced reliable accounts, but rather the schematic forms of fable. Official history has laid down that Moctezuma was stoned to death by his own people, whilst Atahualpa was judged and condemned for being a conspirator and a tyrant. But native Aztec versions claim that when Cortés brought Moctezuma out before the hostile crowd, he was already dead, and that the stones were thrown not against the emperor but against a piece of chicanery, against the Machiavellian manipulations of politics as spectacle,

so to speak. In the case of Atahualpa, the fable performs a different strategy: the priest gives a sacred book to Atahualpa, which the Inca then defiles.
This is the agreed signal for the assault on the Inca and his capture.

Ten months after he was captured, Atahualpa was garrotted. He
was granted this form of death as opposed to being burnt at the stake
because he had converted to Christianity. A year later, in his chronicle
The Conquest of Peru, called New Castile (1534), Captain Cristóbal de
Mena produced the first version of the encounter and also the first sketch
of the fable of the book. As in a religious drama, the missionary, the
priest Valverde, confronts the heretic Atahualpa, who lifts up the book
before throwing it away (illus. 1). Mena gives a military report on the
events, laid out chronologically. He notes the Inca squadrons, their arms
and their conduct, and gives a detailed account of the Spanish manoeu-
vres. Mena states that

> a Dominican friar with a cross in his hand, wishing to tell him of
> the things of God, went to speak to the Inca. And he said to him
> that the Christians were his friends, and that the Lord Governor
> loved him greatly and wished him to enter into his lodging to see
> him. The chief replied that he would not go any further until the
> Christians had returned everything that they had taken whilst
> they were in the land . . .[1]

This claim is intriguing not only because it brings together two different economies, but also because it suggests that the Inca suspected
that these strangers who were so proficient at pillage could not be sent
by the gods of order, but must be messengers of the forces of chaos. The
Dominican friar, Vicente de Valverde, goes on to explain the powers of
God to the Inca with a book in his hand. The Inca asks for the book,
which he then immediately throws away. Mena notes:

> the father gave it to him thinking that he wished to kiss it; he took
> it and then threw it over the heads of his people. The boy who
> was their tongue, their interpreter, who was telling these things to
> him, ran over and picked up the book and gave it to the father
> and the father came back, shouting, saying, 'Come out, come out
> Christians and set on these enemy dogs who do not love the
> things of God: that chieftain has thrown the book of our holy law
> to the ground!'[2]

1. Title-page of Francisco de Xerex, *Verdadera relación de la conquista del Perú* (Seville, 1534).

La conquista del Peru.

llamada la nueua Castilla. La ql tierra por diuina vo
luntad fue marauillosamente conquistada en la felicif
sima ventura del Emperador y Rey nuestro señor: y
por la prudencia y esfuerço del muy magnifico y vale
roso cauallero el Capitan francisco piçarro Gouerna
dor y adelantado de la nueua castilla: y de su herma
no Hernando piçarro: y de sus animosos capitanes
τ fieles y esforçados compañeros. q có el se hallaron

We do not know if the book was a breviary or a Bible. Pizarro's secretary, Xerex, claims in his *True History of the Conquest of Peru* that the book was a Bible:[3] in other words, a canonical translation. Father Valverde would have said to the Inca: 'I want to teach you the word of God, which is contained in this book.' The book had clasps and the priest tried to help the Inca unfasten it, but the Inca rejected his help. Eventually, he succeeded in opening it and then immediately threw it away. After questioning various witnesses, Cieza concluded that the Inca looked at the book repeatedly, and threw it away without knowing what it was. It was believed that Valverde had designed the stratagem with Pizarro, so as to provoke the Inca's blasphemous reaction, charge his forces by surprise and take him prisoner. Hence the importance of the episode and the Inca's behaviour. If one were to agree with Cieza, the episode could not have been sufficient cause to justify the Conquest, since the Inca did not understand what the book was, and in consequence there was no act of blasphemy that needed to be punished.[4]

In 1552 Gómara added the legend that the Inca expected to hear the book speak. Valverde had announced the word of God and the Inca was waiting to hear it. He threw the book away when he could hear nothing. Gómara also narrates the first dispute over interpretation within the encounter: the Inca replied to the Dominican's attempt at conversion with the argument that he, Atahualpa, was born free and was content with his own gods. Furthermore, he could see that Christ had died whilst the Sun and the Moon never die.[5] The official version was very rapidly imposed. Atahualpa came to be seen as the usurper. He had supplanted his brother Huascar as Inca, and had ordered the latter's death even though in captivity himself. At his trial, the accusation of tyranny, as well as those of heresy and conspiracy, decided his fate.

But the debate continues, with a version of events from the other side, one told by the natives. In the course of his extraordinary humanist labours as a compiler of native texts, Martín de Murúa advanced an explanation in terms of a 'prophecy of the end'. According to this version, an oracle had announced to the Inca that messengers would come with news of the divine will. But the Inca believed that those messengers would be from his god, not from another god and another king. That is why he threw away the book. So, he took the book for the word of a god who was opposed to him, a god whose silence announced the Inca's own death.[6]

Guamán Poma de Ayala, on the other hand, maintains that Valverde himself had said to Atahualpa that he was ambassador and messenger of a great Lord who was a friend of God. He advised Atahualpa to worship the Cross and to believe in the Gospels of this God. Atahualpa replied that he would worship no one save the Sun, who never died, and his *guacas* and gods and his own law. In this version, it would have been surprising for the Inca to find news of his world in the book. 'Give me the book so that we can see if it can tell me the same thing', he said. For Guamán Poma, the book's silence was not the Inca's fault, but the Spaniards' for not knowing how to explain Catholic doctrine.[7]

Garcilaso Inca de la Vega comes to the same conclusion. Quoting from the papers of Father Blas Valera (which were lost in the English assault on Cádiz), Garcilaso claims that Atahualpa and Valverde discussed religious matters, but also claims for Spanish sovereignty. It was Valverde himself who threw away the book when the Spaniards charged and even tried to prevent Atahualpa from being captured. For Guamán Poma there was no conquest by arms, but rather an agreement to cede the Indies to Spain, and this agreement is more than a historical fact. It underlies the change of mythical epochs, and signifies the end of one and the beginning of another.

For Garcilaso, on the other hand, violence can be explained only in terms of error. The soldiers charged because there had been a failure of communication. The historical drama of the encounter is conceived by him as a problem of translation.[8] According to him, Pizarro's translator, nicknamed Felipillo, was a bad translator; moreover, Valverde was a bad orator. Valverde occupied himself with explaining the mystery of the Trinity to the Inca, an explanation that Felipillo translated badly. On top of everything, Valverde sermonized, at great length, whilst Atahualpa spoke correctly, sentence by sentence, so that Felipillo managed to do no more than badly gloss the unfortunate priest. But it was not just a problem of communication, but also of complementary mediation. Christian learning is not a product of 'natural reason' but of revelation, and therefore has to be taught. Atahualpa was ready to receive that revelation but Valverde missed his mission. This interpretation is not only more complex, but in a subtle way is properly American. Looked at closely, it replaces the humanist fable of the 'self-taught philosopher' (the child or shipwrecked mariner who can confirm divine writing because he is himself a sacred text) with the more modern reading of mediation in the face of the Other (the evangelizing dialogue requires a shared knowledge).

For both Guamán and Garcilaso, the book represents an authority that fails to communicate. There is a failure in the mediating responsibility between writing and speech, between two types of knowledge. They conclude that had the Spaniards been able to teach, the Inca would have learned. The Inca, who was already outraged by the pillage the Spaniards had engaged in, at last understood that these men were not there to fulfil the injunctions of divine order, but merely to impose their own violence. 'Atac' ('Oh, pain'), he cried out in Quechua, truly desolate.

Both Andean chroniclers deny that there was a conquest. There was a transfer. The difference is a metaphysical choice, but also a political one. It is a question of intellectual legitimation, which reveals the cultural strategies of a civilization pushed to the edge of the abyss. If they had been forced to accept the notion of conquest (put forward by the heralds of imperial hegemony) these first American intellectuals would have had to regard themselves as victims – in the best of cases as displaced and remote products of Spanish expansion. Moreover, this would have condemned their cultures and peoples to the ostracism of defeat, stranding them on the margins of humanist and Christian discourse, precisely where knowledge is constitutive and redemption a promise. On the other hand if there were no conquest, but only the errors of the misguided who exercised violence in opposition to religious and imperial intentions, then there would have to be retribution, since the Indies were transferred by their native lords to the Christian monarchs. Both Guamán and Inca Garcilaso wrote in order to expedite the procedures of retribution, in the name of their inheritances, sons of princes and chief dignitaries. It was not in vain that they believed themselves vindicated by the discourse that equally sustained Columbus's explorations and Pizarro's armed progress in the name of civilization and faith: in the last analysis in the name of the Christian destiny of native culture itself. Guamán Poma took up a teaching that was based on Las Casas's thought. Garcilaso spoke from a discourse that emerged from the utopian political thought of the time, Neo-platonic in form, whose programme was shown to have been fully realized and painfully destroyed in the Inca state. Both were acutely and movingly critical of colonial violence, but they sought to control and transcend this degradation through a superior affirmation of a sort of symbolic re-distribution of Christian and legal propositions.[9] They wrote so as to construct the memory of a present that would include the Andean world as part of a restored future. And so as not to be merely subaltern or displaced, they gave their own regions (Cuzco, Lucanas) a place within the greater map of Christendom, within which Spain was just a different part of a single, narrated world.

Antonio Cornejo Polar has reviewed the accounts of witnesses to the encounter in order to contrast the functions of writing compared with those of oral accounts. He concludes that 'the book says nothing to someone who at that moment synthesizes native cultural experience, with which he (Atahualpa) and his people are subject to a new power, which is expressed in the letter, and made marginal to a history that is also constructed with the features of written language.' Nevertheless, history would be a re-writing that would dispute regimes of interpretation, as well as an oral and legendary re-evaluation of events, a popular saga, different and fragmented but capable of revising the pronouncements of writing. Sabine MacCormack observes that: 'Indeed, Valverde's book, whatever its content might have been, was written in Latin and thus could not have been read by Pizarro and his men. How then could the Inca expect to read it?' More intriguing is the fact that the book was not merely an object for reading but also part of the religious panoply and itself an emblem of Christian doctrine. The first chronicles confirm that the priest believed that the Inca asked for the book in order to kiss it. According to the legendary version of the encounter, Pizarro and the priest had agreed on a signal for the attack: the Inca's disrespect for the Holy Book. How had they been able to predict Atahualpa's reaction? The fable obviously reinscribes itself, and even the most accurate chronicles are a reading (an interpretation) of the events that are already confused in memory (and in the archive). Furthermore, the Bible, if indeed it was a Bible, was already a translation, an actualization of the archive.

As is logical, the meeting illustrates mutual differences until it becomes an emblem of a misencounter. The vision of the Andean intellectuals Guamán Poma and Garcilaso de la Vega suggests that in interpretation, in the discursive re-elaboration of the colonial experience, other negotiations come into play in order to situate the mis/encounter in a wider, more inclusive project or at least one that is not merely disjunctive. It is not only a matter of the historical vision that Garcilaso reveals in presenting Atahualpa as a usurper (a prince from a Quito family, who replaces the legitimate heir, Huascar, who comes from a Cuzco house), nor is it just a question of the most radical difference posed by Guamán in which a mythical substitution occurs with the change of powers. It is a question of the need to situate history inside the complementary discourse of the colonial experience. This discourse is not only Western (for all that Garcilaso fully concurs with the Christian rationality of the Conquest), nor is it just indigenous (for all that Guamán provides a cosmic explanation for the alternative orders). Both accounts in fact require that the profound rupture be contextualized within a form of colonial complementarity, which makes the Indies, with their peoples and spokesmen, into something other than subsidiary and marginal subjects and locations. Rather, they become agents who act and make decisions at the moment at which interpretations are being constructed and reconstructed. This discourse of colonial complementarity serves as an intellectual thesis: it brings together the parts so as to legitimate their contribution, suturing the wounds of the Conquest in order to control violence, articulating events so as to organize its own reading. It thus produces the possibility of reading both worlds. In the same way, Garcilaso and Guamán construct something more than a simple history of events, or even critical interpretation or well-documented denunciation. They manage to elaborate models that accurately process and project the present from its history: the present is built on memory. Their submissions owe as much to the present (chronicle) as to memory (history): to documents (denunciation) as to projection (future good government).

Guamán Poma seems to have been more concerned with the need to organize fluid channels of communication between different ethnic and regional voices, different state and community functions and the many different languages and translations. By contrast, Garcilaso thinks that the quality of communication is at least as important as its truth value, if not more so. He notes that Father Valverde's oratory was inappropriate not merely because it failed to explain concepts that did not exist in Quechua (such as the mystery of the Trinity), but because his preaching 'was very dry and rough, with no softening juices, nor any other taste whatsoever'. These reflections on oratory and eloquence stem from a concern with rhetoric, but they also refer to Garcilaso's project of constructing a superior form of speech, where the dignified refinement of words can be used for mutual education. In Garcilaso's discursive project, the other is constituted by means of the quality of the speaker's address to him. Guamán Poma's communicative drama is concerned with the rights that form the context for speech, and he appeals to an authority that will produce a structure for dialogue. Garcilaso's communicative dilemma is concerned with the protocols of dialogue: form becomes the setting for shared meanings that confer dignity on those engaged in dialogue. For him the incompetence of Valverde's translator becomes a terrible historical absurdity. Even if the content of the message had not been in question, its meaning was lost by the poverty of its expression. If the translator had been more experienced, then the meaning of the Spanish would have been better communicated, and the message of Christianity would have inevitably spread. But this would have required Quechua formality, for which the translator would have had to use 'wisely and discreetly the ancient elegance and manner of speaking that the discreet and curious Indians had'.[10]

Garcilaso Inca's first intellectual work was the translation of the Neoplatonic treatise *Dialoghi d'amore* (1535), written by the Portuguese Jew Judah Abrabanel, known as Leo Hebraeus or Leone Ebreo. It has often been said that Garcilaso took on the work in order to prove his skill with the most literary language of the time and to acquire authority as a humanist. There is a tempting parallelism between the two writers: both were on the borders and had a bilingual education, and both turned to Italian as the source of authority and authorship, and to philosophy and philology (Neo-platonism and Petrarchism) as the most solid traditions.[11] Roland Greene has proposed that Inca Garcilaso's translation is an allegory of his own identity. The discussion of love allows him to situate his own colonial origin in a wider, more inclusive vision, and to define himself not as a child of desire and appetite but as one of possession and knowledge. Greene sums up:

> First the medium of this treatise on the principles of love and desire, then the author of an ostensibly 'similar' account of Hernando de Soto's journey to Florida, and still later the historian of his own country . . . the Inca Garcilaso bids to change his station, from illegitimate son to author – and perhaps, father – of a new emotional and intellectual bond between Spain and Peru.[12]

This is the intellectual work characteristic of the new colonial subject. Rather than representing himself as a mere victim, Garcilaso creates strategies for dialogue, which are radicalized by his demands and proposals. These will endeavour to combine his paternal and maternal inheritances. This project is neither given, easy nor inevitable. It will combine history and biography, genealogy and utopia. Acting as its own archive, it will stage the drama of recovery of origins and their recontextualization within a larger European history. But this is a drama that is also inspired by the disputes of the present. This refracts history through the protocols of rhetoric as an exemplary and persuasive contemporaneity in urgent need of resolution. It is a discourse that articulates one world with another. Whilst based on the chronicles of Peruvian history it is also indebted to oral memory and written testimony. It thus emerges from both the disillusionment created by the breach of the Conquest and the hope of its potential subjects the *mestizos*. These are imagined as brothers and created as readers.[13]

The humanist translator, who pursues philological learning whilst maintaining a taste for fabulous prose, knows that his consciousness of *mestizo* difference rests as much on mastery of Quechua as on the resources of Spanish. The former gives him not merely authority but also the freedom of a double register: it allows for combination or elimination, inclusion or exclusion. He is not simply a bilingual author. Rather he is a translator who combines many things. Even the two languages are combined without being confused, and one works for the other, as its emotional obverse or its reasoned intelligence. They can exchange roles since they are linguistic resources that stem from one common, superior truth. We can often see Garcilaso lingering over a detail or relishing the emotions of a particular tale. At times he approaches the realms of fable, skirting the borders of legend. But in the end he always achieves the final translation, that of the evidence itself. In Garcilaso's books even fiction is put to work to give greater clarity to certainty. Thus he is more than a negotiator, a mediator, more than a literal translator, translating from one culture into another. He is a modern intellectual who creates the subtle and complex mechanism of conversion: he converts terms into others and encourages a dynamic transposition that weaves an exemplary syntax of combination. After the enormous literature that expressed the wonder and horror of America, Garcilaso devotes himself to describing the hyperbolic beauty of Spanish seeds growing in American soil, where fully fledged Renaissance forms take on sensual grace. In the melancholy seventeenth century, America became a superior realization of Europe's potential.

Translation presupposes the interpreter and the authority of the mother tongue. Garcilaso tries to turn this act of mediation into something more than a mere act of service. Translators or 'tongues' were, after all, nothing more than minor servants, badly paid and granted few rights. But with the example of the European humanists before him, Garcilaso realized that his mastery of Quechua gave him both linguistic authority and a unique autobiographical voice. As a translator, he could thus deploy the creative capacity of his own language within the versions he produced of his translated texts. In his own book, the life of this Andalucian native of Cuzco turns into the production of writing. In other words it becomes the projection of a subject forged by a double language, by the difference that establishes one within the other, like the two sides of newly minted coin.

Testimonies from native sources are of a different order. First, we will discuss the anonymous poem 'To the Great Inca Atahualpa', which was first noted down in Cuzco and may date from the eighteenth century, at least in the opinion of the noted author and folklore specialist José Arguedas. The voice of the poem assumes that the Inca's death has just happened, and thus perpetuates it as present memory. It is a mythical vision of events rather than a historical one, and the helplessness that it communicates places the collective cataclysm in a cosmic dimension. The notion of cosmic disorder as the consequence of political disorder is inherent to the worldview of traditional peoples. In the Quechua documents that have come down to us, the story does not recount the hero's tragic destiny at the hands of the gods, but rather the collective vulnerability of a people who suddenly find themselves without a destiny.

These are the first stanzas of the poem:

What kind of rainbow is this black rainbow
Which lifts itself above us?
For the enemy of Cuzco horrible arrow
That threatens.
For wherever a sinister hail
Strikes.
 My heart felt a presentiment
At every moment
Even in my dreams, gripping me
In lethargy,
Of the blue fly that announces death;
Endless sorrow
 The sun turns yellow, night comes,
Mysteriously;
They put the shroud around Atahualpa, his body
And his name;
The death of the Inca reduces
Time to a blink.
 His beloved head is already wrapped
By his awful enemy;
And a river of blood runs, spreads,
Becomes two currents.
 His grinding teeth are already biting
Terrible sadness;
His eyes that were once the sun have turned to lead
Eyes of the Inca.
 His heart has already turned to ice,
The great heart of Atahualpa,
The weeping of the men of the Four Regions
Drowning him.

The poem is a *wanka*, or funeral elegy, and the dominant image situates the death of the Inca in its mythical dimension: it is an event that announces the end of an order. The image is powerful: a black sun dawns. The black rainbow appears to be a metaphor for the cut throat of the king, which is a cosmic wound. The sun's head, like that of the Inca, has fallen. The colours of the rainbow, on the other hand, are associated with the standard of *Tawantinsuyu*. The king's symbolic body, the structuring principle of unity, succumbs. Death scatters organs and attributes: blood, teeth, eyes, heart are fragments of mortal agony.

Moreover, death means that time speeds up: all that remains are tears, which emanate from the four symbolic spaces of the empire and cover its lost axis, the fallen body. Thus in the poem everything is dislocated by death: the cosmic order, the regime of time, the terms in which the world is articulated. The voice speaks in the name of premonitions, dream and omens and weaves the signs of the fragmented body with those of nature out of joint. It communicates, in spite of the rigidity of the poem, the seismically historic quality of the tragic event, the bourn from which there was no return. But above all it expresses with crystalline acuity the helpless subjectivity that is lost in the radical uncertainty of an unknown future. The poem precisely expresses the subjectivity of the modern colonial experience.

The poem, then, rewrites history through its own mythical interpretation. This is the only way is which the image of the beheaded Inca and what it suggests can be understood. Although lacking in historical accuracy, this popular interpretation prevails within the anonymous texts of the Atahualpa cycle, an enormous series of popular dramas, which are still staged in some villages of the Peruvian Andes, as the ethnologist Luis Millones has documented.[14] Everything suggests that this popular version of the death of the last Inca had replaced the historical account, to the extent that even a chronicler like Guamán Poma de Ayala, who had learned of the events through the chroniclers that he had managed to read, preferred or chose to believe the popular Andean version. This becomes explicit in the drawing that Guamán includes in his *New Chronicle* in which the Inca attends his own decapitation (illus. 2). In the syncretic narrative scheme of the emblem, this drawing is the staging of a popular stock image. The event occurs for the first time, and yet simultaneously: it is the repetition of the event and deprives it of any dramatic quality. In a complex mediation that involves the illustrations that appeared in European books of hours and the staging of the testimony of local witnesses, the drawing has a referential character but also that of schemata of allusion. It does not claim to reproduce the event, but only to evoke it, almost like a spectre of popular memory. It is thus relieved of history, but also deprived of myth: it is a drawing that combines different elements and turns them into a stock figure. The choice of this death and not another makes the rationality of myth explicit, just as it confirms that there is a truth superior to historical veracity. It is not a question of erroneous information, nor is it one of metaphor. Rather a certain cultural order is being elaborated. In effect it is a means to preserve information (the system that classifies events so as to give them

94

2. 'They cut
Atahualpa's head':
Felipe Guamán Poma
de Ayala, 'El primer
nueva corónica y
buen gobierno'
(1615).

CONQVISTA
CORTALE·LA·CAVESA·A
ATAGVALPA·INGA·VMATACVCHV

meaning), and one that elects to explain the death of the Inca and the end of a mythic order from a native perspective. By the same token, there is still something more: if it were just a question of a historical representation, it would be unimportant. But by attempting to make a mythical representation, the fact of the end, seen and predicted, then repeated, suggests the recurrence of events: Atahualpa's death does not happen here, it happens again. In consequence, every time it becomes internalized as a cycle, as a final act and inaugurating form. In this logic of cyclical time, in the spiral that it traces realizing yesterday in today, the act becomes an instrument, a moment of instrumental knowledge. Atahualpa's death, when it happens in native terms, is recuperated within a mythical system of thought and is a first act of restitution. The fallen body is reestablished and its lost parts gathered together. The disorder of the cosmos is surmounted. The unity of thought and language that underpins myth is verified in nature.

The question raised by the cycle of plays devoted to the death of Atahualpa is this: why would a people choose to perpetuate a tale that places their origin within a history of defeat? The reply can only be given in terms of Andean messianic thought: the end implies a new beginning, where a new age is initiated. Time has gone backwards and the world is turned upside down. Memory acts on the present speeding up this counter-flow of time. Painful events are as great as those of the promised redemption. Song and theatre produce and advance the cycle, and give us a role in the unfolding of events . . . [15]

The most elaborate version of the cycle is undoubtedly *The Tragedy of Atahualpa's Death*, which was written down in Quechua and translated into Spanish by the scholar Jesús Lara.[16] Although Lara believed that the play went back to the middle of the sixteenth century, the only evidence that we have for the age of the play is the date on the manuscript, 'Chayanta, March 25th, 1871'. However, various elements do seem to refer to the background of Andean myth, even if they do not guarantee its antiquity: we could well be in the presence of an instrumental memory, a past made present. First, there is the experience of uncertainty, expressed in the role played by dreaming in the work: the Inca orders his priest to go to sleep so that he can dream and thereby discover the intentions of the bearded invaders. This scene of a subjectivity threatened by its inability to control events might be a later addition, but it vigorously communicates the unease and helplessness felt by the native peoples in the face of violence. Secondly, the work makes skilful use of a technique used in folk tales, where a question is passed from person to person and in this movement demonstrates that no answers are possible, and that, for the same reason, there can be no end to the questions. This type of story, in which an object or a question includes a whole chain of characters, illustrates the paradoxical historicity of the play: events are in both the past and the present of the story – they always occur in an expanded present. Thirdly, there is a new variation on the theme of Atahualpa's severed head. At the end of the play, Pizarro stands before Spain (which is here the name of a king and not of a country) and shows him the Inca's head, but the king upbraids Pizarro for going too far, and condemns him, then and there, to die at the stake. This may not be revenge, but the symmetry of the cycle has been fulfilled: Pizarro dies in the fire, guilty of regicide.

This re-reading of Atahualpa's end might have as a historical mediation the trial and sentencing to death of the young prince Tupac Amaru, who was decapitated in Cuzco on the orders of the Viceroy

Toledo in 1572. In the words of Inca Garcilaso de la Vega, the sentence was 'against all the humanity and clemency with which a prince of such an empire should be treated' (*Historia*, VIII. xviii. 248). Guaman Poma draws Tupac Amaru as an adolescent overwhelmed by the mechanics of death (illus. 3). When Toledo returns to Spain, the king reproaches him for having executed the rebellious Inca and condemns him to ostracism, to death according to these native versions. Guaman Poma's illustrations of the execution are symmetrical, except for the public character of Tupac Amaru's death, which surely suggests its historical nature.

A more decisive mediation seen in the theatrical works about Atahualpa's death may have been the execution of the last descendant of the Incas, José Gabriel Condorcanqui, a reader of the Inca Garcilaso, who takes on the name of Tupac Amaru II and leads the most important indigenous rebellion in the history of Peruvian vice-royalty. After failing in his enterprise, Tupac Amaru II is condemned to be drawn and quartered by horses in the plaza of Cuzco in 1781. This manner of death, probably rooted in the execution of the first Tupac Amaru, is recovered in the works of the Atahualpa cycle as the other term of a sequence that begins with the capture of the last Inca emperor. Tupac Amaru II is not only a historical personage but also the incarnation of a lineage, a complementary figure that repeats and stages the tragedy of Atahualpa. Between the two deaths, time has reversed and the world has become other. Chayante's play probably fuses both Incas into a single character, which is no longer historical but rather a principle of order within the universe, whose strength wanes so that a new cycle can begin. Tupac Amaru II's sacrifice could be said to incorporate Atahualpa's death and turns it into an emblem that no longer signifies the tragic origin of the present state of things but the renewal of the cyclical order, the promise of a new beginning. Culture thus stanches the wounds of the aboriginal symbolic body and restores the order that has been lost, with all the strength of exemplary memory. Death here works on behalf of life. Even if tragedy prevails, culture functions as a reservoir of strategies to negotiate violence.

Fragmentation (of the body, the Inca's legacy, the characters who undergo interrogation and even language itself) is indeed experienced as dispersion and loss, but it is also the sign and form of a new contextual arrangement, a different articulation of complementarity.[17] Language and writing, for example, are held up to scrutiny. The play is in Quechua and the Spaniards do not speak. They merely move their lips and Felipillo translates for them. The translator is a mediator: he facilitates the course of things and generates meaning. A central moment of this mediation comes when the conquistador Almagro, through his interpreter, gives the priest Waylla Wisa a message to take to Atahualpa. Now there is no name for 'paper' in Quechua and the priest calls it *chala*, a Quechua term that refers to the leaves that cover the cobs of corn. These filaments are similar to a sheet of paper, or at least parchment. The priest looks at the letter and says:

> Who knows what this chala says.
> Maybe I will never
> Come to know it.
> Looked at from this side
> It is a swarm of ants.
> If I look at it from the other side
> They look like the marks
> That the birds leave with their feet
> On the muddy banks of the river.

To which Atau Wallpa asks him: 'Take this *chala* / And give it to the Inca Sairi Túpaj . . . / Ask him, whether perhaps he knows.' Thus a sequence of questions begins, which in the end confirm the premonitory dreams and auguries that have announced that men with beards will come and replace the Incas, favoured by the Sun himself. The unknown writing is thus isomorphous with the tragedy that has been foretold: neither can be controlled, and the impotence of the defeated people is confirmed. 'It is impossible for me to decipher / the language of my enemy. / I am filled with fear by the glint / of his iron catapult', Sairi Túpaj says, equating writing with firearms. Once again, the exposition of events and the confrontation of unequal forces reaffirm the logic of substitution: one order is replaced by another, and writing is as forceful a weapon as war. This exposition betrays the play's probable didactic character, at least its less native and more 'national' aspect, from which these dichotomies are seen as irresoluble.[18] A piece of writing is interrogated by men without writing and compared with elements of the natural world: what is revealed here is the candour with which the *letrados* rather than the natives illustrate the lessons of the first contacts. Nevertheless, this is one of the few documents about the Encounter that acknowledges the vulnerability of Quechua orality and hence proposes that Quechua appropriate writing in order to deal with both the truth of events and the uncertainty of meaning.

Another version of the cycle was collected in Oruro, Bolivia, in 1942, where it was put on as part of the procession to the chapel of the Virgin of Socavón.[19] This version is notable for its syncretic character, the fluid hybridity with which it combines and integrates different forms of information and distinct formats of documentation. What demands attention, first, is its religious function. It is put on as part of the carnival celebrations in honour of the Virgin. La Ñusta calls out: 'Everlasting Lord, make the Young Powerful Inca rise again' and unites Christian hierarchy with native messianism. He also implies an intimate parallel between the death of the Inca and the passion and death of Jesus Christ. Pedro Pizarro noted in his chronicle of the Encounter that 'as he was dying, the Inca Atahualpa had given his sisters and wives to understand that he would come back to the world'. The performance culminates as an epiphany and concludes in Atahualpa's resurrection and triumph. What is less obvious is the rebellious character of the play. In a programme of 1939, the second day of the performance was given over to 'general war', or perhaps this 'war' was understood as another staging of the same cycle. Written in the Quechua of Bolivia, it combines archaisms and anachronisms. It is an archive of the past as well as an inclusive memory of the present. The Inca is strangely dressed (it is Carnival after all) and the Spanish soldiers carry cuirasses and helmets from the sixteenth century, form up in cavalry troops belonging to the nineteenth century, but wear contemporary police uniforms. In various Andean performances the conquistadors are dressed like police officers. The men wear sunglasses and the women wear coloured spectacles.

Almagro appears as messenger and captain, but also behaves like a schoolmaster and gives a lesson on the discovery of America and the beginnings of the conquest of Peru. Immediately afterwards, he acts out the role of a contemporary soldier: 'Shoulder ar, . . . forward mar . . . soldiers, halt'. Synthesizing times and languages, Atahualpa is called 'King Inca'. The episode with the *chala* has a number of variations. The First Inca puts the paper to his ear and comments:

> What chala, what chala is it? It does not belong to the King Inca. If even he cannot solve it with all his power, how am I going understand it? What can I do? From this side it looks like a chicken's foot, split in three . . . from the other side it looks like a heap of black ants: what sort of black water have they splashed this chala with, so that we can't understand it, we can't work out what it means?

And when Apu Inca receives it, he exclaims: 'From here it looks like a viper's tail reappearing; from here it looks like little birds fighting'. But the most contemporary feature is that General Pizarro orders the Inca to die by firing squad. Almagro announces that: 'convicted of *lèse majesté* and heresy, the Inca has been shot in full view of the Spanish army'.[20] Then, going back to the original version of events, Pizarro orders the Inca to be decapitated. But since these are the last words of the play, it is foretold that Pizarro will suffer 'the same death'. The deliberate anachronisms do not correct history by myth but rewrite scholarly texts by means of contemporary reality, that is, they make a political reading of events that is only apparently ingenuous. In fact, the performance, with all its crudity and naivety, puts the native cultural system into play, no longer as mediation between two worlds that explains the dominant culture in the terms of the defeated, but as a negotiation with real powers: Catholicism, the army, the police, elementary education and the regulatory national state. The play is altogether contemporary, and Atahualpa serves as a tribal or ethnic myth, which articulates native knowledge, and a Quechua or Andean identity that is permanently tested by the powers that use it. The translation from one world to another, from one language to another, now becomes the junction of different codes, transposed and superimposed, whose information is a critical exercise in interpretation, an argument over the place of the subject. The day after the Conquest, the post-colonial world began in an act of translation: it appears in the partial versions and crossed readings of events. The subject of the New World who had learned to speak and to read was already a translator. Permanent translation is the gesture that defines the imaginary subject of the Americas.

five

Drawing:
The Wonders of the Caribbean

The representation of the Caribbean has a certain dramatic quality, which is manifest in the tension that emerges between classical models and techniques of representation (including perspective) and the new objects whose abundance and extravagance even exceed the reach of hyperbole. But it is also to be found in the insufficiency of language as such, which fails to stand in for the object found at the limits of language (the Old World) encountered at the same time as the New World itself. Whereas the problem for colonial representations of Mesoamerica and the Andes was to reconcile memory with an anxiety-filled present, the representations of the Caribbean had to process a constantly changing historical flux. The drawings and engravings that form the graphic testimony from the Caribbean go beyond language and frame the object in a manner that is different from that of the encyclopedia, where words and norms legitimize the newly discovered objects. Here the frame is the border of the drawing itself, the transitive unity of the present. Where the maps of the islands look to articulate and the chronicles to evaluate, the drawings from the islands try to fix objects. In the manner of an insular discourse, in which each object is an island cut off from its context, these sequences of images make use of a botany, which separates off and arranges its objects of study. They also make use of a supposed homology where the objects found in the Caribbean garden figure a superior and excessive fertility, where fruits and livestock multiply and concentrate their essence. Nature takes on an exaggerated form in the food produced in the islands. Every drawing is an extravagant island, thanks to the object it preserves. This object is a part of a language in which wonder grasps the panoply of abundance.[1]

Bodies display their activity as if possessed by an urgent and energetic graphic dynamism. The pearl fishers of Margaret Island, for example, are drawn jumping into the water: they are caught between canoe and sea, just on the point of diving in. Botany unfolds as a technology of representation that carries a moral lesson. It tells us that abundance is not just a given, natural force, but also a profit and gain from drawing, from its capacity to give things back their essence, namely their presence here and now. The drawing establishes a landscape. In the drawing the gaze confirms the vivacity of memory, the physicality of the body, the tremor of taste and enjoyment: in short, what was experienced. Vivid colours give the fruit the temperature of duration, the moment of taste. It is as if the fruit resist being converted into allegory: their sensual plenitude and earthly opulence are enough.

The anonymous draughtsmen whom Juan de Tovar instructed to record the recollections of the Aztec people did something similar with their intense colour, rich ornamentation and sharpness of line, lingering over their art so that the smallest page had the maximum register. The 'History of the Coming of the Indians', the 'Relation of the Origin of the Indians' and the 'Treatise on Rites and Ceremonies' (Mexico, *c.* 1558) seem timeless. The texts begin by telling a simple story, but then become more complex reports and catalogues, taking their authority from the native books that Tovar interpreted with the help of indigenous historians. But this truthfulness is exemplified in, and takes form as, the drawings and paintings by native artists, who provide illustrations from memory – characters, monuments and customs, many of which had already vanished. The freshness and liveliness of the drawings give these vanished forms a renewed presence and contemporary quality. It is as though memory were not traumatic and conflictual but a model language, a ritualized recognition. As emblems these drawings represent a latent narrative, following the thread that leads from past to present. This turns out to be an allegorical network and is an entire native discourse, where each colour, form and gesture is connected to traditional learning. This learning is recovered through the didactic possibilities of an art reconfigured by its new context: it is transformed into a book, a supposedly historical source, a deterritorialized memory.

A painting of Quetzalcoatl, for example, pictures the god on a hill criss-crossed by numerous roads. He hardly touches the ground, but prepares for battle, festooned with his regalia of plumed serpent, like an apparition emerging from a space between this world and some other. The hill is crowned with vegetation: this is just traced out in the background, but represents the land as intact and whole. The lively colours of the god's attire suggest present time, as do the muscular movements of his body, his wide-open eyes and the cry that emerges from his mouth. He raises his weapon with his right arm, and battle commences. But perhaps the wind that rustles the leaves suggests that the combat is heading in his direction and that the god is waiting for his enemies – not Walter Benjamin's angel of history turning back to contemplate the ruins, but the hero who confronts the winds blowing against him.[2]

The drawings in the works of Guamán Poma de Ayala are not always subordinate to the text of the *Chronicle*, but rather endeavour to construct a parallel discourse. But if many of them stage the crude violence and cruelty of the Conquest, many others have that exemplary quality expressed by Tovar's draughtsmen. They represent the self-sufficiency of native bodies, their communal work and their labours in the fields, whose seasonal progression is a better measure of time than what has been imposed upon them. Iconographic memory has this pure contemporary quality, powerful in its exemplary character, but fragile just because it is situated in time. The drawings are thus a self-referential gallery, a demonstration of aboriginal wisdom within a present filled with memories. On various occasions Guamán Poma draws self-portraits and does so on the title-page of the manuscript where he establishes the authorities presiding over the drama of communication his work constructs. His Holiness, the Pope, seated on his throne, occupies the principal part of the symbolic quadripartite scheme (upper–lower, left–right in four quadrants) – that is, upper-left. Moreover, the Pope is the only figure who looks to the front, towards the reader. Immediately to the right and towards the centre is King Philip, His Holy, Royal, Catholic Majesty, kneeling before the Pope, in profile, with his crown by his side. Below is Guamán Poma, on his knees and in profile, with his hat in front of him, and self-described as 'prince'. Their coats of arms are aligned hierarchically: in the author's we can see the falcon (*guamán*) and puma (*poma*) of his emblematic name, both looking upwards. These three, in effect, make up a composite figure of authority – religious, political and scriptural – that ratifies the evidence the author calls on in his denunciations, and offers guarantees for the reforms that the book demands. Although Guamán Poma had often claimed in his chronicle that 'There is nothing to be done', his 'Letter to the King' finally leads him to believe that 'We shall soon have a remedy for our ills'. Even though Christian and imperial influence can be felt within native iconography, the hierarchically organized space of the latter supports the symbolic value of the representations. The American subject forms part of a greater articulation in which it recovers its social value, thanks to the allegorical staging that is made possible and even facilitated by the drawing. This horizon of possibility is neither simply rhetorical nor voluntaristic: it is a space that the colonial body occupies in both the logic of power and native rationality. In order to be himself, Guamán Poma de Ayala – prince, author, translator, draughtsman, historian and witness – requires a place as an interlocutor so that his message can fuse all these cultural functions into a single political resolution.[3]

There is an extraordinary sequence of images known as the Drake Manuscript, which is now in the Pierpoint Morgan Library in New York. Entitled the *Histoire Naturelle des Indes*, it consists of 199 drawings of Caribbean plants, animals and Indians, accompanied by short commentaries in French. It is the work of one of the artists that Francis Drake employed during his voyages to the Caribbean in pursuit of Spanish treasure on its way from Panama to Spain. Verlyn Klinkenborg thinks that the treatise must have been produced in the early 1590s, probably by a Huguenot who had fled religious persecution in France. Although there were perhaps two hands involved in producing the drawings and the commentary, what finally emerges is a dialogue between a single author and an Indian. Backed by the voice of the author as witness, the book ceases to be simply an extraordinary collection of plants, animals and a careful portrayal of native customs. It becomes a pictorial account of everyday native life, displaying an admiration for the independence and self-sufficiency of these forms of community. The authorial I that emerges here is novel. Nevertheless, nostalgia for family life and for the apparently natural autonomy of this quasi-autarchic social order produces an exoticizing gaze, and reveals the artist succumbing to an ethnological temptation, the syndrome of positing a desocialized, or at least decontextualized freedom, complete and natural in a setting of philosophical innocence. But it is also a remarkably modern gaze: it sees a rationality in the service of the common good at work in native labours and production, and recognizes the divine favour of shared abundance.[4]

Despite the manuscript being produced 100 years after the Discovery, it represents the Caribbean as though on the first day. It makes a detailed account of plants and animals of every type, as if they had no determinant colonial history. It also illustrates the labours and customs of the inhabitants, Indians and negroes, with no indication of their tribal ancestry, their languages or the colonial regime that brought them there. This formidable task is achieved in the course of its three categories of image. Plants are accurately observed and given in all their rich detail. The fish and other animals are presented in a more stock way, drawn from hearsay, and closer to representations in medieval bestiaries. But the representation of everyday native life, in all its energy, is presented with notable vivacity. The perspective from which the account is constructed is intriguing. In the first place, it is meant to be a report on the natural history of the region, an account of the peculiarities of a different world closed in on itself. It then becomes an economic report on natural properties and productive goods, and, when it concerns itself with mining, on wealth and applied technology. But it is also a contribution to botany and medicine, concerned with tastes, medicines, poisons and remedies, as well as on local foodstuffs and the ways in which the natives prepare them. Last, it pays great attention to the everyday life of the natives – their joys, their management of the environment and their wisdom.

The manuscript could be seen simply as something produced by a draughtsman in Drake's fleet, a fleet dedicated to looting ships and sacking ports in the cause of 'revenge' against Spain, anti-Catholic zeal and desire for wealth. But the delicacy with which it delineates the difference of the Caribbean, the vibrant luxuriance of an extravagant nature, and native skill and industry reveals a more complex relation to an environment rich in goods and full of earthly energy. There is clearly a self-interested quality in the possessive gaze, but there is nevertheless a sympathy evinced for the world that is represented in the drawings, expressed in the diversity of detail, the admiration for the skills of the society and even in the nostalgia for a self-sufficient setting.

In examining the catalogue of plants, what is notable is how the artist has deliberately tried to exceed the traditional botanical format.

Although the drawings of the plants follow the standard technique in which the principle feature, or point of difference, is highlighted so that fruit are often out of proportion to the rest of the plant, or are even much bigger, the artist does not follow a consistent criterion in his annotations, not even distinguishing between native plants and European ones, for example. Nor does he frame his figures, often drawing two to the page. The format seems to suggest that a disciplinary gaze (history, botany) cannot do justice to immediate testimony, and that even the titles of the drawings seem somehow *post facto* or insufficient. Because of this, it is difficult to put the drawings in order, despite the obvious tripartite sequence of plants, animals and Indians. Perhaps there are several formats underlying the account, which come to impose themselves sequentially. First, the manuscript is an illustrated calendar, where the images receive more emphasis than the dates. Secondly, it is a catalogue of colonial merchandise, which lists goods on offer, but not their prices. And last, it is a travel book, a miscellany of images with a minimum of descriptive commentary, which offers a taste of the wonders of far-away places.

Things are given names in the French of the time, these often being versions of Spanish or native names. Occasionally, when the author does not know the native name, he resorts to metaphor, as with the Andean llama, which he calls 'Moutons de Perou', explaining that these 'Peru rams' are pack animals that the Spaniards use to carry gold and silver from the mines to the ships that will transport them to Spain. This suggests that the author had read some chronicles in which, for lack of the Quechua name (*llama*), the animals had been called 'pack rams' or Indies rams. Gómara had already spoken of rams as big as horses, and Father Acosta speaks of both Indies rams and llamas in the chapter devoted to them in his *History*. In 1607 the Dominican Gregorio García was still offering abundant scholarly considerations to show that 'Peru rams' were 'monstrous' as a species, by virtue of their ancestry, descending from the camel.[5] Furthermore, the observation that these llamas were the means of transport for the gold and silver to the transatlantic ports formed part of the information that Drake's men collected in their long siege of the Darién caravan and the Spanish royal fleet. A similar source must have yielded the information that when the animals arrived at their destination they were sold to the captain of the ship as provisions.

Although this 'Natural History of the Indies' is centred on the area of the Antilles or West Indies, the material it refers to traces the course of Drake's movements from the coast of Florida to the coast of Venezuela.

Drake had taken part in slaving expeditions to the Guinea coast at the beginning of 1560, and this brought him to the Indies to sell his cargo. In 1567 he returned with a powerful fleet, and the following year brought 400 slaves to Dominica. The traffic took him to such places as Río Hacha, Cartagena and the Gulf of Mexico. His legendary bravery as well as his depredations are testimony to the struggle between the European colonial powers that occupied the Caribbean amphitheatre.[6] During these wanderings perhaps, Drake's French draughtsman had insufficient time to produce a report after Pliny's model, which would have given a better description of the things that could be found in the West Indies. The Spanish names might well betray or gloss them, and the descriptions that he gives do not always lead one to be sure that he has properly distinguished between the fruits he mentions, or that he has really seen the animals he refers to. However, it is always clear when his curiosity has been satisfied and he is making personal judgements. This personal quality of his explorations is evident in the fact that the book begins with a drawing of 'Ache des Indes' (Indies garlic), which he describes as sweeter than French garlic and having a better consistency. He adds that the Indians make great use of it, and eat it roasted. Some historical and philological research needs to be done for us to decide whether this was a native species of garlic. It is symptomatic, however, that the report begins with a discussion of food and the taste of a favourite condiment. The magnificent figure of these garlic bulbs, with their smooth elegance and delicate skin, looking like leeks or sweet onions, presides over the sequence of images of cultivation. Moreover, the image comprises two bulbs held up by a single stalk, as if nature were doubling its extravagance. This double image goes on to be developed in a large number of the drawings, underlining the fertility of the earth and the abundance of its products.

There then follows a fruit, the soursop, which is described simply as 'found in the woods', although the drawing is quite accurate. The lack of description of a fruit that is placed foremost suggests that image value is at times imposed on use value, even on the personal testimony of taste.

A comparison of this repertoire of images with those that circulated during the period when Drake was in the Caribbean, would take into account the popular books of Gonzalo Fernández de Oviedo (1478–1557). There is the eloquent *Summary of the General and Natural History of the Indies* (1526), and then the first part of his monumental *General and Natural History of the Indies* (1535), both immediately translated into several languages.[7] It is intriguing to observe the agreement between these works and Drake's manuscript. Some of the drawings in the latter could almost be illustrations of Oviedo's detailed descriptions. With regard to the soursop, for example, Oviedo writes in the *Summary*:

> it is a very large and beautiful tree ... and it produces pineapples or fruit very like them, as big as melons, but elongated, and on top it has subtle workings that seem to be scales ... and inside it is full of a paste like blancmange, only, although it is as thick, it is watery and has a beautiful, delicate flavour, with a smooth sharpness, and inside that fleshiness there are seeds ... [205]

Oviedo occasionally feels obliged to correct the observations of Pedro Mártir (1457–1526), whose learning and Latin he resents, accusing him of writing his *Decades in the New World* (1530) without ever having been in the Indies. Father Acosta (1540–1600), with his harsh severity, does not share Oviedo's hyperbole. Rather, he uses his own knowledge of the soursop to correct Oviedo in his *Moral and Natural History of the Indies* (1590): 'The soursop is the same size as the pear, and is somewhat bony and open. The inside is soft and tender like butter, white and sweet and of choice taste. It is not like blancmange, but has a delicate and flavoursome taste, and in the judgement of some it is the best fruit of the Indies.'[8]

The avocado 'is found in the woods', the drawing states, which Oviedo had already indicated when he wrote that the 'pear-trees grow wild' (he did not know the name of the avocado, and pears, like melons, were used in the European languages in a comparative and generic way). For Oviedo the model of the market garden that regulates the catalogues of Indies natural history has another subject: 'God is the principal gardener, and the Indians put no work into those trees at all' (216). Another coincidence with Oviedo's catalogue is the description of cassava, whose poisonous root has to be exposed to the sun for it to be become edible. In the same way, the Huguenot praises the *mamey*, which Oviedo compares with European fruits to the latter's disadvantage. Predictably, the pineapple is discussed with great enthusiasm by Drake's draughtsman, who describes it as 'an exquisite fruit, extremely good and tasting of strawberries. It grows on a tall tree where you can find several of them, and they hang down rather than grow upwards as French fruit do. The Indians eat them raw and salted to avoid stomach ache.' And he outdoes Oviedo, who praises the pineapple in the *Summary* as 'one of the best fruits in the world', so that he even recommends it as a cure for melancholia: 'it returns the appetite to those who are wearied of eating, and have lost their taste for food' (236). Oviedo dedicates chapter xiv, book vii ('On Agriculture') of his *History* to the pineapple, and anticipates the Baroque representation of the fruit, with its luxuriant and exuberant symmetry: 'just as amongst all the birds Nature has varnished the feathers of the peacock, so she has taken the same care in the composition and beauty of this fruit, and more than with any of those that I have seen, so that I suspect that there is no other fruit in the whole world as gracefully and prettily adorned' (1,241). This artistic quality of nature, lavished on its fruit, is an intimation of the Baroque fold and volute.

Oviedo and the author of Drake's manuscript also concur in their description of various poisonous plants, amongst which the most intriguing is the machineel ('Mensenille', folio 27), which the Huguenot describes as 'a very poisonous tree, such that anyone who gazes on it is blind for three hours afterwards. When they are at war, the Indians secrete their arrows in this tree, to make them more poisonous.' Oviedo devotes one of the short chapters of his *Summary* to the tree ('Apples of the Herb'), whose poison is so strong, he says, that 'a man has only to pass an hour in the shade of this tree, that on arising his head and eyes are so swollen, and his eyebrows are stuck to his cheeks, and if by chance a drop or more of the sap of these trees falls into his eyes, it destroys them or at least makes him blind' (223–5). They are also evil-smelling trees, which if burned as firewood 'make your head ache terribly'.[9] On the other hand, the artist points to the medicinal properties of tobacco, but gives no indication that the natives smoke it. He notes that it can eliminate bad humours by virtue of its emetic qualities, and that inhaling it can help to get rid of water on the brain and can help to soothe toothache, and an infusion of its leaves will cure eye problems. Characteristically, the Huguenot spends more time on the practical usefulness of a plant than on the taste of whatever fruit he is discussing. Furthermore, his description includes a guide to its preparation. For his part, Oviedo condemns the use of tobacco with great distaste, claiming that none of its supposed benefits has been proven. He goes on to deplore the fact that the Spaniards are beginning to use it. One of the Huguenot's most characteristic drawings is that of the Royal Palm, which he describes with some enthusiasm. The Indians extract palm wine from it, he explains, and it tastes like perry.

Pearl-fishing provides the occasion for an energetic drawing accompanied by a detailed description. 'Canau pour pecher les perles' (folio 57) shows a Spanish canoe with three sails and six negro fishermen who are probably working for a local master. We are told that they are returning to La Ranchería, where they live, after their day's work. They might be descendants of runaway slaves, but in any case, they perhaps already belong to a space of suburban artisanal work. The artist tells us that the pearls are to be found between the mainland and Margarita, in a space of ten leagues, and that the Negroes swim in the water, carrying baskets that they fill with the oysters that they bring up from the sea bottom, 'And the deeper down they go, the bigger the oysters they find'. They can stay underwater for up to fifteen minutes, he claims, and fish from morning till night. They do this near the island of Margarita, in Riohacha and at Cabo de la Vela. In the *Summary*, Oviedo, who seems easily excited, talks about Indian fishermen who 'are underwater for an hour, some for longer, some for less, depending on their aptitude for the task' (266). The biggest pearls come from Terarequi in the Gulf of San Miguel, he says. He claims on another occasion that what he says is true because he has experienced it himself: 'I say this as a witness to the event, because I have been in the Southern Sea, and I have been particularly careful to find out everything there is to know about these pearls.' It seems that he has bought some pearls and then sold them to a local notable. Oviedo's perspective is verified by his own experience as explorer and trader. Buying and selling reveal the essentially benign quality of things and do so better than the senses of sight or taste. Father Acosta must have been alarmed by this claim for the privilege of experience as the means of establishing truthfulness, since it completely bypasses divine precept and the reasons of faith. It is no coincidence that Oviedo's work was censored in Spain, and only the first part of his *History* was published. His criticism of the abuses that the Indians suffered and the Church's complicity in this were sufficient motive for his silencing.

Garcilaso was more prudent, knowing that verification by his own experience (seeing, tasting, hearing) needed to be supplemented by witnesses at the scene of truth, nearly all of them representatives of power and its institutions. Certainty required not just personal experience and eyewitness testimony but also the sanction of the authorities within the colonial system, which were assigned the role of intermediaries between the spoken word and writing. Oviedo's experience as explorer, colonist, chronicler and administrator authorized his vigorous and picturesque testimony: 'I know this because I have experienced it' he liked to repeat. But this testimony was also dictated by the dynamic of Caribbean itself, by travels and change, and therefore his submission gives vivid testimony to current reality and even prefigures it. The actual drifts towards the potential. When he extols the abundance of pearls, he quickly makes an offer to the king to obtain them for him.

We have been suggesting that the similarities between the Drake Manuscript and the *Summary* and the *History* might indicate that the Huguenot knew Oviedo's books, and that he might have read them in French translation (the *History* was translated in 1555). It is true that the draughtsman is more laconic, but his eloquence lies in the drawings themselves. He looks at fruit, animals and people with the same intense curiosity and empathy that Oviedo's descriptions possess, whose lists, full of descriptive clauses, lay siege to the American object that finds itself uncomfortably positioned within language. For the artist, the focus on the object is decisive. Even its dynamics requires a concentration of the gaze. The gaze has been educated by interest, usefulness, curiosity and educative skill. The artist wants to learn and to teach. This morality of the drawing requires precision from him, an economy of expression that is nevertheless something more than dispossession. It is another mode of testifying to the region's value and wealth. Once the settings of the animals and plants have been constructed, the artist recovers his narrative freedom in his portrayal of the Indians in the various tribes and groupings that he has come to know through his travels. In order to distinguish them, he follows the practice of contemporary Flemish painting, portraying them at work, in the everyday setting of their lives as mothers, farmers, miners, warriors. He draws attention to the work that women do, as well as to the skills of the men. This fit between the subject and his environment, which his work allows him to control, appears to the Huguenot as a lesson in community. His natives are neither natural nor savage, neither slaves nor barbarians: they are formed by their knowledge of their marvellous world and their capacity to inhabit it. It seems as if his Caribbean denizens had already read Montaigne. The title of the manuscript – 'Natural History of the Indies' – suggesting a much more elaborate text, is perhaps a later addition to the collection of drawings. There is some variation in the drawings. Some are rather naive and even crude, whilst others are fine and detailed, which makes it likely that two artists had collaborated on this compilation of images of the Caribbean.

There is not a single drawing of a Spaniard in the collection, although stewards and miners are mentioned. Nevertheless, the colonial presence is there throughout, neither affirmed nor rejected, but simply left outside the island of the drawing. What remains inside is the vision, both individual and collective, of the Caribbean Indians, who transcend the colonial order with their energy and self-sufficiency. Perhaps the silence and exclusion of the colonial world constitute a condemnation of the Spanish colonial regime, even though the negative effects of that rule are also unrepresented. What is patent is the interest in the non-European.

The manuscript does, however, include the author himself, who portrays himself in an emblematic setting. Folio 111 is entitled 'How the Indians had visions of the Evil Spirit', and presents a space as seen from two distinct perspectives. In the first, which opens out from the native point of view, the Indian stands at the door of his hut, and points out to the European man the figure of a demon hidden amongst the trees. The second, drawn from the artist's point of view, shows him in the middle of the scene, acting as a mediating witness between native and European space, in other words, as a sort of spiritual advance guard of the spectator. Thus, protected by the gaze of a superior faith, the native denounces the evil spirit, which, now revealed, flies away. This time, we are given a detailed narrative:

> At night, the Indians are tormented by visions of the Evil Spirit, which they call in their tongue 'Athoua'. They dare not leave their houses at night, only when day comes, and this is so because they have no belief or teaching and have nothing to worship, like the people of Barbary, Guinea and Brazil. One day during the time I was staying in an Indian's hut, I went out at night and the Indian begged me to return to the hut saying that he could see Athoua, that is the Devil. The following morning when he asked me about my daring and lack of fear, I replied that he ought above all to believe in Jesus Christ who was crucified, and that He would free him from his diabolical visions if he believed firmly in Him. Hearing this he said that the one who dwelt above was not good: he only sent them cold, rain and exhausting heat, whilst the one who dwelt below in the earth was good to them and gave them their daily food, like bread, wine, meat, fish, fruit and other good things from the earth itself, and when they died they were buried therein. To which I replied that God is the Creator who has created the heavens and the earth which he warms and that He makes the fruit grow, thanks to which they had their food [269].

The idea that the Devil dwelt in the Indies became an obsession from the very first stages of the Conquest, and was consonant with the idea that the Indian was innocent and primitive, if not savage. The Indian's fear reveals him as victim rather than accomplice, and by the same token, his ignorance redeems his guilt and heresy.[10] But the idea that the Devil took advantage of the Indians because they lacked a consistent religious outlook reveals the hierarchical gaze that the Huguenot employs, which sees religious education as a battle against evil. Finally in this drawing, the Indian and European both appear. Both believe in the demon and both confirm his presence. Furthermore, the artist explains the origin of the abundance of the Caribbean. It is a consequence of the heat that God gives to these lands. The European alerts his immanent interlocutor to the transcendent cause, to which his listener owes his being. The divine favour bestowed on these natives who are otherwise lacking in any great religious education suggests that they are directly descended from Eden, or at least that they are people whose lack of evil makes them ready candidates for redemption through Christian teaching. This scene, then, is a didactic emblem, and the artist includes himself as a witness to the potential of indoctrinating these beings who lack full consciousness of the fact that they are divinely favoured. Whilst Catholics gave themselves to the massive task of saving souls, as expeditiously as possible, even at the cost of their converts' lives, this Huguenot Puritan shows himself to be an individualist and a moralist and gives himself to the task of fighting the demon, cultivating souls and fruit at the same time. With sound good sense, therefore, he observes apropos of the cultivation of life, that monopoly is an anti-natural economy. For, if the Indians, and even the Spanish colonists, had the freedom to cultivate their vineyards, the Spanish crown would do business without profit: 'the land is so fertile that one can find ripe fruit in one's vineyards at any season'. That is, natural logic demands another economy, not only more individual and less state-directed but also more in accord with the dictates of nature itself, which by Divine design is miraculous and lavish.

The image of a native Garden or Orchard realizes the *locus classicus* with its morality of the family and social *economos* (the home). In folio 121 the artist takes great delight in presenting an admiring image of a native man cultivating his garden ('The Manner and Form in which the Indians Cultivate and Plant their Lands'). He is tall, well built, sure and diligent, and he is pictured in the act of sinking his hoe. In European representation, the act of sowing is *prima facie* evidence of culture. The symmetrical tracing of furrows enacts the model of agriculture as the conquest of nature by culture and productive rationality. By contrast, the sown fields of the natives lacked symmetry and their model was the bush rather than the tree. This contrast is shown both in the use of leaves as fertilizer, which covered the furrows, and in the use of riverbeds as seasonal growing land. Whilst agriculture implies the sedentary economy of storage and accumulation, this riverine or island cultivation suggests a nomadic model.[11] The Tainos did develop more stable methods of cultivation, at least on a small scale, but by the time our artist came to portray their horticulture the Tainos, whom Columbus had described as being 'easily given to laughter', had disappeared in the wake of colonization, victims of its violence, epidemics and population shifts. The drawing is of the head of a family cultivating his own garden rather than of an Indian working the land of some master, and from this we can conclude only that the Huguenot is giving us an allegory of modern work, that is to say, of the hero of self-sufficient and harmonious production, producing scant surplus and accumulation. For him, the American subject is thus the man of the countryside, free of the habits of the city, and given over to the tasks that make the land fertile. However, looked at more closely, this Adamic Indian is not engaged in ploughing, or in working poor land. Rather, he is occupied in an elaborate form of propagation, that of the seedbed. In effect, the land enclosed by a wooden rectangle serves as an emblem: it figures an intermediate space, where seedlings are grown, before being transplanted. By the same token, the whole scene is in the first instance an account of the book itself, since the plants that surround the Indian and form his exemplary garden come from the book itself. They are cited here as the forms of a nature that has been transformed into a garden. The various fruits and fruit-trees, bigger than the native Adam himself, rear up with their swollen produce, just on the point of being harvested. The legend that the drawing carries is itself an example of the power of the civil code: 'The Indian cultivates his garden, sowing different sorts of seed in order to raise his crops, and making it look like he works hard so as to please his betrothed, and produce sufficient to feed his wife and children, the land being so fertile that it gives forth fruit all the time' (271).

The reference both to betrothed and to future spouse suggests that the native who so happily cultivates his property is doing so in part to demonstrate to his beloved that he can provide for his new family. The episode suggests that natural abundance is so fluid, circular and periodic that subjects split and multiply as if they had become plural. The whole sentence carries this implication of fluid, complementary plurality, whose source is the fertile land and its lavish fruit. The book ends with this narrative logic encouraging matrimony: 'Having worked as hard as possible to please his betrothed, the Indian puts on as magnificent apparel as he can and returns to the house of his betrothed's father' (271). The last drawing, then, reinforces the principle of the family economy. It combines couple and garden: thanks to the ritual tests of agricultural knowledge the goods of a fertile nature circulate. This circular symmetry includes tribal nomadism: the artist tells us that when the land stops producing, the natives move to different parts of the island and after three or four years return, setting up just as they had done before. This subject of abundance is an agent of his own well-being. We have here an allegory of Protestant modernity.

But before he finishes his agreeable testimony, with its affirmation of the individual skill which engenders both natural good and family well-being, our Huguenot pauses and tells us a fable. Native society is based on the family (the new bride even looks after her husband's parents) and although it is ignorant of writing, it possesses a natural code, which is wise and productive. The drawing 'How Indian messengers carried letters through the country' is a fable about this emptiness of the letter. The description of the drawing is sufficiently explanatory:

> Indian messengers deliver letters to parts of the country where the Spaniards are unable to go on foot. These travellers carry partridges and other birds of prey as gifts for the Governors, as well as packets of letters brought by the fleet that comes to the Indies. These letters are carried in a stick whose point is split, which the natives hold in their hands. In this way, they can swim rivers without the letters getting wet. They also carry a courgette in which they place the letters, then sealing it with wax to keep the water out. Having crossed the river, they take the letters out and put them back on the top of the sticks. When they come across other Indians on their way, these others do not dare approach the messenger carrying the letters, because he tells them that he is carrying a ghost. When the messenger arrives at the place to which he has been sent and hands over the letters along with the birds and the other things he has been given, and they realize that a partridge is missing and that he has not brought what the letters indicate, the Lord or Governor to whom these things were sent asks the messenger for the lost object. The Indian then asks the Lord who has told him about these lost things and he replies that his letters are ghosts and have revealed this to him, which the Indian firmly believes.

The fable of a letter that talks to the master and denounces the native (an allegory of writing) is well-known to us from Inca Garcilaso de la Vega, who cites it in his history of the origin of melons in Peru (see chapter Four). The fable appears in various other versions, always with the same meaning: oral culture is punished by the superior truth of the written law. Apropos of 'Miracles of Conversion' on Hispaniola, Gómara refers in his *History* to the fact that the Indians believed that the possession of writing endowed the Spaniards with 'the spirit of prophecy, since things were understood, without being seen or talked about, just from what the paper said'.[12]

It is interesting that in the version cited in the Drake Manuscript, we have an Indian messenger, a role that dramatizes his intermediary function. Rather than carrying fruit or *hutía* (a small rabbit-like animal native to the Indies) he is carrying letters, but even though he acts as a bridge between the fleet (with its news from Spain) and the lords of the interior, he is not part of what is news: the mere confirmation of the tally of goods makes him guilty. The 'ghost' serves a two-fold function: the messenger uses it to frighten off curious Indians, but at the same time the master uses it as a witness. The Indian, who believes in the ghost's power, is thus encumbered with the weight of his own guilt. By contrast, the master exercises the force of truth (writing) and of the lie (the trap). In the drawing, the messenger is carrying the cage with the birds of prey and a long stick with a bag at one end to protect the letters through a forest opening out on to a road. The messenger is taking a short cut because he is familiar with the lie of his own land. It is hardly surprising that he has decided to eat one of the partridges on the road. And although the fable is told with little humour, it is clear that the pleasure of the tale has overcome mere description. The Indians' simplicity, which Garcilaso saw as a virtue of pre-Christian peoples, is presented here as fear of the unknown. The letter is a ghost, present and absent, and its power is thus greater, just as the submission of the innocent Indian to the guilt of his ignorance is greater. The messenger is the bearer of his own legibility – he can be read through the letter – and is thus left himself without letter, but also without voice, silenced by the evidence. History subjugates him and the fable condemns him. It is only by learning how to use the power of names that he will recover what is his, which is erased from history and made indistinct in the tale. The drawing of this Caribbean Indian who carries the weight of the letter therefore reveals another spectre, equally evident: that of a subject represented as absent, as a character created by colonial roles.

In order to present a full subject, the artist has to free the Indian from this colonial role and return him to his Garden. There his body is whole; he cultivates his trees and his fruit and shows himself capable of love and care for home and family. This Garden emerges from the nostalgia that besets the colonial artist who serves an equally fierce master, the pirate Drake. The liberty that the artist grants to the Indian is partly his own, the freedom of the religious nomad, who has undoubtedly undergone persecution and exile from his homeland. Those wise and adept Indians, consummately in control of their imaginary setting, momentarily reveal the margins of colonization, with their opposing and alternative spaces. The artist is himself a messenger between Drake and the natives, and his book is the ghost of a paradise lost to all.

There is another consideration that seems relevant here. Looked at correctly, this series of drawings with their systematic staging of a rich and full native life and strategic suppression of the colonial context becomes a pragmatic utopia belonging to a particular cultural rationality. It maintains, though never explicitly, that cultural difference is in itself a realized life, and is perhaps self sufficient. Christian revelation, which is not too distant, is all that is lacking in this natural form of government for it to be an allegory of modern humanism. But if we look more carefully, we realize that this cultural proposal is based on the evidence of the new: what is most human and most modern is *mestizaje*, the combination of what is different, so that what most belongs to the region is just what is different and distinctive. This encyclopedia of a non-conflictual *mestizaje*, which is neither hurtful nor traumatic, shows us how to combine the produce of the Indies and of Europe, Natives and Africans, and at bottom, how the Spanish, English and French can be amalgamated – as well as men and women, parents and children, farmers, fishermen, miners; sedentary tribes and nomads; people from the islands and from the mainland. Against this double background – of abundance as social agency and colonization understood as a dynamic process of intermixing – the book concludes with an affirmation of the social: the marriage of the new Caribbean couple. This scene is a small amalgam of values and promises, and as such, an allegory of the New World as a new social beginning. Combining tradition (the father) and the new (the daughter's marriage), the allegory stages the alliance between lineage and economy within the renovation of society. The couple is not Arcadian but utopian, founding communal values on the basis of individual ones. The couple turns the new into family. This will include both tradition and the future. It is thus the beginning of the emergent national romance, forming the germ cell of a native society that combines its own traditions with the colonial inheritance. This *mestizaje* fulfils the cultural dream of the Reformation: the possibility of a secular civilization based on tolerance. Perhaps the Huguenot imagined a utopia in opposition to orthodoxy, as though the Caribbean subject had given society a second chance here in the islands of the Indies.

Despite his imperial vocation, a chronicler such as Gonzalo Fernández de Oviedo cannot but express the contradictions of his Christian universalism and hegemonizing ideology. Faced with the experience of diversity, intermixing and hybridity, the subject refashions itself, and through writing responds to its place in the New World. Historians and intellectuals of American origin experience this consciousness of *mestizaje* as a personal identity (like Inca Garcilaso de la Vega, who made a claim for the historical legitimacy of the term), both biographical and cultural. Furthermore it is a national identity. The *mestizos* were in effect already a nation, as were the native populations: it was just that the *mestizo* nation was one 'born' *a posteriori*, out of the possession of language and the practice of writing. This was why Garcilaso's posthumous work was dedicated to the *mestizos* of Peru, his kinsfolk, that is, a nation already being shaped, where the future dwelled as cipher and reading. Writing, that is intellectual labour, reveals the imminence of this heterogeneous nationality. The same is true of Guamán Poma de Ayala, and other *mestizo* and Creole chroniclers, who felt no compulsion to reject or erase their origins as they learned to write. They allowed the memory of their origins to realize itself as another form of property, co-presence, within writing.

Gerbi reminds us that Oviedo never applied the term 'race' to the natives. In the sixteenth century it was only ever used for animals (401). José María Ridao in his stimulating revision of Spanish hermeneutics *Against History* (2000) sees the term 'race' (used in Golden Age expressions like 'Jewish race' or 'Moorish race') as carrying 'a strong pejorative charge' (43). He reminds us that the term was applied to religion rather than to colour of the skin. Thus one speaks of the 'African nation' because the concept of the nation is more important than that of the state, and against all sorts of ideological rhetoric, more important than that of empire. The notion of empire, Ridao maintains, did not have a territorial sense in fifteenth- and sixteenth-century Spain. Instead of a monolithic unity defined by the universality of its language, empire implied a dispersed aggregate of distinctive nations.[13]

We would add that the American nations were in effect symmetrical corollaries of the dispute within Spain for a redefinition of *mestizo* nationality. Ridao follows the critical thinking of Américo Castro, Francisco Márquez Villanueva and Juan Goytisolo in seeing the forces of *convivencia* and toleration as what was most European about Spain, articulating the experience of Islam and the Arab presence as something close and intimate. These forces were reproduced within the American cultural formation from very early on, often by the Spanish travellers themselves, to form a plural and heterogeneous consciousness. In a self-definition that was symmetrical with that of the Catalans, Galicians and Basques, but also like that of the Jews, Moors and Negroes, American intellectuals, even given historiographical protocols and growing censorship adopted an identity as *mestizo* Spaniards, that is, they saw themselves as subjects forged by ancient nations for a new nationality.[14] Perhaps one could say without paradox, that what is most European in Spain is American. Despite imperial impositions and restrictions, the overseas Spanish nations very soon treated combination as their inheritance, and intermixing as their contemporary reality. In this transatlantic to-ing and fro-ing another map of the modern is constructed. It exists in the space of redefinition that the Spanish language, inspired by many others, creates between Miguel de Cervantes and Inca Garcilaso de la Vega, and between Father Bartolomé de las Casas and Felipe Guamán Poma de Ayala.[15]

six

Representing:
The Language of National Formation

Tradiciones peruanas ('Peruvian Traditions') by Ricardo Palma (1833–1919) is a paradigmatic example of the interactions between literary discourse, national formation and the culture of nineteenth-century Spanish-American difference. We will discuss these interactions from a number of perspectives. First, we will look at the models through which America is represented, then the heterogeneous quality of the new literary genres, and finally, we will offer some reflections on the language of the nation. Palma's work is centrally concerned with the elaboration of an anti-canonical genre, the 'tradition'. Equally important, though, are his ironic and relativized representation of American history and his peculiarly heteroclite and dialogical language.[1]

'Wretched in the midst of plenty' was Simón Rodriguéz's judgement on the nations of Spanish America as they contended amongst themselves during the transition from colonial to republican forms of government.

The Venezuelan thinker (1771–1854) was prompted by his intense republican utopianism to contrast the two great models of the American world: the discourse of abundance and the discourse of scarcity. Like most intellectuals of the period, Rodríguez saw the countries of Spanish America as impoverished and exhausted by war and bad administration. But he also saw them as rich in natural and human resources. Nature had endowed them with an abundance, which was not just mythical and legendary but material and economic. In a single description he managed to encapsulate a widespread sense of the contemporary conflict-ridden process of nation formation. Though it is never made explicit, there is an implied third term between wretchedness and abundance: potentiality. This forms the basis for Rodríguez's constructive proposals. The discourse of potentiality yields the forms of political rationality and communal citizenship through which reality can be reconstructed. Rodríguez and the intellectuals of the early nineteenth century use this discourse to construct their projects for the future, and as a touchstone to assess the dramatic transition from empire to republic.[2]

In one of her poems, as we have seen, Sor Juana Inez de la Cruz states that she was born 'in abundant America', which makes her a 'country-woman of gold / a fellow citizen with metals'. This economic value was sustained by the fertility of a humanized Nature: 'which happens almost without effort / something that happens nowhere else / on mother earth'. At the time, this representation of natural abundance was a staple elaboration of an established Americanist discourse. What was new was the idea that Europe coveted and treated this wealth in an unnatural manner: 'it has been almost insatiable / in its bleeding minerals from America's abundant veins'. Beneath the conventional figures, there is then, a courageous critique of colonial practice. In a characteristic gesture, which displays her mastery of stock figures and *topoi*, she inverts their relationship: the best evidence for abundance is scarcity itself.[3] The representation of a Nature extravagantly yielding its goods rapidly shifts from the old topos of *locus amoenus* (the place of paradise, which becomes a utilitarian figure after Columbus: the place whose abundance can be exploited) to the order of criticism where social rationality is questioned. The new visions and hopes of the Enlightenment were decisive in this process, heralding the formation of the national community.

The debate on the formation of nineteenth-century Latin American culture, in all its processual, heterogeneous and even antagonistic elaboration, can be usefully viewed from the perspective of this horizontal cut in the corpus of its defining discourses. The historically given character of the discourse of abundance and its counter-discourse of scarcity have to be interrogated in terms of the political dimension of the experience of America, and the long, and often uncertain and incomplete process of decolonization. Descriptions of abundance offer images of well-being, fertility and common wealth because they represent an America that is capable of refashioning its colonial condition and constructing its own future. This representation is precisely what is undone by the denunciations of scarcity. Exploitation, poverty, injustice, chaos, ignorance and even the continent's multi-racial character are all seen as endemic evils, which rob the emancipatory project of its future, and condemn the countries of Spanish America to anarchy, *caudillismo*, corruption and political violence. This antagonism, which has shaped the idea of America from its earliest foundation, underlies that third discourse of potentiality and the possible, which offers a programme, a project for a future built out of the heterogeneity of Latin American difference. This is not just a utopian appeal. It is rather a call to concrete, even voluntaristic practice that would affirm collective processes through the formation of a community.

Conscious of this antagonism, Rodríguez decided to dedicate his work to these projects, sketching out passionate and lucid blueprints for a future Spanish American civilization. Andrés Bello, although equally driven by the evidence of post-colonial chaos, turned his efforts to the gigantic task of giving abundance a rationality that would be proof against the depredations of bad government. If Sarmiento thought that the roads of prosperity could be built through the space of privation, José Hernández saw that their foundations were built on violence and that the true origin of the nation was dispossession. Manuel Ignacio believed that the nation was the historical space of abundance, whereas Ignacio Ramírez bore painful witness to the agony of Mexico's historical transition. In the latter part of the nineteenth century, as contradictions sharpened, the countryside could now be seen more easily as the space of scarcity, having previously been the privileged locus of abundance. Well-being was a gift of the city. González Prada mocked bourgeois priorities as Ricardo Palma fictionalized and relativized history from an ironic urban perspective. After 'political independence', figured in the representations of lack and scarcity as incomplete and uncertain, so-called intellectual independence was in reality an extended contestation between models of formalization and reorganization, both political in their concerns with power, and cultural in as much as they concern a plural collectivity, the republican community. Thus at various crucial moments of the nineteenth century something like a Latin American cultural citizenship was produced.

José Martí is one of the modern originators of the Latin American discourse of abundance, developing it throughout his work, but especially in his advocacy of independence. In 'Our America' he offers the traditional image of the American tree as the emblem of a politics of difference, just as Inca Garcilaso de la Vega had offered an image of a graft between the New and Old Worlds. 'Let the world be grafted on to our republics, but our countries must be the trunk.' Abundance is surely more than a catalogue of Nature's produce. It is representation that creates discourse out of nature. Thus the central notion of the tree has an analogical value here, moving the image from one discourse to another. Latin American culture acts as the axis of articulation, appropriating knowledge from the rest of the world, which then flourishes in its very difference. Martí's cultural theory is central to the construction of Latin American specificity, and in this sense is a project, an elaboration of possibility. Independence, decolonization, nation building and resistance all tend in this direction. Martí's political thought is built on this cultural foundation, and very early on he advances the idea that a democratic politics can only grow in cultural difference. To enhance both requires dialogue and association – the community of what is specific to Latin America.

In this same essay he says:

> the good American governor is not the person who knows how the French or the Germans are governed, but the person who knows from what elements his country is made, and how he can guide them as a whole, with methods and institutions that originate in his own country, so as to arrive at that desirable state where every man knows himself, acts, and all enjoy the abundance that Nature has offered to all the people who labour and defend their work with their lives.

In 'Mother America' he says: 'From sun to sun [our America] overcomes everything, through the power of the soul of the earth, harmonious and artistic, created from the music and beauty of the nature in our lands, which gives its abundance to our hearts, and the serenity of its lofty peaks to our minds.' Abundance is the source and the end result, and is expressed both in 'natural man' and in 'the superior politics written in Nature'.

Cintio Vitier has pointed out Martí's preference for terms like 'emerging', 'sprouting' and 'growing'.[4] 'Sap' is another, and Martí talks about 'peoples growing from their bulbs' in 'Ancient Man in the Americas and His Primitive Arts' (1884), where we read: 'The slender stalk ought to have been left standing, so that the whole, flourishing work of Nature could then have been seen in all its beauty. The Conquistadors stole a page from the Book of the Universe!' He is clearly referring to pre-Columbian peoples and the interruption of their history by the Conquest. By the same token the image of the tree is the point of mediation between a fertile nature, an expanding society and a culture in formation. Society and culture are the emblematic 'works' of a Nature that is in turn an emblem of creation, process and difference. The traditional trope of the 'book of Nature' or the 'writing of the world' appears in the final exclamation, this time as a historical analogy. Vitier notes that in 'Our America', the Grand Semí of the Caribbean riding on the back of the condor symbolizes 'the salvation of our America'. It is 'the spiritual sign of a telluric quality, of *a nature that has become history*' (emphasis in the original). It allegorizes the incorporation of the cultural and the natural into an emblem of American abundance (the Semí is the god of fertility). History itself is represented by the language of culture, hence the powerful, incorporating meaning of American (cultural) experience. It is made up of aggregations and appropriations. In 'Mother America' this conviction is expressed in hyperbolic terms: 'we have turned all this [anti-American] poison into sap', Martí writes. In the most exemplary cultural instances, nothing is lost and everything confirms the meaning of life. Likewise, Martí sees this process (engendering) of foundation (independence and democracy) as something in which even negativity ('poison') is transformed into something fertile ('sap'). For this reason, 'the immense new land smiles, drunk on the joy that its children have divined'. This divining is the mytho-poetic and civic intimacy of the communal: the sense of belonging as the source of difference. The community is Mother Earth, whose fertility is shared by her children. Martí could thus write: 'My verse will grow: under the sod / I too will grow.'

It was the Cuban poets who most eulogized the land – its fruits and natural beauty. Their *topoi* and descriptions of the land became motifs within late nineteenth-century civic discourse. They also produced a stock of figures that were used to celebrate the speaker's language, the subject's history and man in relation to his environment. This logic of belonging combined classical *topoi* with baroque inflections, romantic nostalgia with modernist formalism. Once more Martí's poetry richly illustrates how variations within his language are interwoven to produce a synthesis that is both dramatic and pleasing.

In his famous poem 'In the Temple of Cholula', written when he was only sixteen, José María Heredia (1803–1839) produced an extraordinary combination of motifs: classical Mexican topos ('perennial greenery') is combined with Baroque hyperbole ('The orange tree / And the pineapple and the singing banana / Children of a equinoctial soil are mixed together / With the leafy vine and the rough pine'); naturalistic motif ('this land / Grows such rich ripe grain, fertilized / With the blood of men') with Catholic conclusion ('And the superstition you served / Let it sleep at the bottom of the abyss!') and Enlightenment moral ('For our last grandchildren, however, / I know a healthy lesson'). A visionary, romantic perspective that sees fall in the context of a millenarian cosmos underpins these discursive combinations, and whilst it recognizes the beauty and abundance of the Aztec land, it no longer acknowledges the difference and value of its culture.

Joaquín Lorenzo Luaces (1826–1867) was the author of an extravagant, mythological poem, *Cuba* (published in 1882), in which he gave a detailed account in *octavas reales* (a Spanish verse form, with eight lines to the stanza) of the complicated love affairs of Apollo and Cuba. It is a drama about the gods in all their erotic and baroque glory, rescued from obscurity by Lezama Lima, who included it in his *Anthology of Cuban Poetry*.[5] At a crucial moment in the poem, Luaces has the young goddess Cuba stealing two pomegranates from Cupid's garden. Cupid surprises her and as punishment makes the pomegranates become part of her breasts. This is one of the most audaciously hyperbolic uses of fruit imagery in Cuban poetry:

> The tight flesh of the virgin
> Relaxes, extends, swells
> And the divine fruit begins to envelope it,
> Slowly dissolving into its fibres.
>
> xxiv
> As her flesh opened up
> In her essence the fruit transform
> Receiving life and movement
> From the parts they touch.

The analogy supposes that flesh and fruit share the same representational substrate: Cuba. But this personification – a romantic gesture with an almost *modernista* sensuality – carries these *topoi* to a poetic plane in which they are sufficient unto themselves. Thus the poet comes to speak of abundance from within his rhetorical tradition, but gives his classical allusions a national location and a sensual inflection. Lezama Lima is right in saying that Luaces's sonnets 'anticipate Parnassian forms'.

By contrast, Gabriel de la Concepción Valdés, 'Plácido' (1809–1844) – accused of conspiracy and executed by the Spanish – imagined a different type of hero in the shape of Jicotencal, an Indian chief from Tlascala (Mexico). Valdés produces a refined romance, which recalls both Góngora's romances and the native Mexican chronicles. Here the hero acquires an emblematic cultural and political value: he grants the defeated pardon. This different dimension of heroism offers a subtle critique of the colonial administration. Plácido's extraordinary poetry achieves its major syntheses thanks to the refinement and pliability of his formal structures. His *letrillas* ('The Flower in the Café' and 'The Flower of the Cane' are the most well known), another Spanish verse form, convert the floral figure of abundance into a sort of popular metadiscourse. The poet fuses high diction with popular speech with surprising humour, freshness and intelligence. It is as if he has turned the language of botany into that of the man about town, inflected with a proper, Creole tone. In the end, Plácido demonstrates that abundance is primarily a virtue of poetic language. In the move from Luaces to Plácido, representation of abundance has become internalized: it has ceased to be a figure and has become a language. In Martí this refined celebration unfolds as exceptional wit and drama.

For Inca Garcilaso de la Vega, the evidence of abundance in America demonstrated that when Spain and the Indies were combined, intermixed and grafted onto each other, a new cultural paradigm was produced, that of *mestizaje*. Martí's work, however, turns the idea of abundant America into a paradigm of difference. This difference is a real tradition: Latin America has become herself through it, and in it she encounters her own image. 'Our' America is different therefore from Anglo-Saxon America, but also from Europe. But there are also internal differentiations, between those who define their identity in European terms, because of their urban location, and those whose experience is converted into a collective knowledge linked to difference, whose emblematic space is the countryside. Here Martí clearly opposes Sarmiento's ideology of civilization, but he also advances an important thesis about Latin American modernity. To define modernity in terms of difference, in terms of specificity, is to propose a political paradigm of the possible, whose basis lies in culture. For

Martí, this articulation of history, the culture of difference and the politics of autonomy is an articulation of transparent abundance. It is genuine and promises a future plenitude.

The set of emblems – gold, flowers, the tree – that turned American Nature (or better, its discursive representation) into an allegorical metamorphosis, a process that would constantly bring forth the new, also formed part of that reservoir of figures with which to describe what was American. This was the store of information or figuration that writers drew upon to confirm their identity, and in which they discovered the stock figures of their collective representation. In his poem 'Victory at Junín', José Joaquín Olmedo (1780–1847) places the new voices of history over images of abundance:

> The Andes, those enormous stupendous
> Masses resting on foundations of gold
> Balanced by the weight of the earth
> They never move. They, mocking
> Alien envy and malevolent Time
> Fury and power, will be eternal
> Heralds of freedom and victory
> With profound echo
> They will speak to the last age of the world:
> We came from the country round Junín, etc.

The Andes have ceased to be figures of abundance and are now witnesses to history. Olmedo revels in the topos:

> The deep entrails of the land
> Already offer up the long veins of their treasure
> The Sun keeps within them, and our mountains
> Will bathe the valleys with golden lava.

Even though this triumphal history is written in a language of plenitude, the poet has to choose between gold and agriculture:

> Oh Sun, make your land fertile
> And heal the hurts of war.
> Give our fields copious fruits
> And although you deny the sheen to metals
> Give ships to the ports

> People to the wilderness
> Victory to arms
> Wings to Spirit and glory to the Muses.

Welfare requires the choice of agriculture against gold, because different collective needs have different moral weight. Trade and the peopling of the land are the bases for independence and for the arts. In seventeenth-century Spain, Saavedra Fajardo was already advising his prince that he should favour agriculture over mining, since the latter's dominance had so impoverished Spain that it led him to doubt whether the discovery of America had yielded any benefits at all.

When Antonio Raimondi later says that Peru is 'a beggar sat on a bench of gold', the brief hopes had passed. The images of scarcity reveal the paradoxes and contradictions caused by this abundance of gold: the gold is expropriated and society dislocated. The contradictory and antagonistic schemas of abundance and scarcity will underpin the later Indianist and Indigenist novels, with their representations of society as inner disarticulation, in which space is alienated and the community dispossessed.

Andrés Bello (1781–1865) was – along with Martí – one of the Latin American intellectuals most conscious of this defining antagonism. As is well known, he wrote his paeans to agriculture at the moment when his country and most of America were struggling in the midst of economic debacle and depression. His writing is thus part of the first expression of the crisis in poetry, its counter-discourse. But in an early dialogue 'Venezuela Consoled' he is already writing:

> You who in better days
> Saw the beautiful sheen
> With which Nature decked out her power in my dominions.
> Today, to the sad
> Accents with which I tell
> Our universe all my misfortunes, join your cries . . .
> Blessed days
> Of joy and delight
> Season of abundance,
> Joyous image of the golden age,
> To black night swiftly
> You have turned!

'The golden age' is a topos not merely because it provides an 'image' but because it presides over the opposition. The goddess Venezuela is here lamenting the spread of smallpox, but Time brings the good news: thanks to King Charles iv, the vaccine has been brought to America. Bello dedicates another long poem to the virtues of progress. The Enlightened and programmatic character of Bello's representations mean that the names given to Nature in his poem form part of the cultural rationality implicit in agriculture itself. In his 'Address to Poetry' Bello asks her in the name of his 'native rustic home' and because she is 'a nymph of these woods' to leave behind the 'cult of Europe' and live amongst the new valleys and fruits of America. Here, in claiming that the basis of the new culture is the cultivation of natural resources, his practice is parallel to but not identical with Martí's. The civic muse of the new poetry will change the place from which she speaks: she returns to the primordial forest, now the American countryside but written in the language of Virgil, leaving behind the decadent European city of court and corruption. Even if the analogies are never finally resolved, this fragmentary poem includes the promise of natural resources amongst the list of heroes and civil virtues. The political history of the contemporary world promises something new, just as Nature itself produces the new. American poetry recovers diversity within language. However, we are not faced with an Adamic language, or with a different speech. On the one hand we have the Virgilian paradigm, with its harmony between names and things amidst the beauty of natural goods, and on the other, we have traditional Spanish forms with their listings of local riches. For Bello, then, the issue is not that of origins, or even that of process, but of the place of the name within full speech. In 'Agriculture in the Tropics' to give names to fruit in the classical descriptive tradition presupposes their inclusion in the Archive of Universal Nature. Everything has its beginning in the discursive zone of abundance and not necessarily in the 'tropics':

> Hail, fertile zone that circumscribes
> the vagrant course of your enamoured sun
> and caressed by its light
> brings forth all living things
> in each of your many climes!

The land gives birth to living things when it is fertilized by the sun. This image of rational gestation declares the universality of place in the possibilities of language:

> Nor purple fruit, nor red, nor yellow
> In your beautiful glades,
> No shade is absent . . .

The use of every colour here implies the presence of every name. Fruits are listed according to their comparative excellence in the world. The banana tree is chosen to represent natural fertility, since it provides the greatest amount of fruit for the least care – as Bello notes. Given the model of nature, comparison necessarily becomes moral: 'But, fertile zone, though rich, / Why did not nature work with equal zeal / To make its indolent dwellers follow her!'

Contemporary reality intervenes. Men have abandoned the countryside for the city, where idleness, ambition, division and sensuality dominate. To this list of republican ills, Bello opposes the great Virgilian model, Rome itself, governed by 'the strong hand / browned by the sun and calloused by the plough'. Martí would have endorsed this conclusion, not in the name of Rome, but in the name of a rural American experience, which had the capacity to resist the bad times of penury and political crisis. In conclusion, Bello invokes the future on the basis of his own models of discourse: he bids the 'young nations':

> Honour the countryside, honour the simple life
> Of the labourer, in its frugal simplicity,
> Thus you will always have
> Freedom
> And ambition a brake, and law its tempering.

A conclusion that is much more moral than the luxurious beginning of the poem with its descriptions of fruit and fruit trees. But this conclusion agrees with the rationality of a representation of America where the political subject is the culture of the community, the agent that affirms what belongs to it, its promise.

Bello constructs this poetic rationality out of classical promises and sets it against less encouraging contemporary facts: the horror of war, the agonies of factionalism and disunion, the fear of chaos. In his 'Letter' to Olmedo, these phenomena are seen as expressions of lack and negativity, that latent counter-discourse:

> Do you see how in our homeland
> Ambition unleashes its furies, forging once more

The chain for our necks?

Do you not cry out on seeing what the wind blows in
So many burning vows, so much blood,
Twenty years of horror and isolation.

Fields of destruction that horrify the world
Poverty and grief and tearful loss
That raise their cry to heaven in vain.

When Amunátegui was editing Bello's work, he came across the drafts for the final section of the 'Letter', in which the choir of the Muses receives Olmedo in triumph, bringing a poetic resolution to the elaborate missive. The Muses ask Olmedo to carry on writing ('Ceaselessly lend your beneficent light') and tell him that 'ruin will cease in your land / and you will see the people who adore you set free'. This is no mere rhetorical solution, but a display of Bello's civic poetics. Poetry, that is, letters and the virtues of the man of letters, are an antidote to scarcity and work in favour of freedom, progress and the common good. Freedom, concludes Bello, loves the rivers Magdalena and Rimac more than the Tiber and the Garonne. Thanks to the future that freedom will inaugurate and whose first outlines appear in poetry, the 'immortal bards' will recover 'the sky, the water, the wind, the shady forest', that is, the elemental names of native abundance. The realization of art will thus be found in the political realization of society: both affirm the collective good. In his 'Discourse on Venezuela' (1892) Martí invoked Bello as well as Bolívar when he wrote 'like children [we should] venerate the land, which has been given to us by our first politician who was also our first warrior and the most profound of our legislators who was also the smoothest and most artistic of our poets'.[6]

Ignacio Manuel Altamirano (1834–1893) was one of Bello's great admirers in Mexico. Like Bello he was involved in the extensive task of the foundation and redefinition of the state, which he understood politically from a liberal perspective. Liberalism, as José Luis Martínez has pointed out, gave nineteenth-century Mexico its characteristic features. In his 'Mexican Literary Reviews', the first written in 1868, Altamirano elaborated his proposals for a national literature, and did so in terms that bear revealing comparisons with the tradition of rhetoric used to describe nature in America: 'Mexican poetry and literature should be virgin, vigorous, original like our soil, our mountains, our plant life'

(36). It is clear from the terms he uses that nature should be model and reflexive source of writing: literature will be 'reborn', there is a 'task' to be done. He speaks simply but eloquently of a 'superior and industrious' spirit, and so on, implying a long process of gestation within a culture that is rich in voices, intonations and registers, and whose promise is literally the conversion of natural abundance into cultural abundance.

Like Bello, Altamirano rejoiced that 'the poets had descended from Helicon and ascended the steps of the Capitol', although, unlike Bello, public affairs did not seem to him to be a superior calling for the humanist man of letters, but was merely one more labour of culture, where the artist was just another artisan constructing the nation. These various labours as journalist, critic, publicist, chronicler and narrator were all attempts to construct the same idea of the collectivity – what it was to be Mexican. Hence the concerns that were generated by the examples of the other American nations that he knew at first hand, and which with their richness and demands he still could not altogether see in his country's literature.

Altamirano went further than his contemporaries and, imbued with a social romanticism, thought that literature was not the outcome of the common good, but rather its origin: 'Blessed be that change', he writes, 'since it enabled literature to open the way to progress, or better, gave birth to it, since literature had contained the germ of great ideas which produced an enormous revolution. It was literature that spread democracy most passionately' (30). In this perspective, the writer had an equivalent function to other trades, all of them benefiting from the nation's history and the nature that underlay it. He continues: 'Oh, if anything is rich in material for the writer it is this country, just as it is rich in resources for the farmer and the manufacturer!' (34). The language is once more that of natural resources, rich endowments that can be transformed into other useful things. In a similar vein, he states: 'The ancient history of Mexico is an inexhaustible mine.' This optimism about what is possible and his affirmation of the powers of language lead Altamirano to propose that the younger generation should rewrite the past, recover history and reconstruct the narrative of nationality:

> When he sees the smiling lakes of the Valley of Mexico, when he sees its volcanoes peopled with ghosts, whose legends haunt those who live on their slopes, its fertile villages, its enchanted gardens and its century old forests, through which still pass the shades of the ancient sultans of Anahuac and their beautiful,

odalisque princesses, when he sees all this who is not tempted to compose a vast legend about Mexico? [35]

This idea that America is a natural and historical reality in search of a national narrative inspires Altamirano's didactic romanticism. He is the first American writer not to treat the past as a trauma. That is to say, Altamirano believed that America enjoyed a cultural health because of the multiple elements it combined and asserted. It was necessary to create a literary 'epic' that could articulate historical experience and liberal consciousness. This 'American inspiration' was one of the great virtues he saw in Bello. Altamirano writes: 'Because of this his disciples, like the Greeks, always sing about its seas, its mountains, its sky, its sun, its flowers its plains and its virgins. They sing to the fatherland, they sing of freedom.' He then adds:

His songs have the magnificent originality of primitive poems. A perfume of the living forest is exhaled from them; they have the majestic accents of the ocean; they breathe the mysterious calm of the desert nights; they are filled at times with thunder and lightning. Others murmur with the sweet sigh of the canyon, which slips onto the meadows, or with the zephyr that plays through the folds of the hills [193].

Nature here is turned into an American discourse. It is a complete programme of territorial reappropriation. The new literature is a return to what is specific and proper to Mexico. It names, describes and recovers the landscape and the voice of its materials and spirit, of the place itself. This articulation of nature and discourse will be the basis on which the virtues of the civil order will rest.

Altamirano's favours the epic, even though he realizes that the novel is the form appropriate to modern social life. He reviews recent Spanish American novels with equal enthusiasm, but rejects French influence in favour of more native expression. *María* by the Colombian writer Jorge Isaacs fills him with enthusiasm. For Altamirano, the novel is the genre appropriate to the new: 'the nineteenth century novel must be placed alongside journalism, theatre, industrial advance, railways, the telegraph and the steamship. Like all these inventions it contributes to the improvement of humanity and to the levelling of classes by education and way of life' (48). What is new about the genre is thus in keeping with a Faustian view of modernization, typical of nineteenth-century optimism about the democratic possibilities of progress. Altamirano sees the novel as born from the printing press and is thus the form most characteristic of the new times.

In her *Foundational Fictions: The National Romances of Latin America*, Doris Sommer suggests that the didactic form dominant in Altamirano's novels can be explained by the 'national romance' that determines both character and genre.[7] Setting aside the conventional description of his work as 'magisterial', Altmirano, for all his virtues and limitations, illustrates a deeper dilemma of the late nineteenth century. What current genres, or what new ones, could provide present-day voices with a legitimate discursive articulation, whilst transcending their parodic derivation (which is evident in the dominant romanticism). The very notion of the 'novel' is rather protean at this time, and includes within its expansive remit discursive forms of quite diverse origin, generally coloured by a verisimilitude that comes from the chronicle, the mediating genre between the reader and the new literary form. This play of generic form, which becomes self-reflexive both in discourse and in representation, has two famous examples: Esteban Echeverría's *The Slaughterhouse*, and Ricardo Palma's *Tradition*, both of which are discussed below. It is not coincidental that the exploration of form in order to find a generic solution that would accommodate the distinct materials and voices that the authors wished to articulate should produce two distinct solutions (each full and realized) giving narrative form to the national. It is not so much in 'novels' as in 'novelizations' (in the forms of the short story, the serial or the fictional chronicle) that this exploration comes to fruition.

We have still to formulate and study the correlations between the formation of nation and nationality in Latin America and the formation of genres and the resolution of artistic problems within Latin American culture. To do this requires a wider remit than is usual, and needs to go beyond Henríquez Ureña's model in *Literary Currents in Latin America*, where he proposes a grand synthesis of which his book gives only an introductory sketch. His model brings together – without apparent conflict – biographical data, a characterization of the work and the political experience of the author, and sets them within an outline of the evolution of letters and culture, which are understood as forms of historical knowledge. Our task is to discuss the explorations of genre and linguistic differentiation within these representations. This double articulation (national formation / literary formation) can be seen as a process of production, connected to other processes that are asymmetrical and heterogeneous. Henríquez Ureña's model levels these processes, submitting them to schemata of validation and authorization. It offers an illusion of cultural articulation, dissolving the possibility of production and reinforcing control.

In his *Latin American Contexts, Literature and Society in the 19th Century*, Valeri Zemskov endeavours to give a typology of the genres of this period.[8] He states that at the end of the eighteenth century and at the beginning of the nineteenth: 1) 'local cultures and their folk traditions were consolidated' (meaning the cultures of the *llaneros* [plainsmen] of Venezuela, *rancheros* [ranch hands] of Mexico, the gauchos of Argentina and the *guajiros* [peasants] of Cuba), 'but these traditions were not common to all the population of each of these countries'; 2) 'they were not stable and never became the legitimate, developed forms of expression of ethnic consciousness'; 3) 'their active development . . . coincided . . . with the period after independence'. National literatures were formed 'without the support of folk traditions that had been fixed and established over time'. Beginning with the idea that 'the *ethnic universe*' is a series of models that form 'ethnic consciousness', he proposes that 'The core of this ethnic universe is formed by the image of homeland-nature and, intimately related to this, the image of the ethnic hero.' This is another study that needs to undertaken, since ethnic consciousness is not necessarily something that has been realized once and for all, and may well be riven by conflict. It is not just plural but something in process. It is the sensibility of the period, and has various concrete literary and political forms. These have an effect not merely on representation and genre, but also on political projects, and on stock representations of the given.

One such is Montalvo's ethnic trope of making the Inca speak (something that even Bello approved of). Another is Altamirano's ethnic sensibility, which was to become the basis of his version of the national. Another is Martí, refusing to believe in 'race' because local fusions of peoples produced universality. On the other hand, the Mexican Pimentel produced a document that was fiercely hostile to the negroes, and Miguel Antonio Caro saw the Conquest as the victory of a superior race over an inferior one. Zemskov provides an interesting conclusion: 'Creole–Mestizo folklore provides the basis for non-epic genres, that is the minor literary genres mainly of the 17th and 18th centuries, like the *décima, glosa* and *romance corrido* [forms of Spanish verse], which replaced the Spanish romance, formed from the epic tradition.' He ends by saying: 'Both gauchesque poetry and the Cuban romances use the minor genres of the gaucho and the peasant: *décima*, *glosa* and elements of the romance tradition, and in the case of gauchesque poetry forms derived from the singer–dancer tradition.' This variety of genres points to the process of formal exploration and reappropriation of extant repertoires that leads on the one hand from Martí's *Simple Verses* to Hernández's *Martín Fierro*, and on the other from Sarmiento's essay to Palma's 'tradition'.

Echeverría did not leave behind any examples of the popular 'songs' that he planned to write, but his intention was clear when in 1836 he published his curious 'Project and Prospectus for a Collection of National Songs' ('it never saw the light of day', Juan María Gutiérrez noted) in which one reads: 'The Brazilians have their *modinhas*, the Peruvians their *yaravíes*, tender and melancholic songs . . . there is no cultured people that does not delight in singing of their glories and misfortunes, expressing in their poetry and music the fleeting emotions of their existence' (135). Interestingly, he does not give us the popular source of the Buenos Aires songs that he proposed to include, although it is clear that he is looking for the same legitimacy for his implicit national music that he finds in neighbouring forms. The *yaraví* was smiled on by fortune, it has to be said, since Bello also mentions it, and the Peruvian writer Mariano Melgar (1790–1815, shot by the royalists) wrote a series of delicately polished *yaravíes* in which an 'ethnic' sensibility (the intimacy of a regional voice) appears even more starkly because of the dignified rhetoric of his formal apparatus. It should not be forgotten that the imminent domination of the city over the rural universe would disrupt the legitimacy of these voices. The new hierarchies that were constructed by capitalism and pressing modernization would discard indigenous forms with increasing violence.

From this perspective, literary criticism is an encyclopediac form, which offers a synthetic view of the processes of nation formation: historical, political, social and artistic. Altamirano is again an outstanding example. Gutiérrez spends more time on the texts but treats biography as an interesting manifestation of the regional. In her discussion of a volume of critical essays by the Mexican writer Francisco Sosa, Rosalba Campra notes his Latin American literary conception of the 'nation', which he conceives through the Mexican national project, one he shares with Altamirano.[9] Sosa says: 'The world that Columbus discovered shows greater riches in the intelligence of its children than in the gold it hides in its bowels.' This version of culture as the transfer of natural abundance is typical of Altamirano, and is identical with Sosa's critical practice. The self-reflexive dimension confirms the national cultural programme. Sosa, like a good liberal, enjoyed Palma's 'traditions' and the two authors exchanged letters. It was to Palma that Riva Palacio wrote, saying: 'I believe like Seneca that you cannot be a good orator or a good writer without being a good citizen. The reactionaries, those rabid ultramontane zealots, are excited because they think that the world can be turned back to an earlier time' (3 May 1888). Good literature, like the country itself, advances because of the arts. When Altamirano died, Manuel Gutiérrez Nájera's 'Obituary' described him as 'the voice of democracy', who spoke in the name of freedom and progress.

Esteban Echeverría (1805–1851) also saw a distinctive model of national literature in the representation of nature. He writes: '[Poetry] must appear dressed in its own original character. Reflecting the colours of the physical nature that surrounds us, it must be at once the living description of our customs, and the most elevated expression of our leading ideas . . . feelings and passions . . . and social interests' (letter to J. M. Gutiérrez, 1834). Like many people of his time, he believed in the symmetrical development of society and the arts, and in the definition of society and culture in terms of the nation. Thus, he also saw a causal relation between literary and political independence. 'National poetry is the inspired expression, the living reflection of the heroic deeds, customs, spirit – all that constitutes the moral life and the inner and outer mystery of a people' (v, 125).

It is revealing that in being faithful to his poetic ideology, Echeverría created not an Argentine version of the discourse of abundance but precisely its opposite, the most extreme version of the discourse of lack. *The Slaughterhouse* (written between 1839 and 1840 and published in the *Revista del Río de la Plata* in 1871) was the greatest denunciation of the political negativity – 'bad government' – that dominated social and moral reality. This discourse of lack sees reality not merely as badly made but as a form of systematic reduction, which dispossesses and destroys the subject, making social interaction inhuman.

The Slaughterhouse opens by situating itself within discourse, but in an unexpected place: 'Although I am writing history, I will not begin with Noah's Ark and the genealogy of his descendants as the ancient Spanish historians of America, who ought to be our models, were wont to do.' This declaration is obviously ironic. He is telling us that he has good reasons for not following their example, but he is not going to tell us what they are. We already know one of them, however. Every nation must have its own literature. 'History' and 'historians' would lend verisimilitude to the tale, so that refusing their codes means having to find another contract through which to share the truth with the reader. But on the other hand, the historical is also the novelistic (as will be clearly demonstrated in Palma), even if the material of history is still in search of its appropriate genre.

Noah's Ark introduces the first image of crisis and response to crisis. The irony grows with the traditional character of social control: the Church prohibits the consumption of meat during Lent. Right from the start, the weft of images produces a polyvalence that opens up within the associations that reading weaves together. The events that are described belong to the social order (disorder), seen from the point of view of liberal irony (political). The common (biblical) emblem of Noah's Ark is in tension with the Church (traditional). Knowledge is historical (belonging not to history but to historicity), and discourse is born as the moral account of the contemporary. In the second paragraph, the first *federales* appear, the warehousemen, men who obey the Church's commands and are thus defined as belonging to the conservative forces. We thus shift genres from 'history' and a quasi-ethnographic 'picture of customs' to the 'chronicle', a scathing tale about the contemporary world. But in the third paragraph ('Just then, there was a fierce rainstorm') a description of the environment coincides exactly with the beginning of the tale. The rainstorm that turns the city into a quagmire is just one more episode, but in its singularity it also lends a quality of legend to the tale: the beginnings of social disorder are accompanied by cosmic chaos. It is not by chance that the rainstorm seems like 'a new deluge'. This primordial material, this urban mud, corresponds to the beginnings of social organization. The formation and deformation of the collectivity will take place with this malleable material as their base.

From the start, the story makes the reigning powers relative: even the interpretation of natural phenomena is shown to be political. The Flood is a divine punishment provoked by the 'impious Unitarians' and the inundation itself is described as a 'Unitarian devil'. Echeverría drifts towards satire as he sets conscience against the demands of the stomach. The absence of meat so undermines the power of the Church that the populist government can, in a gesture of reconciliation, decree the reopening of the slaughterhouse. We are in a world turned upside down. Reality is perceived and represented as something to be laughed at: its sign is reversed. We can see this in the enthusiasm with which the good news of the reopening of the slaughterhouse is received by the rats: 'the usual joy and jubilation that preceded abundance returned to those places'. Everything in this magnificent tale is inscribed on another inscription. The tale is a re-writing that dismantles the discourse of the social. In this critical-satirical perspective, however, the social is ambiguous: 'From a distance, the perspective on the slaughterhouse reveals a grotesque world, full of animation.' This idea of 'distance' is interesting. Satire imposes a greater distance, with its Enlightened didacticism, which turns the description of customs into moral advocacy. A lesser distance is involved in the fiction, the account of events in the febrile and paradoxical world of human business in the contemporary slaughterhouse. It is the change of perspective from 'grotesque' to 'full of animation'. It is not that Echeverría's discourse is contradictory, but that it is made up of the various tensions that the critical representation of social experience and its immediate political interpretation impose. In the same way, the word 'perspective' is in itself self-reflexive. Between the greater and lesser distance, the subject decides to transfer mediation (a median, mediating distance) from the witness to the testimony (the distance woven by discourse, more impersonal, more objective). 'This could be seen at the beginning of the slaughter', the author says as he concludes his first descriptive picture, giving the impersonal verb the role of factual testimony. And he then immediately adds: 'But as he went forward, the perspective changed.' The tale (in the place of the narrator) advances, reducing distances and soon we can hear dialogue. The horror of the spectacle with its intense animation is warped, producing the effect of a paradoxical vivacity (already there in the jokey dialogue between the gravediggers in *Hamlet*).

The greater distance is then re-established when the narrator returns to the discourse of politics: 'This is a model in miniature of the barbaric way in which questions of social and individual rights are discussed in this country. In the end, the scene represented in the slaughterhouse should be seen and not written.' If the scene is written it will tend to be appropriated by the episodic and the novelistic. When the community of readers presupposed by the discourse of politics sees the scene acted out in the slaughterhouse they can do nothing but follow the horror to its conclusion. Writing grips us with horror, and makes us part of the testimony. The tale imposes itself upon us again, with that individualization characteristic of the novel: 'An animal had stayed behind in the corral'. This whole scene with its festive violence prefigures the political violence of the final scene. But we still sense the double tension of this testimony: popular speech is composed of 'obscene, joking exclamations' (one adjective indicates the lively fable, the other a critical distance). The politico-moral allegory with which the story ends introduces a wider perspective: the victim (emblematic of the *unitarios*) perishes (in a critical parallel) at the hands of the butchers (whose political function makes them emblematic of the *federales*). This political didacticism returns us to the beginning, to the disintegration provoked by the crisis. This expresses itself in violence and ends in the negativity in which the social is usurped by the dictatorial state. After this political conclusion, which the story extracts from its own fabulation, the tale ends with words taken from contemporary reality, that is, it concludes in the name of 'Enlightenment and Liberty'.

It is revealing, however, that the story begins to designate its social space as 'Slaughterhouse' with a capital 's' just at the point when a bull bursts in ('something strange, even forbidden'). This 'change of name' is maintained for the rest of the story. Why does the 'slaughterhouse' of the first part become the 'Slaughterhouse' for the remainder of the story? Lacking all the elements for a reliable reconstruction, we could nevertheless suggest that there is in fact more than one slaughterhouse, depending on the discourse in use. At the beginning we have a concrete slaughterhouse (historical) with its own name and a well-known location. This discourse is that of the 'chronicle' (composed of a description of local customs and the history of the immediate past coupled with political journalism). Subsequently, but only after the central episode of the bull, the Slaughterhouse appears. The discourse of the fable now gives it a resonance emblematic not just of urban and social space but of the place that violence has in the 'natural' geography of the city. The bull that has tried to escape into the city is recaptured by the slaughtermen and butchered. This discourse belongs to fiction, to the fable, which traces a figure of necessity upon the indeterminate, revealing the character of its actors. The young *unitario* appears immediately afterwards, and the Slaughterhouse becomes the space of political violence, at which point the discourse turns into one of national allegory. These three 'slaughterhouses' (belonging to the discourses of chronicle, emblem and allegory) appear through a widening of function and signification. Historicity (the social experience of the political) acquires a discursive formation in this sequence of transformations.

It is interesting that Gutiérrez, the first person to read *The Slaughterhouse*, saw it as a true story: 'If this had fallen into the hands of Rosas, its author would have disappeared on the spot. He was very conscious of the risk he was running, but the evidence of his trembling hand that appears in the imperfections of the original manuscript, which is almost unreadable could be due more to anger than to fear.' He goes on to add: 'the scene of the "wild *unitario*" in the hands of the "Slaughterhouse Judge" [who presides over the inverted world of the torture ceremony] and his acolytes is no invention. It really did happen on more than one occasion during that tragic time.' In the story, this episode in the Slaughterhouse is allegorical: in history, it is a fact. This transformation of an event that might have taken place into an allegorical political figure shows how the fable has worked on its given materials. It shows the necessity of formalizing common knowledge.

If lack appears in *The Slaughterhouse* in the de-naturalization of social space, in the poem *Martín Fierro* (1872) by José Hernández (1834–1886) it is represented as de-socialization. With the poem's equating of biography and song, thanks to the extraordinary poetic solution of the reworked *décima* (Hernández reformulates the standard ten-line strophe, giving it a novel suppleness and inclusiveness), the gaucho is able to tell his life story and make of it the poetic emblem of historical injustice. The narrator speaks in the first person within the legitimate space of his own formalization, through which his voice acquires conviction and persuasive power. So that when he says 'Like those beautiful birds / That jump from branch to branch / I make my bed amidst the clover / And have the stars for my blanket', he makes Nature into man's home, and in this case, the home of the subject of the romance of his freedom, the 'self-taught philosopher' or 'natural man' who belongs to the discourse of pre-social good. But at the same time this natural home is a space delimited by the family house, in no less a natural correspondence:

> I have known this land
> In which the countryman lives
> Where he has his small holding
> And his wife and kids ...
> What a delight to see
> How he spends his days

This self-sufficient and Arcadian order also presupposes the intimate conversation that underpins the knowledge of place ('I have known') and the agreeable passage of time. The voice of place is idiomatic conversation, whose roots in the local region give an order to the verse, articulate its sequences and construct its discursive models as natural. Thus the freedom of the open spaces is in keeping with the internal and domestic harmony of the subject within its environment. Both orders are made unnatural and are deterritorialized by the pressing expansion of the state, which seeks to incorporate both geographical and private space. Echeverría uses a mordant irony in putting the incongruous word 'barbarian' in the mouth of an authoritarian power: Hernández uses the gaucho to throw it back at the agents of civilization:

> The gaucho was secure
> On his land
> But . . . what barbarity!
> Events went so awry
> That the poor man spent his life
> Fleeing from authority.

The exclamation mark signals the reversal of values, the world turned upside down. And for that reason it sustains the heroic voice of persecuted reason, which is here embodied in the victim of an arbitrary law. The idea of a 'lost good' refers to a specific historical experience (but within the Latin American tradition of lack): 'At peace I lived on my land / Like the bird in his nest'; 'All that was left was the unhappiness / Of lamenting the good that was lost.' The fullness of this good makes present scarcity incredible: 'Whoever sees me now so poor / Perhaps would not believe all of this!'

In lines 1069–80, there is a powerful image that reflects how place itself has been orphaned. The singer imagines the things his children lack, as they are turned into social orphans. For the persecuted, displaced gaucho the desocialized marginality to which he is condemned becomes a radical negation of his humanity: 'His home is the scrubland / His lair the wasteland', we read. Space itself has been denaturalized and turned into the enemy. All that is left are the margins. This inversion of space robs it of meaning: 'Without goal or direction / In that immensity / the gaucho wanders like a spirit.' At the end, when the song becomes a conversation with the arrival of Cruz, 'they cross over the frontier'. 'And following their true course / they enter the wilderness.' The 'course', that tracking through open space, becomes their guide in that nameless space, which in its turn unnames: it is the space where the song and the poem can only cease. As Ludmer has suggested, 'Hernández wrote the most radical text of oral autobiography and threw it at his political enemies. The text showed that there were two juridical orders, one of which differentiated by means of language, and put the other outside the law. The law creates criminals'.[10] The gaucho's order is that of popular culture, the bearer of natural law. The hero of this persecuted culture is turned into a fable of the place that has been lost. The state, its judges and soldiers occupy space by force, a space that they then denaturalize by their inhuman and anti-democratic culture of violence. Martín Fierro is a true allegory of cultural difference as it appears historically under the paradoxical form of coercive civilizing modernity. He is not just that civilization's first discontent, but also a living document of its violence. In this sense, the affirmation of language and place is paradoxically phantasmatic. The poem is rooted in the materials created by uprooting; the model of community is constructed from its loss. The Other's song within a community of intimate address is formed out of the fragments of an inverting mirror, where the voice is a brief dialogical indication of a vulnerable humanity.

From Echeverría's utopian socialism to Hernández's social romanticism, we can see how the formation of the nation becomes a question of the shaping of genre and the production of narrative. Both writers give an account of nation formation in the very act of reformulating the genres in which they write. The one is expressed in the other, and this discursive option is part of the very texture of cultural nationality. This is a (non-nationalist) nationality that works on the voices of identity and plurality, voices that cross the frontier. It works on the historical and the discursive, on geography and on the page. For a moment, the national is just this social life – often tense, polarized and full of conflict – affirming its spaces and contesting them with the dominant orders. Discursive historical consciousness, often partial and incomplete, is also the articulation of a nationality at once universalized by its humanizing political ideals (even if in tension with its own civilizational programmes) and particularized by its cultural subjectivity, through the networks of the community of difference.

Palma's version of the national narrative, the 'Peruvian tradition', has been many things to many people. His detractors have attributed to him the ideology of a section of his readers (those in the oligarchy who read him, neither his only constituency nor even the largest), and even more naively have seen his work as the expression of an ideological worldview rather than a discourse *on* ideology. Palma elaborates his 'tradition' from a great variety of sources: the romance, the chronicle, the legend, the description of local customs, the sentimental tale, the romantic serial, the historical novel and linguistic investigations that are both documentary and lexicographic. The 'tradition' is thus a 'Peruvian' (national) solution to the problem of genre, whose plural discourse is in itself one of anti-canonical multi-lingualism. Its popular language produces a version of the national that relativizes a traumatic history and an arbitrary social stratification. How can we recuperate Palma's literary and cultural work and his 'tradition' within the process that produced the discourse of nationality? Undoubtedly, we need to go beyond ideological or sociological criticism, which perpetuates the naive belief that nineteenth-century liberal writers were merely the instruments of the power of the 'Liberal State'. Working on the critical plurivalence of the 'tradition' we need to reconstruct the inner voices that subvert the authoritarian rhetorical edifices of the Tradition. This monological, canonical and anti-democratic authority was destabilized by Palma's irony, relativism and tolerance, and by his subtle transgressions of a social code, which was even more authoritarian as it presented ideological representations as natural.

Most importantly, the 'traditions' must not be read in the episodic form in which they were written and published. Rather, the corpus needs to be reordered so that different networks of articulation can be produced: historical, popular and legendary traditions, social and ideological representations, traditions devoted to love . . . (It should be said, however, that the author's relation to his genre is very interesting, and remains extremely flexible, as the genre develops and expands in the process of its own creation, generating its form and the ways in which it is to be read.) The traditions devoted to love are nearly all gruesome: passion comes and goes with neither rhyme nor reason and lovers end up like those of melodramatic serials, but not without some breach in the social code, a gesture that is the very basis of Palma's narrative method.

Palma was a liberal sceptic, conceiving his public task as a cultural mission, so much so that he saw his fictions as only one element in a whole array of historical and documentary works. He felt that he was forging a knowledge of the national, working on its discourse in appropriate places – the library, the archives, lexicography and narrative. At the same time, this work was informed by a social conception of art, in which the artist speaks for his community, preserving its knowledge and lore. What he produced was a highly crafted synthesis of form and information. On the other hand the relativism that is typical of the 'tradition's' multi-perspectivalism has the consequence that nationality becomes the dissolution of these different versions: nationality is at times just this disarticulated differentiation. Although Palma relished his image as 'archivist' or 'lexicographer' surrounded by yellowing papers with no relevance to the present, nevertheless in the version of versions with which he wove the discourse of his 'tradition' he created another

channel for the voices of the popular. In his 'traditions' the popular is a
form of humour. It is also a way of evaluating and preserving information as lively, immediate material that will survive in spite of crisis and
codes. It is a centre in displacement, with its own legitimacy, wisdom
and capacity for life. Many voices speak within this comedy of nationality, and they do so from the intimate contradictions between individual
and institution, between new and old, between prejudice and irony,
between norm and breach, between code and licence: in the end between
law and its transgressions. Using the materials of the Tradition, Palma's
'tradition' carries out a veritable deconstruction of constructed forms
and given content – the substance passed on by cultural tradition.

In Latin America in the nineteenth century historicity pervaded every
discourse with its paradigmatic representations (abundance / scarcity /
potential), its explorations of genres (the modified *décima*, the multi-genre
narrative, the didactic pamphlet) and its theories of literary language (a
unifying Spanish, a purist Creole, a regionalism stressing difference).
Historicity is thus not merely a narrative of history, but above all one of
culture. It thus ceases to be pure frustration, traumatic crisis, violence and
loss. If politics all too often confirms this pessimistic account (to which
both Bolívar and Sarmiento succumbed), culture is the space where historical experience can be transformed as discourse, process and elaboration.
And this creation (no simple punctual and causal foundation but a process
unfolding over time) informs the best stories and poems with their deep
narrative structure and their combinative diversity of form. In fact, even
the 'historical novel' is less 'historical' than the texts of Echeverría,
Hernández and Palma. The quality of the novel (novelization, the fable of
history) precipitates out more easily in these great moments of genre differentiation. In this variation of difference, a discursive plentitude gives
formal representation to a full nationality. The nation is produced by
articulation with its internal elements and with its external equivalents.
Most novels of the period, by contrast, reveal the inability of the genre
to effect this articulation, and surrender to didacticism or regionalism.

The 'tradition' is exactly this novelization without a novel. In the
emblematic case of Peru in the second half of the century, the country's
national narrative emerges more easily in this hybrid genre, which
brings together literary and historical discourses combining an appeal
to veracity with the persuasive power of community art. Often, the pure
pleasure of narrativity prevails within the 'tradition': the story about the
story, the genre's reflection on itself. The historical is processed by literary art, by way of a transference that saturates the historical with a

familiarization, suturing the traumatic with an ironic relativism and treating the ills of society by demonstrating their absurdity. Thus the subversions that the 'tradition' achieves do not constitute an Enlightened political programme, as in Echeverría, or a challenge to the legitimacy of the system, as with Hernández's critique of cultural hegemony. Rather they form a thesis about reading, a hermeneutic of the formations and deformations of the national, produced inside a culture that is plural – popular and Creole. A culture, in other words, that is composed of common sense, the will to survive, the conservation of collective knowledge and critical rationality. The 'tradition' does not partake of some essence, be it one of character, determinism or national identity, but rather allows the instruments of nationality their operative effect. These functions and episodes construct a 'surface', a rich human material, as durable in its knowledge (in culture) as it is precarious in its spectacle (in history).

It is hardly coincidental that a conservative writer like Miguel Antonio Caro, whilst writing his apologia for the 'Conquest', should launch an attack on Palma. He condemns the 'witty writer' who 'with the deliberate intention of making the facts more interesting alters them . . . as he does in his *Traditions*, something which is so much more dangerous in societies that have not yet fixed their history'.[11] But this is exactly the point: if history were fixed, the 'tradition' would be meaningless. It is because history does not yet have an authorized and normative version that the 'tradition' can co-inform it, as an account within a nationality in process, a *becoming-nation*, creating it with all the ambiguities, tensions and dramas that are evident in Palma, but with the pleasure of its telling and the intelligence of its own dialogical relativism.

In Palma, then, the dilemmas of representation have been transferred to the drama of form. Genre and writing are the literary corpus and the place where historicity is turned into a plural conversation in which the readers also engage. The 'tradition's' horizontality suggests that interpretation, at once relativistic and tolerant, is a democratizing act: it affirms civil society in affirming the common memory of culture. Hence literature would be in the last analysis a means to generate meaning, fertility and creative articulation, opposed to the arbitrary events of history and the hierarchies of society. Palma is not resigned to the world as it is, but subverts it with irony, letting the reader play his part in the critical allegory that he must articulate. Even if the world is constituted by lack, interpretation, reading and the reworkings elaborated by writing provide a subsequent network of meaning.

The plurivalence of the 'tradition' can be explained in part by the fact that it does not impose restrictions on itself by a binary polarization of society. It goes beyond the satires produced in contemporary Lima, examples of a genre typical of a polemic, pamphleteering spirit. Their immediacy makes them a rich testament to the general discontent with the state and the organization of politics and public affairs. The founder of this genre was Felipe Pardo y Aliaga (1806–1868), an aristocrat and conservative, who brilliantly satirized local customs, politics and democracy – the very form of the republic. Satire is a literal discourse of lack, but its function is predominantly political, which accounts for the way it reduces social complexity. This form of literature is exercised with a prophylactic and didactic justification, which legitimizes its negativity. In 'The Minister and the Candidate' Pardo himself reduces politics to the sphere of the state: 'You've never had it so good / Love spreads to order. / The Exchequer runs smoothly' says the minister, whilst the candidate replies: 'Let the Devil take it / The Exchequer's bankrupt.' In the discourse of politics, abundance and scarcity are just different ways of manipulating reality, an antagonism organized by power. In 'Political Constitution', an extended sermon, whose anti-democratic, authoritarian and frankly racist cast cannot be overlooked, Pardo criticizes the administration of the Exchequer from a conservative and patriarchal perspective. It is an intervention in a long-standing debate about public loans, secured on the national wealth, which were under constant discussion at the time. Martí himself intervened in the debate about the free trade treaty between Mexico and the United States. There was recurrent public discussion throughout the century on the relative merits of economic liberalism, which would open up national markets, and state protectionism, which would regulate them. These options had real implications for the future of the post-colonial republics. Pardo claims that sudden wealth (in this case *guano*) just confirms endemic scarcity:

> What will become of Peru, when, the mine
> Exhausted, it suffers in poverty,
> Because its people have not learned,
> To create a common wealth?
> By a natural path, you could have
> Risen, young nation, to greatness,
> Then came the guano and it left you
> Prematurely aged by vile dissoluteness.

Jorge Basadre saw the Lima satire as revealing the sceptical oligarchic spirit, and it is true that the authoritarian eradication of the Other is a long-standing political practice not just in Peru. This ideological loss of the Other is also the loss of natural and cultural otherness, which the city–country antagonism will provoke. The de-nationalizing consequences of modernity reproduce the old dualisms and the endemic domination of the interior by the coast. The literary responses to the debate and the permanent crisis of the post-colonial, dependent capitalist sub-system would claim one or other of these two spaces as the source of cultural legitimacy, as *the* cultural and political model, or as an alternative discourse. At the beginning of the debate, when difference was still represented through the model of local ethnography, Carlos Germán Amézaga (1862–1906) produced 'La Pachamanca', a description of native customs from the point of view of the city: 'I was there, pulled by a joyous mood / like a child of the coast, a man of another world.' He compares the Peruvian countryside, with its ignorance and poverty, and the injustice of those 'silent, destitute mountains', to 'the Russian steppe'. Manuel González Prada (1848–1918) in his 'Le tour du proprietaire' comes to the following assessment:

> Nature, in vain
> Do you preserve your syrup, beautify your beauty,
> And with queenly gift offer men
> Your glorious, Olympian nakedness.
> The bourgeois, the duo of Harpagon and Tartuffe,
> Do not understand you, mother without hypocrisy –
> You, divine prodigy,
> You, great pagan.

If Amézaga assessed the Peruvian countryside in terms derived from the Russian novel, González Prada mocked the city dweller from the point of view of Molière's theatre. These dualistic reductions generate a comic stereotype, which reveals the centrifugal antagonisms within the national narrative. With the advance of modernity the story becomes impossible, riven and full of tragedy.

Juan de Arona (1839–1895) is one of Peru's greatest satirists. Like Pardo he was educated in Europe, and was inspired to construct a national literature by the example of the European romantics, and in doing so he set out to describe the reality of his country, heretofore excluded from literary discourse. Once he set down to his task, it was the landscape that became the central theme of his writings, and he would give detailed descriptions of Peru's coastal scenery. The poor semi-desert of the coast slowly led Arona away from poetic eulogy to satire, but a reasoned satire, lacking in malice, not unakin to Byron's episodic commentary in *Don Juan*. But the human landscape failed to fill Arona with enthusiasm, and he became its fervent critic. His intention of creating the literature of the nation is defeated by the lack of connections that would be less obvious when mapping the national setting. There is precisely no subjectivity elaborating his inter-action with the environment as there is in Palma and the 'tradition'. This subjectivity of the nation in process is truncated by the antagonistic political rationalism deployed by the satirists, whose accusatory discourse is entirely lacking in the resources provided by dialogue and a fluid rela-tion to the social and cultural milieu, on which it nevertheless relies. Arona finally became a political pamphleteer, and in the end mentally ill. One of his best works was the *Diccionario de peruanismos* ('Dictionary of Peruvian Words and Expressions'), the compilation of which he began in London at the end of the 1850s. After publishing examples in various papers and journals, he published it as a book in 1883. A sort of encyclopedia of the Peruvian nation as revealed in its distinctive forms of speech, the book had the virtue of documenting one of the differences that the period saw as characterizing the national. Philology becomes more than a discipline within the humanities, and turns into a multi-faceted activity of cultural creation. Interestingly, Arona gives examples of usage through his own poetry, in a sort of self-referentiality that moves from popular to literary language via the mediation of the encyclopedia. Language is above all an eloquent but nevertheless indulgent discourse, which its chronicler must correct and reform in the name of Enlightenment. Thus an encyclopedia of differences becomes regulated by a code. Arona comes to condemn licence in usage, judging it from the standpoint of what is 'proper' and 'correct'. He spends 40 years collecting these echoes of popular wit and invention, but when the time comes to evaluate them, he reveals his own unease with the national narrative, and takes up an institutional position from which he delivers his condemnations. Palma, by contrast, more fully immersed in the differences within the national, argued for the legitimacy of regional language forms, even using the Academy as war-rant. He made prolific use of them deriving a great deal of his writing from ephemeral oral forms.[12]

In the prologue to his *Gramática de la lengua castellana destinada al uso de los americanos* ('A Grammar of the Spanish Language for Americans'), Andrés Bello laid out what he considered to be the catastrophic development of Spanish in the Americas. Exaggerating for didactic purposes, he warned of the danger that the languages of America would separate off from Spanish in the same way that Romance languages did from Latin. This was at the beginning of the independence movement, and he had the example of the United States in mind, whose language, he claimed, was already different from that of England. Emilio Carrilla discusses the issues involved in the chapter devoted to 'The Language of the Romantics (Attitudes to Language)' in his book *El romanticismo en la América hispánica* ('Romanticism in Spanish America') of 1958, but nearly all aspects of this fundamental question of the self-consciousness of the national narrative remain to be properly formulated and discussed. The dictionaries of regionalisms are one source of primary materials for analysis, and the work of Bello and other linguists are another. As with the previous question of genre, what is involved here is a wide-ranging discussion of values, norms and models, of which Bello's famous polemics and those of the Argentine exiles in Chile are just one chapter. Bello says in his prologue:

> But the greatest of all evils, and one which untreated will slowly deprive us of the inestimable advantages of a common language, is that of the constant production of neologisms, which flood into and muddy a great deal of what is written in America, changing the structure of the language, and turning it into a multitude of barbarous dialects which lack norms and order. They are becoming the embryonic forms of new languages, and in the course of time what happened in Europe during the dark ages of the corruption of Latin will happen in America. Chile, Peru, Buenos Aires and Mexico will all speak their own language, or worse, languages, as we see in Spain, Italy and France, where certain languages predominate but, side by side with them there are others which pose obstacles to the diffusion of enlightenment, the execution of laws, state administration and national unity. A language is like a living body: its vitality does not depend on the constant identity of its elements, but on the regular uniformity of the functions which those elements exercise, from which derive the form and features which distinguish the whole.

He concludes: 'Whether I exaggerate the danger or not, it has been the principal motive for my writing this work, which in so many respects is beyond my capabilities.'

Here we have another example of how genre creates the writer. For these first linguists, there was no other route by which to organize grammar than this somewhat anxious devotion to purity and proper usage. It was ironic that Bello should refer to the 'dark' ages of Latin's 'corruption', when he himself had devoted a number of studies to the period. Bello's notion of grammar belongs, at least in this instance, to the eighteenth century. At that point, the 'barbarous' constructions that he attributes to 'South American writers' and that so annoy him were in fact Gallicisms and rapidly came to be part of the common language. Bello's concerns must have had another motivation, and not merely a corrective one. He states it clearly himself: it is a question of the unity of the nation (and he uses the term to refer to the Spanish American nation) and the capacity of the state to legislate, administer and manage progress. This 'reason of state' is sufficient for him to consider that the dominance of one language over others is something desirable and a good thing in itself. In consequence, he forgets the actual native multilingualism that distinguishes Spanish America. Bello, Montalvo, Rufino J. Cuervo and other 'grammarians' find linguistic purism and propriety the basis on which to affirm not just a linguistic unity but also the political unity of America. So much so, that Caro makes Bello into a defender of 'Transatlantic Iberia' and 'Young Iberia' (America): 'If language is a second homeland, every people that speaks the same language belongs, in a certain sense, to the same nationality',[13] albeit Caro is not referring here to a new nationality of difference, but one that derives from Spain.

This grammatical conservatism played an important role within the nineteenth-century cultural formation of Latin America. The preservation of stable usage was promoted in the name of easy communication. The conservation of grammatical norms was defended not in the name of a superficial purism but because it promoted a common, linguistic identity. Finally, unity of language guaranteed geographical and political unity, with its emerging state and enlightened modernization. Different emphases gave rise to different polemical positions: Juan María Gutiérrez proposed a definitive break with Spain and the adoption of other European languages; Manuel González Prada refused to write in Spanish metres, and suggested that metric structures of other literatures should be explored, and so on. But the call to linguistic norms had another function beyond that of cultural conservation. It defined the cultural legitimacy of the state. However, from this one cannot deduce a mechanistic sociology with the *letrado* condemned to define his public function solely within the 'ideological state apparatuses'. This functionalist interpretation superimposes political ambiguities on textual formations and thus abandons the formative and creative meaning of the discursive and intellectual operations of nineteenth-century writers. Other critics have preferred to subordinate the extraordinary and discontinuous textuality of the nineteenth century to one or other dominant opposition (nearly always binary: history / fiction; civilization / barbarism; city / countryside). The challenge for criticism is to rework the cultural network, so that the discourse of the founding fathers is more than a simple liberal–conservative opposition. It is an unintentional jest that Latin American criticism has made nineteenth-century liberals more and more conservative.

Altamirano could claim Bello for the Americanist project even as he disagreed with Pimentel, despite the fact that the latter dedicated himself to studying Mexican indigenous languages. Democracy may be defined not by a levelling pluralism but by the antagonisms that are possible and can be tolerated, but this also implies that, given the lessons of political history, it is prudent to acknowledge the rationality of the conservative position and its institutional role in the process that formed the various cultural networks. To believe that only progressive intellectuals counted in the formation of nationality would be a naive error and an acute loss when the time came to draw up a balance sheet of historical influences.

This is clearly important with regards to current conceptions of the nineteenth-century state. Criticism derived from a dogmatic Marxism framed by the simplistic vision of 'the failure of American independence' sees the national state as something bad in itself, forming part of the means with which the established metropolitan powers effect their domination and that of the local bourgeoisies. As an agency in the service of anti-popular interests, the state co-opts the intellectuals into its ideological apparatuses, making them organically 'official' with respect to 'popular' forces. This conception of the 'ideological' national state is in keeping with contemporary criticism that neo-liberal thought is produced by the state. What is obscured here is the role that the nineteenth-century national state played in the management of the processes of modernization. Its control by power blocs within the national and trans-national bourgeoisies provides an illustration of unequal modernization (modernization without democratization) that characterizes the forms of dependent capitalism in post-colonial Latin America. But in some countries, the cultural configuration of the state – its definition in terms of a politics that translates theses about identity and practices of social combination and representation – has been defined by its mediating role between modernization and civil society. As Stéfano Varese has suggested, it is the weakness of republican national states that explains the survival of indigenous ethnic groups that could not be subordinated to projects of national unity, where they would be designated as *mestizos* in the name of 'integration'. But now as then, culture continues to respond with its own articulations and appropriations to the different forms of violence inflicted on the social fabric. What is lacking is any attempt to rethink the social role of the state from the perspective of its negotiating function. There are various instances of a type of popular socialization of the state. Popular organizations have often created their own mechanisms of participation from within civil society so as to 'supervise' and 'reactivate' legal discourses and to generate a different form of state out of their dispute with it. Thus the mechanistic assessments of the 'market' are in need of a profound revision.

With the *modernismo* of the 1900s, Spanish America would demonstrate its capacity to generate the sorts of discourses in which art and artistic consciousness produce a superior form of social experience out of aesthetic experience. Certain aspects of its figurative repertoire correspond to forms of bourgeois life, to individualist forms of urban experience and to the spread of communications. Other aspects presuppose processes of desocialization and imply a criticism of 'parvenu' bourgeois domination and aggressive imperialism. But *modernismo*, prior to its public life, is first and foremost the possibility that art might construct a universal language, where culture would be expressed as an aesthetic plenitude, as formal skill and rigour, and as something different from the extant repertoires of the West. These fairly basic facts have to be established before we can go beyond a critical sociology that would attribute *modernismo* to export-based monopoly capital, and turn it into a document of the alienation of the artist domesticated by his audience. Clearly, the *modernistas* were anti-bourgeois – in the moral-aesthetic sense in which they were 'anti-materialist' – even as they benefited relatively from bourgeois modernization. It is also clear that their aristocratic credos were less symptoms of their class position than forms of a traditional aestheticizing *hidalguismo* (the cult of the gentleman, with a disdain for material work). The conflicts they had with their times (in an environment of optimistic and authoritarian positivism) led them at one and the same time to a cosmopolitanism and to an Americanism. The first had to do with the most characteristic mechanism of Latin American cultural formation, that of reappropriation, the recoding of signs and their incorporation into new and heteroclite orders. The second was concerned with the intellectual need (as advanced by Rodó) for a redefinition of what was American in terms of a conflictual modernity. This was part of an elaborate process, full of contradictions and ambiguity, and at times messianic elitism and elementary sociologism.

But in the first place, in the *modernismo* of 1900 we have an array of excellent poets (Martí, Darío, Casal, Díaz Mirón, Lugones, Herrera y Reissig) whose works were extraordinarily diverse and possessed of a powerful capacity for renovation. We have figures who are politically contradictory, even tragic, like Salvador Díaz Mirón, a follower of the treacherous general Huerta, and the frankly authoritarian Leopoldo Lugones. There were public men like José Martí, who made the greatest demands on themselves, and aesthetes like Julián de Casal or José Asunción Silva. And finally there is one of the greatest writers in Spanish, Rubén Darío (1867–1916), who while singing about the end of the old days also announced the capabilities of art to forge the times to come. In the second place, *modernismo* astonishes us with a complex version of Latin American subjectivity. Society and history are mediated by the senses and emotions, the light and shade, of a subject that now speaks in its own voice. It burnishes the poetry of its own narrative, as if to gain its rightful place in the myth that constitutes its revelatory discourse. Culture no longer belongs to the past, nor to the future, but rather to the realized present, a privileged imagined synthesis of all the ages of Latin America. It is this present that art bears witness to, recreates and projects into the future.

Of the many versions that deal with this fertile difference, we will examine a single page of Darío. In his article 'The American Novel in Spain' (in *España contemporánea*) he says the following: 'Although we share blood and tongue, the links that tie us to the Spanish do not make fusion possible. We are other(s).'

'Blood' here is a metaphor for 'race' (another metaphor that at the time suggested peculiarity, a different form of sociability, outside tradition) and although the 'blood' here is in part Spanish, it is not completely: we have blood from other sources that separates us from the Spanish and prevents 'fusion'. 'The tongue' supposedly provides the unity of a 'second homeland' but even though it is another link to the Spanish, we are still not the same: this tongue already expresses something else, something that is ours. 'Links' undoubtedly refer to our common history, but they too fail to produce unity. 'Fusion' is a lack of distinction: it is neither necessary nor desirable. On the contrary it seems impossible. Here is the revelation of *de jure* and *de facto* diversity. Hence, 'We are other'. This must be read as Darío's definition of Spanish American *modernismo* but also as his implicit cultural theory, no less rigorous for being subjective. We are other(s). But who? This is the question that emerges in the light of traumatic historicist consciousness, when culture is conceived as a project, 'in search of its expression'. But Darío's cultural theory already expresses a non-traumatic version of history (just as the cultural theory of Lezama Lima and Fuentes will subsequently), since the judgement 'We are other(s)' asks no questions but simply affirms. We are the others, the Other, that is inter-locution, the moment of dialogue. This fullness of identity is, obviously, a cultural myth, and in *modernismo* we are dealing with a discourse where abundance is articulated through a combination of Americanist representations, the genres of poetic subjectivity and the language of American reappropriation. When he asks, without irony, the famous, doubly rhetorical question '*Qui pourrais-je imiter pour être original* I say to myself, everyone', Darío is making a cultural assertion of independence, relativizing the meaning of comparative terms (imitation, originality) in order to sustain dialogue, parody and incorporation. Darío goes on: 'Even in intellectual matters, even in literature, San Martín's sabre stroke cut through the binding of the dictionary. It fractured grammar a little.'

We are other, thus, because language is other. Political independence meant intellectual independence. Above all it meant the crisis of normative language. Freedom and democracy are at the origin of this new capacity for language to say more. The arts universalize a language or a culture. In them, society finds its source of recognition, realization and celebration. If the dominant genre of Spanish American *modernismo* is poetry, it should not be forgotten that its language is also made up of forms derived from contemporary reality. The chronicle and the novel feed poetic narrativity, a fact that lyricism cannot hide. Darío in fact acknowledged that the 'French short story' inspired *Azul* ('Blue'). As for the theory of language, the openings of *modernismo* towards other languages show that the nineteenth-century grammarians' concerns were unfounded. Perhaps the linguistic emblem of *modernismo* was the Salvadorean Francisco Gavidia's project of a new, universal language based on Spanish, which, in a typical gesture, he called *Salvador*

('Saviour'). Gavidia eventually produced a grammar and a dictionary for his new language, which was in fact a lexicon of terms of Latin derivation whose similarity in Spanish, English and French would allow one to speak three languages when one spoke in *Salvador*. This optimistic allegory of multilingual communication blazoned the faith that *modernismo* had in words.[14]

Palma's long battles with the academicians of Madrid to get them to include his 'Peruvianisms' in the *Dictionary of the Spanish Language* took place at the beginning of this process of the redefinition of Spanish in America. The conversion of 'Peruvianisms' into Spanish *lingua franca*, and the conversion of Spanish into a universal *lingua franca* in Gavidia's radical project are two memorable instances of an identity forged in the plurality of dialogue.

José María Pereda had published a letter in Madrid asking for a wider distribution of the American novel in Spain. Darío replied to him in his article, expressing some skepticism. There is not a lot to show for the American novel, he replies. Apart from *María*, there are very few. He mentions Eduardo Gutiérrez, 'the first American novelist and the only one to date', and adds:

> This barbarous, hair-raising serial, this confusion of legend and national history written in a free and easy Creole manner is, in the very abundance of the work, the sign of the times in our literature. This literature about the gauchos is the only one up to now to attract Europe's attention. It is a natural product, indigenous, in all its savage wildness . . . the soul of the land walks through it. The poet of this embryonic moment is Martín Fierro, and here I am absolutely in agreement with Señor Unamuno.'

He sees things with great clarity. American difference is a free, abundant language, homologous with its distinctive nature. The model of nature is the matrix of language. Contemporary history is the embryo from which the new will grow. Given such a promise, even the notion of 'barbarous' acquires a positive connotation. 'Barbarous serial' is almost an oxymoron, because it means the following. We have a Latin American narrative, a different language, whose 'new-born' strength takes possession of a popular genre whose origins lie in the newspaper and comes to inscribe its own account on the palimpsest of genres, on the textuality of the novel, the image of modernity. The 'natural' world is transposed

into writing as its product and these images refer to the parallel formation of discourse and nationality, of one in the other.

The novel, then, is the future of discourse in process, but its theory
forms part of the account of those formations, where the 'I' is produced
from the Other, this we-as-other of which Darío speaks, with such high
expectations. He speaks in the name of what is becoming, and together
with the voices that work the cultural potential of the new, that utopia
intrinsic to what is Latin American.

seven

Judging:

The Paternal Desert

Pedro Páramo (1955) by Juan Rulfo (1914–1986) is the shortest of the major Latin American novels, and yet at the same time, it is a veritable encyclopedia of modern narrative – not because the Rulfo's novel includes all such forms but because it meticulously decentres them.[1] It is written against the demands of the novel's expansive economy, sub-tracting from it and representing the world as lack. Rulfo set himself the task of transcending the representations of the given and the known. His project is one of radical negativity. As the novel begins, the young man who is looking for his father is already a ghost confined within the tale. He is dead and eventually discovers that his father is also dead. But this reduction of knowledge comes about by means of a process of elim-ination within the narrative: representations and subjects leave only their names behind. We only discover the origins of this village of ghosts in the unfolding of a story about endings, as told by a classical chorus from beyond the grave. There are no longer explanations only rumours, the voices that are the residue of writing, its frail roots. The story unworks the representations of the world from the standpoint of the radical negativity of death and becomes in Rulfo's hands the most refined form of the novel, the genre that is born of printing and modernity. It confirms the terrible power of the father, the tyrant who voids the life and the death of his children without origin. It is the novel's assertion that after the various historical attempts to construct legitimate authority, ranging from the programmes of independence to the populist and revolutionary projects of the twentieth century, authority has succumbed to the unrestricted use of power, and that this unfounding has fractured social life and the very sense of what it is to live as a community. There are few examples of a novel making such unrestricted use of hostile landscapes. The primeval Garden of Eden becomes the terminal desert and patriarchal paradise becomes a hell without memory: the natal village becomes a graveyard. These reversals are given within a rigorous system of narrative and symbolic equivalences, which turn the novel into anagrammatic discourse. Pedro Páramo becomes the 'desert stone' (Pedro / *piedra*, 'stone'; Páramo, 'wasteland'), that is authority without articulation, the self-destructive power that annihilates things, eroding their form and meaning. The novel is the clearest version of the discourse of lack as the unmapped background of the American myth of abundance.

The ideological code has a powerful representational function within the novel: it manifests the worldview of popular Catholicism. Rulfo uses the hybrid content of popular Mexican Catholicism to construct an enigmatic reality.[2] Arguably, the characters in *Pedro Páramo* perceive the reality of the world only in ideological terms. The world exists only within the systematic codification produced by rural culture. Whilst a novel in which all its characters are dead hardly prompts considerations of verisimilitude, the experience of the author's family nevertheless does inform it. As a child Rulfo experienced the violence of the 'Cristero War' (the struggle over the post-Revolutionary government's attempts to suppress Catholicism during the 1930s), in which rural groups rose up against the Revolution in the name of their Catholic faith. Various members of the author's family, including his father, died during the uprising. The representation of lack demonstrates its power in laconic coherence and formal rigour. The confirmation of the desert's existence seems to require the strictest canons of beauty. But we can also see an ironic and paradoxical demonstration of how the systematic deployment of ideology produces a world that is full of melancholy, even absurdity. Perhaps this is because every ideological construction carried to its extreme, to the point where it replaces reality, comes to exemplify its unastonishing exceptionality and displaced strangeness. When ideology postulates a literal reality (as if it were a map of the other) it produces only a vast alienation. The world represented as ideological is an alienated world since its limits are in the subject not in reality. The representation to which the subject has paid tribute and of which it is the victim is only the ghost of the real.

More properly, representation is a ghost of language. We could say that ideology functions as linguistic compulsion. It is a terrifying, closed discourse in which the subject of lack embodies and disembodies its world, that same alienated subject that has constructed the tradition of modern criticism, which reproduces the system that makes it victim. The novel takes on this critical lineage but with a sharp, paradoxical irony. Its documenting of hell turns our extant knowledge (the genealogies of moralities) into a *reductio ad absurdam*. We witness the destruction of subjects, and it is arguable that *Pedro Páramo* is a metaphor for the end of the world (or the world turned upside down) produced through ideology. In this sense it is a political novel, even a subversive one, since it denounces the language of alienation. It is a novel that deploys the discourse of myth in order to destroy myth. To challenge the function of the ideological code presupposes that one can see how the critical production of the novel works. Or better, on what ideological instances (or agencies) the novel dwells in order to question and finally overturn them. The novel is a meticulous and passionate work of demolition. Rulfo puts every ideological institution into question: the family, private property, fatherhood, the Church, power. The institutions that shape society's superstructure are systematically undermined by a precisely controlled rebellion. Language is stripped down to its minimal statements, whose economy is such that they hollow out rhetoric by means of an eloquent restrictedness. It is language that withdraws to the elemental name.[3]

The novel shows how an ideological superstructure produces social, political and economic structures, which in turn reinforce it. Power and the exercise of violence have a structuring capacity because they give real form to representation and produce a particular system that does not require legitimation and in which social relations are vitiated. In large measure, the novel tells us that society is impossible. This is because the ideological institutions that support and name it are inhuman. The novel thus offers a radical parable of reading: to take on the excess of negativity that is death itself and to judge everything from the point of view of death. *Memento mori*, the novel recovers a world just at the moment of its disappearance. It makes literal Flaubert's view of writing as the extreme paradox of impersonality: writing as if the narrator were dead.

Thus the ideological code is literally materialized in institutions (equivalent to Althusser's ideological state apparatuses), and these in turn distort a sort of latent natural law.[4] This innate norm is not inscribed in the novel but in the reader. The norm or natural code defines human relations as those not imposed by violence. This 'natural' world is absent: there is a void in its place. By the same token, not only do human relations become distorted but society itself ceases to have a proper grounding. This leads us to another level, that of the symbolic. From the space of the ideological, generated by social relations, we pass to the level of meaning.

At this level the search for the father is the most traditional form of the hero's search for himself. The hero who searches for his father is searching for the patriarchal paradise. He follows the trail of a primeval abundance, which the hero's mother has repeatedly told him has been stolen by the enemy, that obscene, distant paternal authority. But through the stages of his journey, the son is also seeking his own identity, which is displaced and deferred. He thinks he will discover his own face through the various masks he dons, all of which serve as mediations. His identity is not composed of the facts he acquires, accumulates and hoards, but is an ever unknown horizon. In the novel, identity is always deferred, until it is finally refused: it is a search that was doomed to failure even before it began. Few heroes have such little identity as Juan Preciado. He finds none of the objects of his quest, and only finds himself in death. He does, however, discover the privileged point of view of death from which he comes to know everything. In popular culture, death is seen as the point of view which resolves everything. The search for the father, therefore, must end with his death, after which everything can then be read. The Oedipal framework in which the son makes an alliance with his mother to sacrifice his father becomes a journey back to the origin of things, which unfolds along the road of cognition and recognition: memory is restored and completed. The only natural order is the truth of death. The father becomes a body turned into rocks rather than dust: he belongs to the desert, to the ruined. Passing through negativity, the novel concludes with the possibility of the subject's liberation: the murder of the father becomes the novel's true meaning. Killing the father and so destroying the institutions that represent his symbolic value constitutes a rebellion that costs the rebel's life: it becomes an allegorical sacrifice. But where is this patriarchal consciousness that knows everything? It is to be found in popular culture, which reproduces the forces of alienation, but which also produces a collective knowledge. On the symbolic level, the point of view of death supposes a certain transgression within the novel. Since we are in a 'world turned upside down', communication is impossible between the living. Ironically, it is perfectly possible in the world of the dead.

How can that world speak, how can a non-existent people be given a voice? If that world is a fantasy, what is it that we are seeing in the novel? Revealingly, we see only what words refer to. What we know of the world is only the referential immediacy of denomination. The 'reality' we see is a mirage of 'language', a powerful language of location. It defines, fixes, reveals and shows, and is clearly representational. Its evocative power is as sensuous as it is enigmatic. It says 'it is raining', and we feel the rain falling in that other world. Language is nominative, discourse substantive. But it is also a discourse of dialogue. We see the sequence of alternating dialogues, but at the same time we also see the internal dialogues, the sub-dialogues, the snatches of dialogues and the floating monologues, and the fragments that criss-cross in search of a lost chorus. Thus the polyphonic spectacle is made up of various inter-cut voices, which spread out and transform to the point where the present dialogues produce evocations and echoes of a larger story. The texture of oral narration corresponds to a collective narrator who does not need to say 'we' but is a species of alternative voice within the collective narrative space. Voices mark a discontinuous temporality. Time is ordered by conversation. Hence the self-referential gesture of dialogue ('as I was saying to you . . . '). This is a language that continuously quotes itself in order to mark the space of consensus. Popular culture refers to itself in a space constituted by proverbs, sayings and pieces of common knowledge that all imply a sort of common recognition. But there is no romanticization of the popular here: quite the reverse. It is as if popular culture had given everything of itself, only to be negated by the institutional powers that subjugate it. The common figures of speech thus become the skeleton of the dominant ideology. The language of clichés becomes fossilized and its contemporary relevance is better explained as denunciation, as a loss of instrumental power.[5]

How do we understand the ideological network, the inflexible order of this arbitrary world? Let us recall that the *cacique*'s judgement ('we will make the law') indicates that disorder, not order, is the prevailing social form of power. This disorder is the arbitrary rule of local chiefs but it is also something more: the distortion of social existence and the loss of individual identity. Power subjugates: it empties out meaning and does violence to the networks of collective life. Hence the paradox: the codes that produce social experience are the ones that deny the very meaning of the code as a system that reorders consensus. The social is only maintained by its destruction.

In Sarmiento de Valladares' *Tractatus de Hispanorum Nobilitate* (1579) we can find a systematic formulation of two of the most important codes that determine social representation in *Pedro Páramo*: property and legitimacy. These are the dual foundation of seigneurial ideology and control over land and inheritance. The treatise gives a historical account of the forms of ancestral land and the legislation concerning entailment and the rights of 'a person of standing'. These provide the codification of the status of illegitimate children. It is around this distant, but nevertheless persistent and enduring axis that the intimate disharmony of the novel revolves. Ownership of the land is what sustains power and conveys legitimacy. The deep-rooted arbitrariness of this disorder is revealed as violence, inverting supposedly 'natural legitimacy' into unnatural illegitimacy. All the sons are illegitimate: they are denied recognition by the 'illegitimate' father. (Juan Preciado, the 'legitimate son' does not bear his father's name, even though Miguel Páramo, the illegitimate son, does.) Thus the novel enacts the ecclesiastical sources of traditional power, which are internalized within the culture, but in doing so reveals their greater illegitimacy, and their social and human absurdity. In the light of this criticism, property and legitimacy are revealed to be codes that usurp and distort. Lacking the discourse of the law they are revealed as arbitrary violence.

Every reading of *Pedro Páramo* is an interrogation of an enigma. But it would appear to be an enigma entirely lacking in mystery since everything is said in the novel. In offering a reading of its codes we must presuppose its extreme legibility. But this is a tale whose legibility attests to its mysteries, which nevertheless lack resolution. It would be naive to imagine that because *Pedro Páramo* is composed of a series of codes, it thereby loses its capacity to pose questions. This is because its enigma is mythopoetic, not a calculus of probabilities. Still less does the enigma consist of some hidden fact exterior to the novel. There are indeed texts that seem to be enigmatic because they cannot be decoded. But this secret dimension is not because of some concealment of information, as in 'suspense' novels. If the narrator hides the identity of the murderer, he leaves us with a limited enigma that suggests that everyone is guilty. But if everyone is guilty, there is neither guilt nor enigma. In *Pedro Páramo* the elements that form the enigma, or what is indecipherable, are presented at the end, in the constitutive codes, as we have seen. But the enigma is not thereby solved, because there is neither sufficient reason nor total meaning through which to resolve the dilemmas that confront us. Once the world has been unmade, it lacks the wherewithal to begin again: it is exhausted and closes in on itself. Nothing continues on. This 'world turned upside down' is a mirror of history, and its radically hyperbolic quality is an allegory of the discursive construction of the real. At this level of the enigma, the novel becomes a theatre, a mediaeval mystery play in which the end and the beginning occur at the same time. It is therefore a mystery, which represents the enigma as the lack of explanation for the son's status as orphan, for the subject's lack of pronoun, for the voice of the uprooted.

The mother sets the novel in motion, sending her son in search of his father. Juan arrives in Comala, the patriarchal paradise. But the development of the mystery becomes an inversion of terms since it is based on the discovery of death and the 'world turned upside down'. Juan Preciado's death then is part of the contract, because in order to know what part he plays in the enigma he has to die. This pessimism presupposes that truth is impossible and can only be revealed outside life: to know the truth one must die. When Juan Preciado dies he is incorporated into the development of the story as his own witness. Only then can he know the end of the story, that is, the death of his father. The mother dies and the novel begins: the father dies and the novel ends. Between these two points, the quest and the contract allow Juan Preciado to experience the complete enigma, as if it were the setting of the subject. The subject is just this blank axis, this child without a face, without a name. He is *preciado*, he is priced, but he has no other value than that of a sign without a proper nature, a pure interrogation constructed through negativity and critique.

If the enigma is that of identity, then the book would be a question: 'who am I?' To know who I am, I need to know *why* my mother died and *how* my father died. These two questions are the basis of identity, but from the privileged point of view of death (where all the voices are on stage together) the subject experiences not merely the enigma of his origin but that of his own interrogation. That is, he is present at his birth in his very negation. In the end, the subject of the discourse of lack is the one who, precisely lacking explanations, learns to ask the most pertinent questions, those that expose the artifices of lineage as arbitrary and that dismantle the inflexible forms of the social. He learns the redemption of judgement – not the millenarian Last Judgement, but a this-worldly judgement, achieved through the redemptive truth of language, with its capacity to hollow out words and discover names. Dispossessed of his original garden, the child of scarcity veils and unveils the father and mother in the language with which he is freed from his own identity.

Pedro Páramo is a short history of Latin American hermeneutics. Each generation of readers finds another interpretation within it (mythical, allegorical, social, political . . .). The novel also shows how systematically constructed its world is, how there is no other world possible within its terms, and how that presence owes its being to the language that articulates and explains its experience through its normative codes, against which there is no appeal. The notion of the real as untouchable and beyond appeal underlines the melancholic character of the novel, the lack of consolation that lies in the distance perceived between reality and desire, between evidence and illusion / hope, and between the contingencies of life and omnivorous death. But in the very movement in which the novel demonstrates the power of the established order, it goes beyond it, as if to reveal an implicit disorder. Power conceals fragility: behind tragedy lies the irony of its telling. When all is over, only the words remain. They give no answer but do bear witness. *Pedro Páramo* is unlike those novels whose enigmas are resolved like puzzles that suddenly reveal their hidden figures. Rather it is a sort of inclusive fragmentation. One voice is quoted within another voice, one history emerges from the bottom of another history, and time splits so that the past appears as the future revealed. Thus the form of the novel is not that of montage, but of de-montage, dismantling, because it functions as a sort of continuous subtraction that reduces the account to a question about itself. The possibility of a complete narration of everything that it comprises has been lost and all that remains is a stoical language, asking questions with no hope of reply.

Pedro Páramo grows in its re-reading. We return to the beginning as though we were following on from the last page, as if the novel itself had returned to include us in its interrogation and subtraction. In place of an implied reader, the novel has an implicated re-reader. Each time we retrace the road of the son Juan Preciado like a pilgrimage to the sources of reading and each time that our question remains unanswered we sharpen the tools of investigation. Everything grows on each page. Juan Preciado becomes more adult for us; Pedro Páramo older, more magisterial and millennial; Susana San Juan less mad and more free. Even the cemetery seems bigger, the dead augmented every day, since the cemetery does not represent the past (that is, the present of the tale) but the present of the reading, that is, the contemporary reality of history.

The novel is formulated in conflictual terms: its representation is problematic and meaning remains unresolved. It questions us because it begins by interrogating itself and placing a void at its centre. Its subtraction is a process of search, missed encounter, disillusionment and lack. Its systematic character is a sort of thesis. It appropriates the vision of the world characteristic of popular culture: it assumes reality to be exactly what the people believe it to be, so constituting its natural referential horizon. This is the discursive ideological articulation of the novel and at this level there are various enigmatic beliefs. For example, do the souls or bodies of the dead suffer? These beliefs often have a pre-Hispanic origin (life as originating underground) but sometimes a Christian one (that same underworld as the kingdom of the dead). Rulfo has made use of a sophisticated modern instrument, the novel, in order to reconstruct a primordial state of social relations, which are here impossible. It is as though the contradictory spirit of the novel had made the people of the *hacienda* into universal representatives, by giving a local form to the Bible and classical Greek culture.

One of the central enigmas of the novel is the nature of representation. Here the name fails to account for its object in the world, or to put it another way, a name subtracts from language the trace of the thing. In the economy of the novel, the world has been dispossessed both by the reductive system of scarcity, which strips meaning from social existence and by a laconic nominalism, which entrusts the name with the full echo of its object. By the same token, these few names resist in their pure verbal horizon the violence and damage to which they are equivalent on a social and historical plane. Writing which here makes present becomes that which unworks representation.

Comala has disappeared, and all that remains are its names. At the beginning of the novel, it is only this evocative power of the name that keeps Juan Preciado alive, since later we discover that he has been dead right from the first line. The novel's first readers thought that Juan Preciado was alive at the beginning of the novel, later dying alongside the incestuous couple. Later readers, preferring to believe in the superior coherence of death, had Preciado dead from the start. The first reading is more novel-like, refracting the dramatic notion of a comprehensive knowledge achieved through death. The second reading is more symbolic, and perhaps more consistent even if it leaves unresolved the question as to who buries the last people to die. This becomes a historical question. Today, our reading is more ambiguous: although the characters may be dead in history, in discourse they are very much alive.

More significant and decisive is the enigma of the son, the subject born to be an orphan. As in César Vallejo's poetry, the son here assumes the voice of the uprooted and is therefore a subject without a pronoun. Everything happens as if the return to the origin, to the shadow of the origin, were a projection of the subject's own constitution through the symbolic acquisition of speech. After all, this flawed hero registers – in a way which if not mute is at least pre-verbal – his own coming to be, refracted in the story by his revelation as the dead son. And this is clearly a characteristically mid-century Latin American definition of the problematic birth of the subject, since its very resolution is dramatized by the subject's control of language. He is born to language when he dies. Between the narrative quest and the symbolic contract (from the mother to the father as we have seen) his enigma as orphan without horizon is resolved into a greater dilemma, that of recognizing himself in the patriarchal tale as in an empty mirror: not his living face but his gaping tomb. But this allegory of the subject is not just analytic. It is rather a narrative hypothesis. Hence the force of its interrogation culminates in negativity, a potential gesture of criticism. History, which rejects him, in the end reaffirms him, granting him the knowledge with which, in turn, he can reject the world that has offered itself as the only possible reality.

Pedro Páramo is also made up of various paradoxes, organized around symmetrical terms, or binaries: death / life, son / father, fertility / desert. These polarities formalize the drama of the profound cut within Mexican life, which Rulfo represents through the major paradox that life is only legible from death: in order to know you must die. This conviction belongs to popular culture and conveys a basic scepticism about the possibilities of truth. But these symmetries are not just antagonistic, for all that the novel is a treatise on disillusionment. They support the exercise of negativity, which works from a position of refusal, denouncing the naturalization of power. Passing into the beyond (which lacks meaning of its own) it can dismantle an ill-founded here and now.

This character of revelation, of self-discovery through a *via negativa*, comes from the very relativizing nature of the novel, the genre that is the ironic discourse of critical modernity. This brings Rulfo's novel close to the intricate tragic meaning of Faulkner's novels, and to the imperturbable lack of consolation in Beckett's work. On the other hand, *Pedro Páramo* comes from a traditional worldview, of pre-Hispanic origin, which conceives reality as made up of cycles of alternating sign. The world the right way up, where order, justice and abundance prevail, is followed by the world turned upside down, where violence, disorder and scarcity rule. The idea of the world turned upside down derives from popular messianism and has different formulations in different cultures and times. *Pedro Páramo* makes use of this model (inverting all forms of order: Divine, human, legal, filial, etc.) in order to construct a radically critical representation of our world, a world that is still constructed as the reverse of order and justice. If the modernity of the novel, its analytic strategy, allows us a clearer view of the meaning that the traditional world has lost in the negation of community, the circular form of the narrative returns us to another tradition, that of myth, which in this case figures the world turned upside down, but also allows us to read it, implicitly, as also reversible. If the sons of *Pedro Páramo* can no longer see another world, we who are the children of reading can imagine one.

eight

Interpreting:
The Authority of Reading

Of Love and Other Demons (1994) is a novel that brings its readers to the verge of tears. García Márquez's previous novels gave rise to laughter, criticism or nostalgia: this novel wants us to cry. For the Spanish Renaissance poet Garcilaso de la Vega, on whose model of expression the novel is based, tears are sublime ecstasy and it is the greatest feat of eloquence to evoke them. But in the novel's rhetoric of tears, the agony of love becomes something else: the end of time, the end of the known world. This takes place as the moral catastrophe of colonialism unfolds, when the landscape of scarcity replaces the language of accumulation. What dominate now are plague, prohibition and death.[1]

The five chapters of the novel are equivalent to Garcilaso's five love poems. They move the reader by their rapid, dramatic alternation between the destinies of his helpless characters and the overwhelming events leading inexorably towards the fatal outcome, against which

170

there is no appeal. This is a fable, delicate but steely, based on history, or legend – or so the author's prologue tells us. But it also has its sources in the author's own journalism, deriving from a story he wrote in 1949 about the discovery of a grave in the convent of Santa Clara at Cartagena. But unlike *The General in His Labyrinth* (1989), where fable is inscribed within history to fill in the blank pages of Bolívar's last days, here the fable turns its back on factual history, and tells the extraordinary story of a twelve-year-old daughter of a minor aristocrat who is sacrificed by the fanaticism of its unreal times. The strategy of the fable is to de-socialize the girl, turning her into an unwanted, illegitimate child, who is saved and adopted by black kitchen slaves. Writing frees her by means of poetry and the fleeting discourse of love that grants her humanity even as she undergoes Church-sanctioned torture in her convent prison. The novel contests the fact that history lacks a court of appeal: it sets its tale within the graves and cloisters of the past in order to rewrite and gainsay such a history. But the novel also contends with ideology (in this case a religious and superstitious one) over the approved reading of events, revealing the purely constructed character of a reality that is as artificial as it is ferocious. History robs the girl of her short life, but religion takes her body, her desiring body from her. And even though it confirms the facts only after testing its own power to question, the novel is a rare achievement of a classical goal: turning suffering into beauty. This desolate strength, this fierce agony, becomes transformed into the ecstasy of poetry, limpid yet passionate.

In *The Incredible and Sad Tale of Innocent Eréndira and her Callous Grandmother* (1972), García Márquez had already recounted the story of a young girl as a version of the master–slave relationship, but had felt obliged to do this through the mediation of irony and parody, with a humorous distance that allowed the episodic rawness of the abject to be made palatable. According to Kristeva, there is no subject in the face of the I that exercises abjection, only the object, the fetish.[2] By contrast with the version of Cinderella and the carnivalized exchange of prostitution that form the axes of *Eréndira*, here there is an distilled, immaculate writing that reveals the history of mentalities behind the social codes, a history that is real, but senseless. The novel insists that here, for once, the violence of the real will win out over the revisions of fable.[3] In opposition to the closed space of mentalities, poetry must try to subvert, through its epiphanies of love, the dark, codified readings of a single truth and a universal authority.

As if this short novel were itself a complete course on the history of the novel, a sort of companion to the art of narration, it begins a narrative reading *par excellence*, confirming the world as social, historical and cultural overcoding. This sceptical vision of 'disciplinary society' (Foucault) is characteristic of the social pessimism of narrative modernity. But it is also characteristic of the contemporary practice of dislocation and fragmentation of the postmodern and post-colonial account. In any case, from this perspective, the very genre of the novel always presupposes a rupture of the code, thus revealing the constructed and arbitrary character of the latter. In *Of Love and Other Demons*, García Márquez deploys a variation on this tough definition of the genre and exercises his talent for creating a narrative storm in a historical teacup to tell the story of the brief blossoming of a transculturated life. The novel is an arabesque of love in a convent, the parable of a life that inhabits both the Caribbean and colonial worlds. In the end, it is a tale of a gentle love told through clear and crystalline speech, a fable of a girl who contradicts all the codes of authorized knowledge in a closed colonial society. She is a propitiatory victim, her body sacrificed, innocent both in life (classical, Renaissance) and death (Romantic, serial-like). At the end she is free as though she were walking on the waters of reading. As if in a cryptogram, García Márquez has rewritten the book of nature with the resources of the book of society, as if both in fact belonged to the book of fables. Reading is the true space of transmutation, the place of abundance, of propitious interpretation, where all books become pages within a perpetual reading.

We should say more about the shaping functions of the code. We are dealing here with the structuring code of Latin American historiography, which designates the centuries of Spanish colonialism as the 'dark ages'. In addition, we have the social organization of slave society, which in this portrait of seventeenth-century Cartagena is centred on religious power. Spanish political power, on the other hand, is en route to Enlightenment. Finally, we must add the detailed socio-cultural codification that produces the Spanish colonial hierarchy, on whose margins lies an Afro-Caribbean hybridity. Let us say that the institutional disciplinary religious code of America presupposes the truth of the dominant colonial discourse. American difference is perceived as the enigma belonging to an untamed nature, a conundrum that God has imposed to test the interpretative capacities of the doctors of the faith. The most important signs of authority are religious and thus turn 'exorcism' (more abject than programmatic) into a test of its evangelical mission. The battle with the demon is not just spiritual but cultural, since the devil represents American entropy, the chaos of the African and native heresies, the non-culture which has to be incorporated or eliminated. Alejo Carpentier saw the Caribbean as a laboratory of history (the enigmatic amphitheatre of Wallace Stevens's poem), but García Márquez introduces a variation within this figure, which is more novel-istic than polemical. Here we have a Creole class in decline: it has no future within the national discourse of the family romance that nation-alism will impose. In Latin America nationalism is the creation of modernity, and not vice versa. (That is to say, modernity emerges more slowly in those countries that lack the nationalist or regionalist energies produced by the Enlightenment and the struggle for independence from colonial power.) The ill-matched parental couple sacrifice their daugh-ter. She moves from her loveless home to the slave quarters where love is freely given. Finally, she encounters the priest's Petrarchan love, derived in part from his love of literature: however, this cannot save her. She is sacrificed in order to show just how precarious the social network is, perishing without understanding her own role as sacrificial victim.

This overcoding turns the world into a text, which is literally inter-preted, in every sense of the word. The reading of codes is always a misunderstanding, which not only loses touch with common sense and the certainty of things, but turns life itself into something arbitrary. Without the possibility for free will, human life is subject to a reduction-ist interpretation, which requires it to make sense (nonsense) through the (demented) rationality that forms and misdirects it.

This is perhaps the reason why Sierva María's parents – the senti-mental but charmless marquis who is unable to read his own place in the tragedy, and Bernarda the wild and horrifying mother, drowning in disillusion – cannot love each other and fail to understand their daugh-ter, whom they first abandon to the slaves as a social orphan, and then have confined in the convent claiming she is possessed by the Devil. Radically other, the girl is disinherited from the discourse of the family, and her de-socialization (almost emblematic of the romantic captive, saved by the natural philosophy of a subaltern culture) makes her the victim of every code. Like the eponymous hero of the romantic tale (the rebel subject who grows through his stubborn struggle against a society that rejects him), the innocent girl reveals the aberrant nature of the code, the social void of any alternative cultural destiny for the orphans of order, those whose identity is no longer Spanish. As though in some inverting mirror, the world that condemns Sierva María becomes a sinister, cruel and absurd spectacle. As in the classical historical novel (Dickens, Tolstoy, Dumas), the laws that produce the world are untouchable and create nothing but misery and unhappiness. The tragic heroine of the novel becomes the anti-heroine of discourse: her tragedy contradicts the discourse that seeks to explain her at every turn. Her breach of the code is equivalent to a refutation of the world. She is in possession of the impeccable logic of a character in Calderón, but also of a worldly irony, which in its refusal to dismiss horror is worthy of Cervantes.

Everything is supported by interpretation, and is therefore decided by reading. Such a conclusion is already present in García Márquez's work. In *No-one Writes to the Colonel* (1958) he produces a parable of reading as an enigma of social and political history. Faith in the distant code of a victorious authority supports the Colonel who is a tragic reader, believing in the truth of the letter, with only the fighting cock that belonged to his dead son as emblem of an illegible chance. *One Hundred Years of Solitude* (1967) constructs the world as an act of multiple reading, to the point where the novel is written as if translated aloud, and the reader reads over the shoulder of the character who is reading himself revealed. *Chronicle of a Death Foretold* (1981) is the deliberate attempt to decipher the code that has imposed its sacrificial letter, more through fatality than conviction. *The General in His Labyrinth* is an exaggerated Cervantine metaphor for reading. It is only after an exhaustive reading of Bolívar's history that the Narrator decides to write the pages that will make the hero legible.

In *Of Love and Other Demons* we witness the spectacle of reading as construction, the production of different versions that struggle over the world. It must be said that at the end of the novel (the reader can ascertain this in his or her own reading community), we feel uneasy: what has been read is a fatality (someone dies cruelly) and yet something precarious (the code that kills her, exercises its violence in an utterly arbitrary fashion). The girl dies during the fifth session of exorcism, and we stop reading at chapter 5. We are moved by the cruelty of her treatment, but the internal reading of events remains unresolved within our own reading. Symptomatically, the reader goes back over the pages he has read looking for the traces of his own reading, as if the anxiety of reading could find some other route between different paths of interpretation. He discovers that in some way the whole history has the character of a re-reading. Its characters are derived from history, from the author's own narrative background and from colonial mythology. The novel itself refers us back to Petrarchan poetry: those who are 'faithful in love' already formed the horizon of Florentine discourse, as can be seen in the allusion to them in the title of *Love in the Time of Cholera* (1985). But we are also referred back to Golden Age drama – to the stern codes of Tirso de Molina and the fervent eloquence of Lope de Vega. The crafting of the world as a weave of changing readings finally, of course, refers us back to Cervantes. The trope of the disinherited subject confronting the world stems from nineteenth-century romanticism. The cyclical form of the novel, where the narrator, the equivalent of national memory, shuffles the order of interpolations, is modern. The radical dismantling of what is represented as pure relativity is post-modern. This is the author's most passionate work: it is also his most literary.

But what is new is this miraculous, epiphanic activity of novelized reading: reading the world like another novel and producing a history through the readings that the novel's characters introduce. If this ironic gaze belongs to the tradition of Cervantes its fable-like framework is altogether Márquez's own, belonging both to this world (America) and the other (poetry).

The author must have experienced something other in his own reading of the novel he was writing: on finishing it he would have had to read it again in terms of his own history. The introduction that García Márquez dates 'Cartagena de Indias, 1994' could only have been written after the novel, which was first published in April 1994. The purpose of the prologue is to establish a triple discursive origin for the tale: in recent journalism, in popular memory and legend, and finally in the enigma of the speech of death. This gesture of inscribing the origin in the end shows that writing (the powers of fiction) prevail over the contingencies of history, the tyranny of ideology and the vulnerability of life itself. Written in opposition to the normative inflexibility of the Law, the novel is also written against a history that naturalizes violence: it is tantamount to a poetic act against death. Hence the surreptitiously emblematic character of the prologue: the Narrator is situated within the everyday contingency of a latent reading ('Have a walk around there and see what comes to you', the paper's editor says to him). His account of that day, 26 October 1949 when they emptied the crypt of the colonial convent of Santa Clara, thus presents the emblematic vision of the novel:

> So the first thing I saw when I entered the church was a long line of bones baking under the terrible October sun . . . and with no more identity than a name written in pencil on a piece of paper.

Even half a century on, I can still feel the shock and astonishment that this terrible evidence of the annihilating passage of
time produced [10].

One of the tombs belonged to Sierva María de Todos los Ángeles
('Servant María of All the Angels'), who had been dead for 200 years,
and whose hair unexpectedly 'measured twenty two metres, eleven cen-
timetres'. The Narrator then remembers a legend that his grandmother
had told him about the twelve-year-old daughter of a marquis. The girl's
hair was also extremely long. She had died of rabies and was now 'ven-
erated in all the villages on the Caribbean for the many miracles she had
performed'. He finishes up, in a sort of symmetry, by saying that 'the
idea that the tomb could have been hers was the news I wrote about that
day, and the origin of this book'. Thus the tale is born of death, through
the mediation of a matriarchal account (also at the source of *One
Hundred Years of Solitude*), but the attribution of the legend to history
(and infantile memory to the ruins of the past) is already a form of
reading, of associative interpretation, which becomes an allegory of origins through the combinative power of writing. The vision of bones
crudely named by bits of paper already suggests a funereal alphabet,
where the fragility of the living is established through moral lesson and
poetic figuration. If the lesson is traditional, the figuration is the first
gesture of a poetic reading ('shock', 'astonishment', 'evidence'). In the
end the anonymous legend acquires a name in the language of the dead.
The tomb gives a name to the story: reading once more makes possible
the associations and figurations of writing. This is a poetic act, which
reads the bones and the tomb in order to represent astonishment at
human lack and to respond imaginatively, with the (imaginary) life of a
girl who would subvert the historical order. The pre-text announces that
the novel is a complex act in the formidable business of writing and
reading, reading in the inscription of the account the decipherment of
the world, unleashed by death and retraced by fiction.

The poetic persuasion of the novel even decides the fate of representation. The world is historical only in the para-text: characters can
exist only in legend, and events are inscribed in the mythic resonance
that triggers them. Everything is fiction, even certainty itself. Everything
comes from literature, from the discursive matrices that dictate intelligible forms, the protean space of the letter and the radically poetic
character of the name as the attribute of the thing that has been
invoked. In this exercise in association, every episode turns out to be the

coded language of another discourse, as if fiction took pleasure in manifesting itself through the variations of its combinatory alphabet, as if the world were not different from the novel that transforms and fixes it in and through its re-namings.

The first scene, where a rabid dog bites Sierva María, installs the principle of disorder in the fable. The sick dog 'overturned the Indians' stalls, the tables of fried food and the lottery tent, and as it ran riot it bit four people' (13). In the tradition of chaos, with which the accounts of scarcity and sacrifice, guilt and expiation begin, this image is immediately followed by an 'inexplicable loss of life' in the slave ship, which raises 'the fear that there was an outbreak of some African plague' (14). The same day the governor buys a beautiful Abyssinian slave girl 'for her weight in gold' and the novel suggests that the slave trade is the source of prosperity. Even Sierva María's mother seems marked by this economy, both literal and symbolic: 'Nobody had been sharper than her in the slave business.' We will see later that social relations themselves are frustrated by a regime that prevents the recognition of the Other, and therefore the reconstruction of one's own identity. The symbolic economy of slavery is another disorder, which denies difference and produces lack. It is no coincidence then that Sierva María's parents' house is next to the 'women's mental asylum', which is another metaphor for the disturbance of community. These references form the basis for interpretation. Sagunta, 'a wandering Indian woman', something between a witch and a fortune-teller, announces that there will be 'a plague of rabies'. Her vision is challenged by the girl's father, the Marquis of Casueldero, who has a different interpretation of the facts: 'I don't see why there should be a plague ... There has been no news of comets or eclipses that I know of' (23). Sagunta replies that in March 'there was to be a total eclipse of the sun' and in fact this eclipse does happen in the novel. These signs of disorder invoke representations of the end of time and the world turned upside down. Plagues and eclipses are homologous with the decadence and aberration embodied by the parents, but also with the fanaticism and violence represented by the Church.

Abrenuncio, the free-thinking doctor, is a privileged reader. Although his science is full of guesswork, he is a man of the Enlightenment who promotes reason and common sense. He at least protests against the marquis's decision to confine the girl to the convent. When he examines the victim, we read that 'The only thing that he could not interpret was the smell of onions in the girl's sweat' (45). However, we know from another reading of this incident that she smells this way because she has taken various herbs that the slaves had prepared for her in order to exorcise the evil.

Even before she is born in Cartagena de Indias, Sierva María is born in the new world of discourse. She is an American sign, heteroclite, emerging from a regional language. She is a sign that is irreducible to the dominant discursive logic, and because of this she is almost pre-social, untameable, wild. The canonical interpretation of this is that she must be demoniacal, possessed. Her definition as possessed by demons is a consequence of the mistaken interpretation provoked by such an ambiguous sign rooted in hybridity. Her silence and illiteracy suggest a renunciation of the very communication that would make her legible and identify her. When she has to reply to questioning, she opts for lies. But as she must be controlled by the code regardless, the interpretation that she is possessed proves the power of the dominant reading, whose conviction carries unto death. The unexpected signs of a subaltern culture can only be explained or erased.

It could be said that the distinctively American is only born at the price of its extinction, and becomes legible only at the cost of its loss. Sierva María's parents already betray a lack of love, a lack of Eros that is monstrous. When the love between the priest and the captive girl erupts it can only consume them. They are the parents who engender the end of the world, the world turned upside down, the very lack that the leader creates in making the cosmos lose its meaning and its goods.

We find the first illegible sign in the symptomatology of rabies. In fact, the child who has been bitten by the dog shows no visible signs of illness, but she is condemned to death by all and sundry, including the enlightened doctor, who is the most important reader of the ills of the body, just as the monks are of the readers of the ills of the soul. The girl's father attempts to protect her, but is incapable of making his own decisions. When the Church sees signs of possession in the girl, her father surrenders her to the convent. The nuns have no doubt. They take the appropriate steps to verify that she is possessed, and cannot even discern whether the child is playing or exaggerating. They interpret everything as a language of malignancy. They believe her to be a necromancer, invisible, a wild animal, a blasphemer and a heretic. She is the Enemy, the radical other.

But even when Sierva María's parents come to regard the rabies as an affront to the honour of their house (although in fact they had already lost both honour and house), their apathy and decadence are such that they abandon her to the convent without further ado. The

Creole is hollowed out from the inside and deprived of any future within the nation. The family romance has its terms inverted, becoming a subtraction of meaning. The listlessness of Sierva María's father would have confirmed Hegel in his view of the Creoles as apathetic.

Sierva María is born as a genuine sign of enigma. She is premature and her umbilical cord threatens to strangle her. Rejected by her mother ('she hated her from the very first time she nursed the child'), the girl learns three African languages, learns how to drink cock's blood and how to slip through the world without being seen. As an American version of the 'self-taught philosopher', the child refuses to be socialized: she rejects writing. Her education is pre-modern, ethnic and African. She has no social destiny in a milieu that condemns her to semblance, since she stands outside the disciplinary space of her times. But her marginality is incorporated and she has to submit to the space of seriality. Even the doctor Abrenuncio exercises the full authority of his faith in reading upon her: 'He could see her future after just one look' (67). The totalizing capacity of reading is the best illustration of its modernity.

Abrenuncio believes that all that can be done is to wait for the symptoms of rabies to develop: the disease is incurable. Other less prudent doctors carry out terrible treatments based more on superstition rather than science, leaving their patients writhing on the floor 'screaming in pain and rage'. This crisis of the body leads him to agree with the other authorities about the girl's supposed illness: 'Even the bravest *curanderos* [practitioners of traditional medicine] abandoned her to her fate, convinced that she was mad or possessed by demons' (71). Rabies, madness, possession: there is no appeal against such diagnoses. Sagunta, who has in the past has performed spectacular cures, confirms the worst. The bishop, who knows about the case only through hearsay, has already made up his mind: 'It is an open secret', he says to the girl's father, 'that your daughter rolls about on the floor in the grip of obscene convulsions howling the imprecations of idolators. Are these not the unmistakeable symptoms of possession?' Her father, horrified, asks, 'What do you mean?' The bishop replies drawing on the analogical vision that equates the crisis of the body with that of the spirit: 'One of the many tricks that demons use is to take on the appearance of a common illness so as to insinuate themselves into an innocent body' (76).

A difference opens up here between the respective reading authorities. On the one hand, Abrenuncio is dismissed as a necromancer, fortune-teller, pederast, libertine and atheist. That is to say, he is a monster of the Enlightenment. On the other hand, Cayetano Delaura is a true son of Mother Church, her most competent interpreter, once a student at Salamanca, a librarian, scholar and devout believer. The marquis attempts to defend the doctor, but the bishop makes this pronouncement: 'Although your child's body is lost, by good fortune God has given us the means to save her soul' (79). This radical division between body and soul reproduces the sequence of antagonisms through which the dominant reading loses sight of the real, inflicting violence through its reductionism. The bishop's pronouncement is already a sentence of death: 'Leave her in our hands', he concludes, 'God will do the rest.'

In this absurd logic (the order of the world turned upside, the disorder of the law) the marquis, moved by his daughter's predicament, discovers a sort of parental love and feels 'the novel pleasure of loving her in a way he had never loved before', only immediately to hand her over to the convent, letting them 'take charge of her life'. It is Palm Sunday and the girl is dressed in her grandmother's outlandish attire. Her father asks her: 'Do you know who God is?', and 'the girl shakes her head, answering "no"'. She is the perfect victim, utterly ignorant of the sacrifice that will lead to her death. Wisely, the Narrator does not act out the compulsions of his characters. He does not offer to read the girl, nor does he claim to know everything about her. On the contrary, she is a sign full of meanings attributed to her by others, not by the Narrator, who tells her story from a suitable distance, somewhere between his memory and our alert gaze. Thus in the crucial passage in which she is condemned to the convent, 'The Marquis watched her move away, limping with her right foot, and with her slipper in her hand. He waited in vain for her to show a rare moment of pity and turn round to look at him' (84).

Chapter 3 is the apotheosis of reading. Reading is the intelligible material of the world: mutual, equivocal, normative and fanatical. But as it is the reasoned form of the world, its historical texture, in permanent dispute with the real, reading often goes astray. The cultural character of the real is thus revealed through the ironic distance that the novel creates, as is the implacable fundamentalism inscribed in every epoch. As the chapter is based on a chronicle of the eighteenth century, it first gives the history of a closed convent. The map of the cloister reproduces that of a closed society, where, in a 'corner of oblivion' Sierva María is locked up. The account requires this referentiality because it needs to place the evidence that supports its positions within the realm of credibility. The novel will use fable to effect a moral demonstration of the facts, opposing interpretations to evidence. The Narrator will suggest that his omnipresence in speech includes history, the 'we' and the 'here', thus making himself more credible, like the pilot of the ship of reading (of the madness of an exemplary world, homologous with the contemporary world, where truth is lost among fiercely contending interpretations). Inevitably, the Narrator from the common language of the city, whose literature is endorsed and inscribed in history becomes slowly novelized by his own fable. He is not a character but an ironic accomplice of the (dramatic) reader in the (tragic) denouement of events.

The convent novices who try to communicate with Sierva María conclude that she is a 'deaf-mute' or 'German', since she does not share their code. Sierva María refuses to take on a legible identity, and to avoid doing so makes use of silence, or when matters become pressing, lies. Lying is simply being other, and it is no coincidence that Abrenuncio thinks that perhaps she will become a poet. But she recognizes her subaltern identity when the slaves speak to her in Yoruba.

By contrast, the abbess has a solid identity: she is a fanatic, nourished by everything she rejects. She is a stranger to doubt and has already come to see the girl as 'the spawn of Satan' (92). Inside this convent prison, writing is law. They record the signs of possession, and the testimony of the novices takes on the value of truth. Once more, the letter maintains the power of those who control it, those who divide good from evil by separating the legible from the non-legible. Records (writing) turn superstition (speech) into truth. Nevertheless, the girl pollutes the convent's order with her legend, and her supposed powers become an exaggerated metaphor for communication, as when they ask her 'to be the Devil's courier'. This brief moment of humour has interesting implications. Sierva María ('absolutely illiterate') imitates 'voices from beyond the grave, voices of the murdered, voices of Satan's spawn'. Orality is the formless margin, the other, the entropic. The novices read literally, but Sierva María, less bound to repetition, hegemony and similarity, is a sign that can fracture the principle of identity and the principle of non-contradiction. Elsewhere, she is said to imitate the language of birds, and we already know that she speaks three African languages. Hegel believed that American languages imitated the language of birds, but the girl exercises her oral polyphony, freely and parodically, revealing her status as an alternative American sign, produced by the culture of differences.

A follower of Petrarch even in his name, Cayetano Delaura promotes his office as reader ('his dignity as reader') as much as the tradition of reading itself (the library he runs is in the centre of the palace, which is

otherwise in ruins). But one afternoon whilst he is reading ('that historic afternoon') he stumbles, and a page comes free from his book. The
bishop, noting the mishap, asks him: 'What were you thinking about?',
and Cayetano replies: 'About the girl'. Like a force prior to the letter, but
subsequent to the literal reading, the girl interferes with the routine of
reading, like a stammer, or a blank page. Delaura has dreamed about
her, and the emblematic dream (he is eating a bunch of grapes, consum-
ing the time he has to live) will be dreamed twice more by the girl, the
last time just before she dies. Thus the prophetic dream appears as a
vision within the space of hermetic reading. To read the dream is to
enter into a greater enigma, since the grapes become an emblem of deciphered reading. The novel cites itself inside the dream, and is dreamed
as the ultimate truth. Unsurprisingly, when Delaura visits the convent,
the abbess shows him the garden of abundance: 'He was equally alarmed
by the garden, which seemed to flourish with such vigour that it seemed
unnatural . . . there were flowers of quite unreal size and colours, and
some with intolerable scents. In the garden, the ordinary seemed to take
on a supernatural quality' (108). In the Scholastic tradition, abundance is
a sign of excess. In authoritarian representation, this abundance must be
removed through a form of asceticism in the name of a moral teaching
of scarcity.

The malign sign of the girl thus takes on a pagan value as fertility
goddess. The abbess reads events literally: the monstrous reveals the
operation of the Devil, 'what we can see speaks for itself'. Delaura takes
on the role of Devil's advocate: 'Some times we attribute things we don't
understand to the work of the Devil, without taking thought that there
might be things that God has created that we don't understand.'
Appealing to St Thomas Aquinas, the abbess replies: 'We should not
believe demons even if they are telling the truth' (109). Delaura introduces the value of non-knowledge as well as the principle of doubt. To
read from a position of doubt is to contradict literal interpretation.

But the eclipse and the signs of disorder leave no place for doubt:
'Thereafter, nobody in the convent was under any doubt that Sierva
María had sufficient powers to change the laws' (117). When Delaura
manages to communicate with Sierva María, however, she is quite capable of speaking humorously, even exaggeratedly: 'I'm more evil than
the plague', she says to him, applying to herself the demoniacal identity
ascribed to her through this drama of reading. A child of the letter,
Delaura turns to the poetry of Garcilaso, which is the place where he
discovers his freedom, and answers her with lines from his poems. The

conversation between them becomes amorous and intimate (if the book was not gallant then the hendecasyllable was), and in the secret depths of the convent, they experience the impossible scandal of the eclogue.

But the drama of reading comes to a head. Delaura challenges the bishop over the punishment of the girl. The bishop replies: 'the Lord's cards are hard to read'. Delaura dissents: 'I don't believe that child is possessed.' Two different readings cannot be maintained, and tragedy ensues. Trying to save her through his love, Delaura abandons her to the bishop's mercies.

But there are still more agencies of reading to emerge, which will temporarily hold back the unfolding of events. The new viceroy is an advocate of Enlightenment who believes in education: the time has come for renovation. Abrenuncio's library like that of the Wandering Jew has a copy of *Amadis de Gaul*, the book that Delaura failed to finish as a child. Another monk, Father Aquino, teaches the girl that the demons of Europe and America are the same, 'but their allegiance and behaviour are different' (179). Disillusioned, Sierva María realizes that their freedom depends 'only on themselves', on their fragile bond. Delaura does not hold with flight, and waits for some legal way out. He himself will come to be seen as possessed. The bishop concludes that Sierva María's diabolic powers demand all his conviction, and the final confrontation between the girl and the man of God is the last conflict in a novel that has alternated its play of oppositions to reveal the irreducible character of the greater tragedy: that of understanding possessed by the demon of a single truth.

With a lyric passion that is both precise and committed, the novel finally comes to inhabit its heroine. It cites itself in the girl's last dream, as if in writing the dreaming poem of memory could recover a relationship of intimacy with the girl-victim, and hence save her through words and reading, but without waking her.

Another miraculous quality of the novel (this short treatise on the art of storytelling) is that every page is better than the one before: more accurate, more moving, more fatal. A child of poetry, Sierva María de Todos los Ángeles is a propitiatory victim of this fable of reading, which the novel turns into a lesson of love and a poem of consolation.

In the end, the radical relativism of interpretations does not entail that reality is dissolved by the rationality or irrationality of a particular discourse. On the contrary, however absurd it might be, the reasoned version of the real is projected as the one with the greatest truth value, and therefore the most authoritarian. This sceptical parable about authority is also a disenchanted reflection on the present time, with its new fundamentalisms and new victims. If truth is impossible, and life is in the hands of authority and its capacity for violence, it means that the existence of many readings does not imply a principle of freedom but only one of scepticism. Melancholy is not nostalgia but loss, a state of mourning. The novel is perhaps telling us that at our *fin de siècle* truth is nourished on lies, to the point where they cannot be told apart, or only by their victims. Perhaps history has stopped telling their stories, but the novel refuses to be resigned to those readings that discount them.[4]

Conclusion

We have reconstructed the cultural history of the Spanish American subject by looking at some of the mechanisms that confer its identity. This sequence demonstrates that the subject is constituted between the European gaze and the testimony of Americans themselves. From the very first accounts of the New World the native is perceived through European interpretative repertoires and schemes of classification: it could not have been otherwise. But what is also true is that these representations have been challenged right from the beginning. The nature of American man is constituted by this conflict of interpretations, constructed through different representations that struggle over his origin, place and destiny. Theology, philosophy, history and politics seek to stamp the authority of their interpretation on America, but time and again the subject escapes this catalogue of resemblances. This is not because it opposes a repertoire of differences to the authority of the

185

gaze, but because it is situated on the restless margins of the array of normative disciplines: its place is constantly displaced. This supplementary place allows the native to be perceived first as 'Natural Man', then as 'the Noble Savage'. But the native is always in transition: innocent and sophisticated, a simple soul and a cannibal, pre-Christian and pagan. It is a subject that is constructed as such in the course of its own education, that is, in the recognition of its own humanity.

If the critical consciousness underlying this judgement nourishes Montaigne's discreet relativism, it also impregnates the mythology of the Other as radically different in Shakespeare's last play. But the fact that 'On the Cannibals' and *The Tempest* are parts of this discussion of the character of the Native American indicates that the choice between 'Noble Savage' and 'Natural Man' concerns not just the man of the Indies, but also the European subject itself. The debate reveals the first suspicions that the latter's own otherness is shaped in the place of the Other.

The richly complex accounts of Montaigne and Shakespeare that represent the American subject in its similarity (rational objectivity) and difference (spectacle of deformity) are echoed in the responses of Guamán Poma de Ayala and Inca Garcilaso de la Vega, the greatest *mestizo* American intellectuals, who conceived the subject in terms of reading and writing, the alphabet through which its past is deciphered and its future discerned. Reading and writing are the great appropriations that the New World Subject deploys in order to pass from its subjugated condition within tradition to its rebirth in faith, modernity and individuality. Its character as subject requires the control of these techniques in order to convert ethnic memory into contemporary critique. Their deployment shows that oral culture is capable of anticipating the dominant political philosophy with its own communal wisdom and superior order. If Cervantes questions the modernity of seventeenth-century Spain, Garcilaso seems to suggest that the modernity of Spain lies in the Indies.

The debate opened up by this field of studies is relevant to contemporary cultural history. One set of concerns leads to a historicizing of the processes of change and crisis that occur within the systems of classification and normativity of colonial culture. These fractures within the system of control (which legislate, legitimate and sanction) occur when American difference resists the reading and processing that stem from colonialism. We can see this in the limits of perspective, in the different temporal register and in the opposing linguistic structure. The fissure inside the norm possesses a conflictual force, which reaches the subjects of both cultures equally. This cultural history of tension, intermixing, syncretism, hybridity, reappropriation and negotiation shows how the grammar of colonialism functions. This grammar attempts to reorder the world in language, through the syntax of the new. In addition, it maintains the interpolations and grafts of a process of transcoding, synthesis and allegorization, in which the syncretic languages of culture exceed the archive of genealogical consolation and open out on to the future and the potential of difference. This practice gives impetus to the programme of the new American culture, which is composed not of harmonious combinations but from the subtractions that it then recombines, that is, the transitions of the post-colonial drama of the modern.

This drama takes place on the shore where Spaniard and native repeatedly encounter one another. In the paradoxical temporality of the Colony, the scene of encounter places the origin in the future, and the scene is endlessly repeated as ritual. Over and over again, the genealogy of the historical account is recomposed by the need to re-enact this encounter. That is Atahualpa, the last Inca, and Pizarro the conquistador continue to meet each other in order to exchange information, signs and values: whoever invokes them produces the setting for their own reading. The historical event might owe everything to chance, producing conquerors and victims, but its cultural history (the long debate over its interpretation) belongs to the present, to the other shore of this first encounter, where the place of the subject is once more decided. Memory is thus made contemporary in the cycle of plays based on the death of Atahualpa. The past is incarnated as a staged body in the public square during fiesta: here its future meaning will be decided. But it is not just a question of a 'history of mentalities', of a memory differentiated by its ethnic space, but rather of a collective history of a present, which is extended by the pressure of the past. In this inclusive present, the representations that are articulated in popular culture are selected by an apparatus that exchanges, processes and preserves the information that maintains the life of the concrete subject. This selective memory is an allegory of the synthesised present and its horizon of possibility.

To study the processes of transformation that select the representations of the new, we have chosen the syntax of the 'discourse of abundance', that is, that paradigm that represents the American as fertility, extravagance and inexhaustible wealth. The other paradigms of representation (the discourse of scarcity or lack, and the discourse of potential) have not been examined systematically, although we have pointed out their salient and differential features. These three modes do not follow a logic of opposition, although the rhetoric of their contrasts is well known. Rather, they correspond to the figurative complementarity of metaphor in the way in which they are articulated simultaneously as process and crystallization. I mean that these discourses are the figures through which the New World is thought: they are not literal documentations of the goods, ills and promises produced by some balance sheet of the New World. They have to do with the semantic field of representations that articulate and contextualize the interpretations, which seek to crystallize consensus and social practice. However, they are not merely figures of civic or state rhetoric: as open signs they take on the meanings of those who deploy them. They thus construct the field that produces symbolic values, making the social diagram of power visible and revealing how institutional control, the art market and consumption operate. But in addition, these modes of representation constitute the first allegories of the American 'imagined community'. They are thus forged and developed within the cataloguing endeavours of the Colony, but are diversified, disseminated and renovated in the explorations and choices of the nineteenth century, and underlie the long debate on the formation of the nation. Abundance, scarcity and potential acquire new emblematic, referential and allegorical functions within literary texts and art objects. We see this in the forms of the Baroque and Magical Realism, in the reductions of scepticism and nihilism, and in the spaces of subjectivity and subversive action. They are not mechanical models but shaping processes, which act as a reservoir of knowledge for a conflictual present. They also serve as palimpsests on which to rewrite history. Some of the great contemporary accounts of Latin America (those of Rulfo, Lezama Lima, García Márquez, Fuentes and Eltit) seem to us to be inspired by a desire to elucidate the vulnerability of the subject of wonder and fortune, the offspring of the popular saga, the displaced victim living on the edge. In these stories the subject becomes the culture hero of his own historical memory: he provides lessons in stoicism, furnishes an example of rebellion and offers the wherewithal for creative production. Social injustice and political and ideological violence turn this subject into the creature of poverty, ghost, orphan and marginal. He is recuperated by the national post-romance, becoming the first citizen of an unfinished modernity. Once more he acquires the identity provided by his American vocation: to reconstruct the grammar of beginnings.

When Diego Saavedra Fajardo dedicated Enterprise 69 ('Ferro et auro') of his treatise *Empresas políticas* ('Political Enterprises') of 1640 to a balance sheet of the discovery of America he could only conclude that the Conquest had been too costly. This was a topos that emerged in seventeenth-century Spain. The crisis and poverty that the country was suffering was a consequence of the scarcity whose origin lay in the New World. Saavedra Fajardo, the prudent courtier, instructs the prince on the advantages of agriculture compared with mining, the false promise offered by America. The obsession with metals and the efforts that Spain expended in exploiting them has been a passing euphoria. The gold and silver flowed for a long time but finished up in the hands of the Flemish bankers. 'Their abundance' has thus been 'damaging for men', Saavedra Fajardo concludes. The argument appeals to the discourse of abundance, to the extravagance of its natural history: 'Did not perhaps Nature give fruits so prodigally everywhere, and soak gold and silver into the deepest bosom of the earth . . . ?' (789). Only he confused effects with their causes: it was not the abundance of metals that has been 'damaging' but their regime of exploitation.

The implicit subject of this abundance is the poor man: the 'poor' Christian of Las Casas and the 'poor in Jesus Christ' of Guamán Poma de Ayala. That is, the primitive Christian seeks his church amongst those who worship the golden calf. Poverty is in itself a state that implies criticism of what produces it: it casts doubt on the justifications of imperial discourse and its doctrinaire good faith. Thus, the numerous natural histories and their commentaries implicitly raise the paradox of an abundant nature inhabited by natives condemned to servitude. Las Casas refuses heaven to those who exploit the Indian and eloquently explains the absurdity of a conquest that leads to extermination. Guamán Poma and Garcilaso de la Vega suppose that there will be an imminent restoration or transfer of power from the usurpers to the rightful heirs. Both are alarmed by the destruction of the Conquest and both denounce it in their different ways. They also give an intellectual form to what will become the strategy of the defeated culture under colonialism: the negotiation of legitimacy within the spaces of control, which allows them through the appropriation of European assets (writing being the greatest asset) to reaffirm Andean memory and mark out their own spaces. This is a not just a network of survival and resistance but also one that consolidates and expands what is their own through the appropriation of the new. Here, as in their scepticism with regard to the outcome, they were modern. We have sought to demonstrate that their cartography of the natural world (the processing, exchange and preservation of food and their fables of politics) is an allegory of reparation. The language of food parallels the interconnections that writing effects in the hands of the *mestizo* chroniclers. Here we are dealing with one of the most consistent mechanisms by which the natural world and social practice are rearticulated in accounts of the New World. In these native chronicles, the culture of the New World contends by means of a post-colonial rationality: its project is to exceed the imperial map. So with the instruments of the discourse of abundance, these writers give critical scarcity a context through which what is potential might dissolve conflict. They do this by discussing fruit-trees and fruits, seeds and harvests, voice and letter, body and memory: thus in writing they can expand the limits of the present.

After political independence from Spain at the beginning of the nineteenth century, the emblems of abundance, the ghosts of scarcity and the expectations of possibility acquired new meanings and values. The dispute over their meaning, however, might now be seen as the process by which a national referentiality was constructed. It was a dispute over the different representations and interpretations of the process of modernization. Martí thought that the subject of the new republics would emerge from the countryside, whilst Sarmiento thought that this subject would be the citizen of the town. These choices produce antagonistic conceptions of the state and the production of the nation: they differ over the role of the state in the inevitable modernization. Bello, for his part, realized that the institutions of the state would be grounded on juridical rationality and a common language. But if criticism has exacerbated these oppositions, today it seems ever more clear that the thought and practice of these intellectuals is part of the self-recognition of Latin America and its modern definition, produced within the secular language of criticism and the forms of a culture renewed by its communicative capacity.

The fact that many contemporary authors (Rulfo, Lezama Lima, García Márquez, Fuentes, Eltit and others) have gone back to rework colonial representations from a post-colonial perspective precisely suggests that the options and redefinitions of the modern are the dreams of Latin American rationality. They are often nightmares and fantasies that distort communal life and increase injustice. The seeds that have been sown in the earth have died in the radical representation of Drought that Rulfo offers as an allegory of colonial power. In Lezama Lima, by contrast, American fruit-trees are fertile because they grow through reappropriation of the Baroque Image as an analogical axis. García Márquez has maximized the figuration of abundance and the reductions of scarcity, but in his reworking of eighteenth-century New Granada the metaphor of the Plague is interpreted by different subjects from within their own disciplines, revealing how colonial truth is only the most authorized version, the one with the greatest power. In the sagas of Fuentes, the seeds of the Orange Tree, in their turn, come from everywhere and represent the plenty that belongs to the *mestizo*. Fuentes rewrites the history of the first encounter from the point of view of contemporary encounters, expelling tragedy in the celebration of culture. For Diamela Eltit, the potential Community is the work that is carried out at the margins and in marginality, against the exclusions of a new, monstrous, neo-liberal and military modernization.

In 1866 the Mexican writer Luis G. Pastor, Professor of Literature at the College of San Juan de Letrán, published a profusely annotated translation of *Iconologie par figures; ou, traité complet des allégories, emblemes, etc., ouvrage utile aux artistes, aux amateurs, et pourant servir a l´education des jeunes personnes* (París, 1791). In its four slim volumes, the work included 350 well-worked and richly detailed figures produced by the famous engravers Hubert-François Gravelot and Charles-Nicolas Cochin. In *Iconología o tratado de alegorías y emblemas* Pastor reorganized the figures so that they follow a new alphabetical order: after Abundance, the presiding figure of the volume, he places the allegory of America. He thus establishes a correspondence that if not causal is at least demonstrative: it is already a convention by the middle of the nineteenth century that America is the 'granary of the West'. The caption for the personification of Abundance runs: 'Allegorical divinity, which the iconologists represent as a nymph crowned with flowers. One hand holds a sickle and the other the horn of Amaltheia full of fruits that Abundance scatters. She is crowned with flowers because these announce her presence. The caduceus, the emblem of trade, is also an attribute of *Abundance*.' This characterization reveals the novel functions of the allegory: it corresponds to Saavedra Fajardo's advice elaborated in the *Enterprises* volume. The notion of work is new: abundance is no longer a cause but a product. Perhaps lauding agriculture as the source of true wealth suggests not only that mining is a risky and arduous industry, but also that agriculture is associated with the ideals of the village as opposed to life at court. It may also suggest the self-sufficiency of the least advantaged colonies. In a treatise that criticizes both Alciato and Ripa, these allegories also have a tendency to self-reference. It is interesting that the language speaks of an 'allegorical divinity' represented by a 'nymph', implying a stage figure: the nymph is not Abundance but its environment, but this very 'divinity' is neither religious nor mythological but 'allegorical', that is, it belongs to the realm of the decorative or applied arts, which are said to have a higher artistic status than engravings. Whilst the figures have a pleasingly theatrical eighteenth-century French aspect, the updating makes them allude to poetry. It is no coincidence that we have two engravers (on Gravelot's death, Cochin carried on the work) dedicated to using their art to celebrate the memory of humanism. The subtle use of the nude also makes it of its time: the nude had been censored in the seventeenth century as had the worldly setting of subjectivity and the emotions.

The representation of America follows the conventions established by Ripa's editors and engravers: '*America* is represented by an olive-skinned woman: her head and part of her body are covered with feathers, an adornment peculiar to the peoples of this continent.' It includes the sign of 'the inhumanity of the ancient inhabitants of this part of the universe', that is, the severed head of a victim killed by the woman who embodies America, who is seated by a banana tree, with a bow in one hand and quiver over her shoulder. The translator inserts a footnote here to recall that Ripa represents America 'by means of an almost naked, with fearsome and menacing features'. The drawing of the peace pipe is interesting since some wings have been added to it. The somewhat eccentric figure is thus a syncretic amalgam of America and Europe: it turns the American peace pipe into a caduceus (the laurel leaf with two small wings, the sign of Mercury). The last sentence warns that the New World 'in spite of having doubled the riches of the old, has not made it happier'. It is no coincidence that a congress had been held in Paris on the subject: 'Was the discovery of America beneficial or unfortunate?'[1]

Although the allegory of America is a melancholy woman resigned to the work of fishing and hunting, which her little children confirm, the Mercury's wings bring trade into the picture. This equation of trade with the promise of peace and wealth suggests the modern faith in progress and exchange of goods and products. What is signalled here is the end of the heroic age of abundance as a model of nature and the potential of a collective good, and its new functionality as an effect of work and trade, an effect of exchange value. Abundance now refers to bourgeois values and liberal economy, to the market and consumption. This is why Professor Pastor yokes Abundance to America. The sequence becomes didactic, but also a confirmation of the reordering of the *topoi* of America. In addition, the contemporary significance of a notion of American abundance becomes political: speaking of Equity, Pastor cannot help but note its associations with his own times. He writes: 'In agreement with the common meaning of the word equity, it is this motto that the emperor Maximilian the First adopted in his coat of arms: "EQUITY IN JUSTICE", meaning that his government would be based on the moderation with which his laws would be applied.' But these lessons in classical culture aimed at a Francophile Mexico City are soon overtaken by the collapse of the French intervention. Juárez's rebellion is victorious and the naïve emperor Maximilian is shot in Querétero in 1867.

When they started building the Palace of Communication in Mexico City in 1904, under the direction of the Italian architect Silvio Contri, the building was to be the final emblem of the cult of progress endorsed by Porfirio Díaz, one of the generals who had won the struggle against Napoleon III's empire. The work on the palace, which was a mix of Florentine Renaissance and French Neo-classical, only finished in 1911, ironically the same year in which Díaz, the patriarch who had governed for 34 years, was overthrown. Now we are in the middle of the Mexican Revolution: what is required is a new repertoire of emblematic forms, which can allegorize current events and organize future memories. Native versions of abundance, scarcity and potential replace the figures from classical rhetoric in the Mexican Mural, that idiosyncratic form of public debate. David Alfaro Siqueiros (1898–1974) expresses the growing strength of the revolution against a cosmic horizon. Diego Rivera (1886–1957) replaces the placid plenitude of the Renaissance fresco with a pre-Cortésian social abundance, where peasants carry baskets of flowers rather than cereals. In his mural for Dartmouth College Library, José Clemente Orozco (1883–1949) traces the cultural history of the Americas, born out of the epic of migration. The United States is represented by an allegory of abundance: wheat, the town council, the severe schoolmistress – even though there are no black people or Indians in the frame and the subjects of this welfare appear too similar, taciturn and grey. Latin America is represented by an allegory of scarcity: a revolutionary peasant, the representation of the people armed, is about to be stabbed by a sinister group of bankers and generals. The Americas have now become opposed to one another, culturally different, but equally constituted by their cultural politics.

In the Palace of Communication, now the site of the National Museum of Art, it is worth lingering over the decorations in the *grand salon* on the second floor. The ceiling roses brought over from Italy are a magnificent example of the first industrial art. They are similar to 'Liberty style' and didactically bring the allegorical sequences up to date, expressing the promises of the new century. Along with the figures of labour, the emblems of the seasons and the images of progress there is a classical figure of *Abundance*. It is unsurprising that this came to Mexico from Italy to illustrate the welfare of a dictatorship that maintained power in the name of the ideals of the Enlightenment, science and order. One year before, the extravagant and extensive celebration of the centennial anniversary of independence turned General Díaz into a master of allegory: Mexican history was represented as a theatre of spectacles. From the re-encounter of Moctezuma and Cortés to the march of Iturbide as first president, the great allegory of Mexico consecrated the authoritarian state. As the minister for propaganda made clear, lies about history and the forgetting of its details are essential factors in the formation of the nation.

On the walls of the palace, the Neo-classical and industrial versions of the memory of humanism illustrate the long history of its primary function: to be an instrument that operates on a contemporary reality that is paradoxical and often contrary. The cultural history of *abundance* is produced through this conflict and reworking of interpretations. The allegory is initially an account of natural wonders, then a setting for ethnic intermixings and syncretic forms, and finally a decoration with didactic, nationalist intent. It represents a restless version of American experience, its expectations, promises and asynchronies, and does so on that shifting strand where the Old and New Worlds continue to encounter each other. Here it recounts the adventure of the American Subject – heroic and joyful, tragic and ironic – that is produced as it sets out from the margins to rename and recover its own world and its own time.

References

Introduction: *The Subject of Abundance*

1 Las Casas writes in his second conclusion to the Eight Treatises addressed to the king:
'All the infidels of the world are in the first place Christ's sheep; they are also his asso-
ciates; they are potential subjects as Christ is shepherd, head and priest to the infidels.
Each in their way. So the Pope, the Vicar of Christ, is shepherd, head and priest to all
infidels.' *Tratados* (Mexico City, 1965), vol. II, pp. 927–41. The legal organization of the
colonial world has been studied by Mario Góngora in his *El estado en el derecho indio:
epoca de fundación, 1492–1570* (Santiago de Chile, 1951). That doctrine and the extension of royal power were freely discussed is shown by the reports that were requested
from monks and jurists. Fray Juan de Váscones, for example, justified his demand
that the Spaniards enslave the Chilean Indians they captured with the following
(amongst other tortuous reasons): 'Although it is true that by warrant of Charles V
of glorious memory, it is ordered that no Indian be taken slave, this is not to be understood as involving those from Chile, since at the time of the establishment of said
warrant matters in the said kingdom were not in the state they are in at present, nor
had those barbarians committed the evils that we have referred to' (1599), in Agustín
Millares Carlo, *Cuerpo de documentos del siglo XVI: sobre los derechos de España en las*

Indias y las Filipinas (Mexico City, 1942), pp. 310–12. Fray Toribio de Motolinia is a good example of the impact of las Casas's accusations: in his letter to Emperor Charles v (2 January 1555) he complains of the virulence of these accusations, and in passing presents Hernán Cortés as a tortured sinner who is redeemed by Christian teaching: see the Letter in his *Historia de los Indios de Nueva España*, ed. Edmundo O'Gorman (Mexico City, 1984).

2 To violence should be added the well-documented infections and epidemics that rapidly reduced the native population. Although calculations of the original native population have been the subject of long polemics, the question has been largely resolved in the studies by W. Borah and F. Cook, *Essays in Population History*, 3 vols (Los Angeles, 1979). Carmen Bernard and Serge Gruzinski conclude the following: 'The 25 million Indians of Moctezuma's Mexico were barely 2.65 million in the New Spain of 1568; Atahualpa's Peru was populated by 9 million people in 1532, but only 1.3 million remained by 1570. And this collapse continued for several generations.' In their *Historia del Nuevo Mundo, del descubrimiento a la Conquista: la experencia europea, 1492–1550* (Mexico City, 1996), p. 479.

3 Antonio Benítez Rojo, *The Repeating Island: The Caribbean and the Postmodern Perspective* (Durham, NC, 1996).

4 See the treatment of this topic in my book *El discurso de la abundancia* (Caracas, 1992). The essay in which I discuss perception and perspective in Columbus and Garcilaso as axes of representation is translated as 'The Discourse of Abundance', *American Literary History*, IV/3 (Fall 1992), pp. 369–85.

5 Juan Bautista de Avalle-Arce on the contrary thinks that the references to 'another Rome' and 'there is only one world' show that Garcilaso had assumed a Spanish identity, and had come to reject the Inca world and to see it as part of an imperial and Catholic history and philosophy. In his 'Ideological Profile of Inca Garcilaso de la Vega' in *Primer encuentro internacional de peruanistas: estado de los estudios histórico-sociales sobre el Perú a fines del siglo XX* (Lima, 1988), vol. II, pp. 285–92. Although Avalle-Arce's proposal is well argued, it overlooks the fact that Garcilaso signed him-self 'Inca' Garcilaso de la Vega, and referred to himself as 'the Indian'. He was regarded as Spanish just like the illustrious members of his family, which included the poet Garcilaso de la Vega, but at the same time he was regarded as other, someone from the overseas provinces who spoke Quechua, and as someone else, someone from an Italian humanist culture, who translated from Italian and Latin. Doris Sommer sees the very name of 'Inca Garcilaso' as an oxymoron in her suggestive study of the complex *mestizo* texture of the Inca, 'Mosaic and Mestizo: Bilingual Love from Hebrero to Garcilaso', in her *Proceed with Caution when Engaged with Minority Writing in the Americas* (Cambridge, MA, 1999), pp. 61–91.

6 Sor Juana Inés de la Cruz, 'Aplaude lo mismo que la Fama en la sabiduría sin par de la Señora Doña María de Guadalupe Alencastre, la única maravilla de nuestros siglos', in *Lírica personal, obras*, vol. I, ed. Alfonso Martínez Plancarte (Mexico City, 1951), pp. 102–3.

7 Inca Garcilaso de la Vega, *Comentarios reales de los Incas*, ed. De Angel Rosenblat (Buenos Aires, 1945), vol. II [Book 8, chapter xxiv, 213]. José Antonio Mazzotti sug-gests a reading of *mestizaje* in Garcilaso as a Cuzco oral and choral practice in his *Coros mestizos del Inca Garcilaso: resonancias andinas* (Lima, 1996).

8 In his essay 'La conciencia coetánea de crisis y las tensiones sociales del siglo XVII', José Antonio Maravall argues that there is a political and economic crisis that exacer-bates every kind of violence and authoritarian tendency. His hypothesis that the Baroque is the literary and artistic expression of those social discontents now seems mechanical, but the array of symptoms that he documents supports his thesis about generalized conflict. See his book *The Culture of the Baroque: Analysis of an Historical*

Structure, trans. Terry Cochran (Minneapolis, MN, 1986). For a critical history, see John H. Elliott, *Spain and its World, 1500–1700* (New Haven and London, 1989).

9 Antonio de Solís y Rivadeneira, *Historia de la conquista de México*, ed. Edmundo O'Gorman and José Valero Silva, 2 vols, 3rd edn (Mexico City, 1978), p. 27.

10 Luis Arocena has made an exhaustive study of Solís's work in his reliable *Antonio de Solís, cronista indiano: estudio sobre las formas historiógrafas del barroco* (Buenos Aires, 1963). For recent studies on the Baroque, see Bolívar Echeverría's compilation, *Modernidad, mestizaje cultural, ethos barroco* (Mexico City, 1994).

11 Beatriz Pastor Bodmer has suggested a persuasive analysis of utopia as a project implicit within colonial history in her book *El jardin y el peregrino: ensayos sobre el pensamiento utópico latinoamericano, 1492–1695* (Amsterdam and Atlanta, GA, 1996).

12 'But at the end of the matter there is no reason to throw into oblivion the care that Divine Providence had for the conservation of the species of all corruptible things, and especially plants. For which He provided two things, the first that there was such an abundance of seeds that every plant produced, that there could never be a lack of seed such that the plant could not be produced again. The other was to have put such a marvelous virtue into each seed, that from a grain or a pip would grow a great bush, which would also produce that great abundance of seeds for its renewal . . . In the same way, from a melon pip would grow a melon vine, and in every melon there was such an abundance of pips so as to repair and conserve this species . . . Nor was the Lord himself silent, when he said "I came into the world to give life to men, abundant and plentiful life." *Introducción del Símbolo de la Fe*, ed. José María Balcells (Madrid, 1989), pp. 252–3.

13 Gregorio García, *Origen de los indios de el Nuevo Mundo e Indias Occidentales*, ed. Franklin Pease (Mexico City, 1981). This is a facsimile of the 2nd edition (Madrid, 1729). Jacques Lafaye has given it some attention in his study *Quetzalcóatl y Guadalupe: la formación de la conciencia nacional en México* (Mexico City, 1981), pp. 84–9. Fray Toribio de Benavente Motolinia was also concerned with the religious sense of the Indians of New Spain and suggested that conversion was the final point of the Conquest; his testimony to native Catholic ardour appears in his *Memoriales* (1527–41); see the critical edition produced by Nancy Joe Dwyer (Mexico City, 1996).

14 Marcel Bataillon, 'La herejia de Francisco de la Cruz y la reacción antilascasiana', in his *Etudes sur Bartolomé de las Casas* (Paris, 1965).

15 On the representation of nature in the emblematic rhetoric of the period, see Fernando Rodríguez de la Flor, 'Mundus est fabula: la lectura de la naturaleza como documento político-moral en la literatura simbólica', in his *La península metafísica: Arte, literatura y pensamiento en la España de la Contrareforma* (Madrid, 1999).

16 F. José de Acosta, *Historia natural y moral de las Indias*, ed. Edmundo O'Gorman, 2nd edn (Mexico City, 1962).

17 José Antonio Maravall, 'El descubrimiento de América en la historia del pensamiento político', in his *Estudios de historia del pensamiento español*, 2nd series: *La época del Renacimiento* (Madrid, 1984), p. 404. Maravall is one of the first social historians of the Spanish Renaissance and Baroque to study American history as a contributory element to Spanish political ideas.

18 Richard Fletcher, *The Barbarian Conversion: From Paganism to Christianity* (New York, 1997). There is a discussion of a counter-acculturation in the peculiar phenomena of syncretism in R. Po-Chia Hsia, *The World of Catholic Renewal, 1540–1770* (Cambridge, 1998). On the complexity of syncretism and religious hybridity in the New World, in addition to Lafaye, *Quetzalcóatl y Guadalupe*, see also Robert Ricard *La conquista espiritual de México* (1932; Mexico City, 1986); David A. Brading, *The First America: The Spanish Monarchy, Creole Patriots and the Liberal State, 1492–1867* (Cambridge, 1991); Sabine MacCormack, *Religion in the Andes: Vision and Imagination*

in Early Peru (Princeton, NJ, 1991).

19 Even when themes and images produce a repertoire that functions as a topos, as a commonplace, these references have the quality of agreement with an already established evaluation. This occurs, for example, in what passes for a commonplace in the following quotation from the Anonymous Conquistador: 'The country is very fertile and abundant and produces whatever one sows, and in many places yields its fruits twice or three times a year' (*Relación de algunas cosas de la Nueva España y de la gran ciudad de Temestitan México*) to Nélida Piñón's novel *La república de los sueños* (*The Republic of Dreams*) (1984), where a character says of Brazil: 'Not even the Mediterranean sun could compare with it. And from what they say here not even the Aegean sun could put it in the shade. As for the land, it is so lush, that things flower three times a year' (p. 81). Nature is the same, but the discourse has shifted: from colonial topos to national memory. On the counterpart of this representation, the narrative discourses of failure and rebellion, see Beatriz Pastor, *Discursos narrativos de la conquista: mitificación y emergencia* (Hanover, NH, 1988). The paradigm of scarcity is applied by Luigi Invernizzi to the Chile chronicles in his 'Trabajos de la guerra, trabajos de hambre: dos ejes del discurso narrativo de la conquista de Chile', *Revista Chilena de Literatura*, no. 36 (November 1990), pp. 7–27.

20 Felipe Guamán Poma de Ayala, *El primer Nueva Corónica y buen gobierno* [1615], ed. John V. Murra and Rolena Adorno, trans. Jorge L. Urioste, 3 vols (Mexico City, 1980).

21 See his *La vocación literaria del pensamiento histórico en América: desarrollo de la prosa de ficción siglos XVI–XIX* (Madrid, 1982). Other considerations and perspectives on the question of *mestizaje* and Garcilaso Inca's rhetorical strategies can be compared in the works of José Antonio Mazzotti, *Coros mestizos del Inca Garcilaso: resonancias andinas* (Lima, 1996); María Ramírez Ribes, *Un amor por el diálogo: el Inca Garcilaso de la Vega* (Caracas, 1993); Claire Pailler and Jean-Marie Pailler, 'Une Amérique vraiment latine: pour une lecture "Dumezilienne" de l'Inca Garcilaso de la Vega', in *Annales, Economies, Sociétés, Civilization* (Paris, 1992), pp. 207–35; Doris Sommer, *Proceed with Caution when Engaged by Minority Writing in the Americas* (Cambridge, MA, 1999).

one Speaking: *Caliban*

1 *The Tempest*, ed. Frank Kerdmode (London, 1954). We considered also *The Tempest*, ed, George Lymann Kittredge, revised Irving Ribner (Lexington, MA, 1967), and *The Tempest*, ed. Barbara A. Mowat and Paul Werstine (New York, 1994); the latter edition pays attention to post-colonial readings of the work.

2 Anthony Pagden has studied the transposition of these images and ideas in his *The Fall of Natural Man* (Cambridge, 1982). A broad conspectus of European ideas about America, from Columbus to Hegel, is found in the work of Antonello Gerbi; see his *The Dispute of the New World* (Pittsburgh, PA, 1973).

3 Antonio Eslava, *Noches de invierno*, ed. de Julia Barella Vigal (Pamplona, 1986).

4 The various accounts of the famous shipwreck were popular in Shakespeare's time. Lyman Kittredge writes: 'On June 2, 1609, a fleet of seven ships and two small vessels sailed from Plymouth to Virginia. The flagship, the *Sea Adventure*, carried the new Governor (Sir Thomas Gates), the Admiral (Sir George Somers), and Captain Christopher Newport. On July 24 a terrible storm scattered the fleet. It arrived at Jamestown in August, but the *Sea Adventure* was missing. She had run ashore on the Bermudas in July 28, but without loss of life. Gates, Somers, and the rest – some 150 in all – remained on the island for about nine months . . . In 1610, soon after their arrival [back in England], three narratives of these adventures were published . . .

More important, however, is a long letter from William Strachey, another of Somer's companions ... The resemblance between Strachey's letter and *The Tempest* can hardly be accidental' (Introduction, *The Tempest*, xii–xiii).

5 The argument that the *mestizos* were the owners twice over of the land of America because in addition to being their maternal inheritance it was a conquest by their fathers is deployed as a challenge. In official reports on colonial life this challenge was considered as proof that the *mestizos* were unruly and dangerous.

6 Michel de Montaigne, *Essays* (Baltimore, MD, 1958) Cap. xxxi. 'On the Cannibals', p. 230.

7 Montaigne also says: 'These nations, then seem to me to be barbarous only in that they have been hardly fashioned by the mind of man, still remaining close neighbors to their original state of nature. They are still governed by the laws of Nature and are only very slightly bastardized by ours: but their purity is such that I am sometimes seized with irritation at their not having been discovered earlier, in times when there were men who could have appreciated them better than us', ibid., p. 232.

8 Stephan J. Greenblatt, 'Learning to Curse: Aspects of Linguistic Colonialism in the Sixteenth Century', in his *Learning to Curse: Essays in Early Modern Culture* (New York, 1992), p. 28.

9 John X. Evans observes this in 'Utopia on Prospero's Island', *Moreana*, xviii (1981), pp. 81–3.

10 John G. Demaray, *Shakespeare and the Spectacles of Strangeness* (Pittsburgh, PA, 1998), p. 117.

11 Barbara Baert, 'Caliban as Wild-Man: An Iconographic Approach', in *Constellation Caliban: Figurations of a Character*, ed. Nadia Lie and Theo d'Haen (Amsterdam, 1997).

12 Edward Everett Hale, *Prospero's Island* (New York, 1919), Series Discussions of the Drama, with an introduction by Henry Cabot Lodge.

13 Roger Bartra in his *El salvaje en el espejo* (Mexico City, 1992), pp. 162–4, calls Calibán 'the first modern man'.

14 David Norbrook, '"What cares these roares for the name of king?": Language and Utopia in The Tempest', *The Tempest*, ed. R. S. White (New York, 1999), pp. 167–90.

15 Howard F. Cline, 'The *Relaciones geográficas* of the Spanish Indies, 1577–1586', *Hispanic American Historical Review*, xliv/3 (August 1964), pp. 341–74.

16 José Enrique Rodó, *Ariel*, ed. Gordon Brotherston (Cambridge, 1967).

17 See Maarten van Delden, 'The Survival of the Prettiest: Transmutations of Darwin in Rodó's Ariel', in *Constellation Caliban*, pp. 145–61.

18 Nadia Lie studies the impact of this essay in 'Countering Caliban: Roberto Fernández Retamar and the Postcolonial Debate', in *Constellation Caliban*, pp. 245–70. Also see the discussion provoked by the Afro-American experience Houston A. Baker Jr, in 'Caliban's Triple Play', in *Race, Writing and Difference*, ed. Henry Louis Gates, Jr (Chicago, 1985), pp. 381–95; the author tries to transcend the play's dualism between Prospero and Caliban.

19 Michel de Certeau, *Heterologies: Discourse on the Other* (Minneapolis, MN, 1986), reads Montaigne's essay as strategically developing discursive sequences that support the cannibal's own speech, the speech of the other. He says: '"Of Cannibals" is inscribed within this heterological tradition, in which the discourse about the other is a means of constructing a discourse authorized by the other', p. 68. This strategy presupposes 'the circularity between the production of the Other and the production of the text'. These three phases correspond to the travel account, to testimony about savage society, and finally, the return of the savage himself, who 'returns in the text', pp. 69–70.

two   Reading: *The Children of the Letter*

1   Fray Luis de Granada, *Introducción del Símbolo de la Fe* (1583–5), ed. José María Balcells (Madrid, 1989).
2   José Antonio Maravall, 'Nature and History in Spanish Humanism', in his *Estudios de historia del pensamiento español*, 2nd series: *La época del Renacimiento* (Madrid, 1984).
3   I have discussed this in my *El discurso de la abundancia* (Caracas, 1994).
4   Inca Garcilaso de la Vega, *Comentarios reales de los Incas*, ed Aurelio Miró Quesada, 2 vols (Caracas, 1976).
5   Gonzalo Fernández de Oviedo, *Sumario de la natural historia de las Indias* (Mexico City, 1950).
6   In his *Peruvian Traditions* (3rd series, 1875) Ricardo Palma includes one devoted to this fable, though without quoting Inca Garcilaso as a source. In the first edition he set the story in the 'melon grove of Pachacamac', but in the subsequent ones he preferred 'the melon grove of Barranca', to the north of Lima. The 'tradition' is entitled 'The Letter Sings' and maintains that Antonio Solar was 'in 1558 one of the most comfortable residents' of Lima, owner of 200 *fangedas* in the valleys of Supe and Barranca. Palma erases the native name that Garcialaso offered and preferred the more historical one, although the attribution of the fable to Soler and Barranca is no less fable-like. In any event, this version suggests to us that the designation of Pachacamac in the Commentaries is not fortuitous. Ricardo Palma, *Tradiciones peruanas*, ed. Julio Ortega and Flor María Rodríguez Arenas (Paris, 1993), pp. 123–6.
7   Hermannvs Hugo, *De prima scribendi origine et vniversa rei literariae antiqvitate* (Antwerp, 1617). The quote comes from 'Preface to the Reader. Of the marvellous nature and usefulness of writing'. Hugo (Brussels, 1558–Rhinberg, 1629) entered the Jesuit order in 1605, taught Humanities at Antwerp, and was prefect of studies in Brussels. He accompanied the Duc d'Arschot to Spain as confessor, and on his return to Flanders was in the household of Ambrosio Spinola; he died in one of his campaigns, a victim of plague. Two of his works have been translated into Spanish, *Pia Desideria* (1624) by Padre Pedro de Salas, and *Sitio de Breda* (1627) by Emanuel Sueyro. John Wilkins in his *Mercury: The Secret and Swift Messenger* (1707) quotes the fable of the Indians and the figs, giving Hugo's treatise as its source. In *Interpretation and Overinterpretation* (Cambridge, 1993) Umberto Eco goes back to Wilkins's fable and speculates on what 'figs' might mean, but fails to refer to Hugo and Inca Garcilaso, whose 'melons' might well have put his system to the test. In passing from De Gómara to Garcilaso and Lope de Vega, from Hugo to Wilkins and Eco, the fable ceases to be an oral tradition (a memory of writing) and becomes writing (a rhetorical variation): between the two, in fact, the interpretations vary, but the meaning is the same: it is the Indians who are the offspring of the letter. Inscribed within the discourse of verification (that is, as subjects of literality), the Indians are the natural users of an instrument for recognition and recording that they will soon make their own in the cycle of new beginnings.

three   Writing: *The Alphabet of Abundance*

1   Felipe Guamán Poma de Ayala, *El primer nueva corónica y buen gobierno* (1615), ed. John V. Murra and Rolena Adorno, 3 vols (Mexico City, 1980). Here we quote from this edition. The historian Franklin Pease edited the book, in two volumes (Caracas, 1980). Discovered in the Royal Library in Copenhagen in 1908, the work was published by Paul Rivet in a facsimile edition (Paris, 1936; reprinted 1968). Within the works devoted to the author, the following are fundamental: Juan Ossio, ed., *Ideología*

mesiánica del mundo andino (Lima, 1973); Rolena Adorno, *Guamán Poma: Writing and Resistance in Colonial Peru* (Austin, TX, 1986); *Cronista y príncipe: la obra de don Felipe Guamán Poma de Ayala* (Lima, 1989); Mercedes López Baralt, *Icono y conquista: Guamán Poma de Ayala* (Madrid, 1988); Rodrigo Cánovas, *Guamán Poma, Felipe: escritura y censura en el Nuevo Mundo* (Santiago de Chile, 1993).

2 Franklin Pease in the Prologue to his edition of the *Chronicle* brings out the encyclopedic and totalizing character of the book: 'it wants to embrace the totality at the same time as it shapes an idealization of the universe that it presents and aspires to. It oscillates between the "there is no remedy" which colors the author's laments, and the concrete recommendations and prescriptions which would remedy those ills, guarantee his role in the old and new societies, heal the authority of the King to whom he appeals against the evils of his officers, and achieve in large part the good government of the Indies to which he aspires' (xvii). In effect, Guamán inscribes the signs of abundance within the signs of lack and absence: with great acuity he documents colonial violence, but at the same time, with great rigour and conviction, he argues for his 'prescriptions' (which he even formulates as 'ordinances', putting himself forward as someone to rewrite the laws with decrees for the common good) as anticipated remedies for ethnic memory amidst the anxieties of the present. Thus the most speculative writing restructures his cultural world with the most empirical of lessons.

3 The extraordinary impact of orality (both Quechua and Spanish, perhaps 'Spandean') expands and unfolds in this work in a fertile fashion thanks to writing, both Spanish and Native, becoming 'oralized', turned into contemporary speech; in the course of this mixing it becomes hybridized as it seeks its own discourse. One good example is that of the name 'Indias', 'Indies' – Guamán hears not one but two words in the name: 'in dia'. Confronted by the five vowels of Spanish, Quechua, with three vowels, registers the phoneme 'e' as 'i', and these two words are understood as meaning 'the land in the day' because the Indies are nearer the sun, and therefore correspond in the cosmic order to the upper world, whilst Spain corresponds to the lower. Guamán therefore depicts them as complementary opposites. As Brian Stock points out: 'A text does not cease to be structured discourse, obedient to the laws of grammar and syntax, simply because it is spoken aloud. And oral exchange, if recorded, may still preserve many of its original features, for instance, formulae, repetition, and encyclopedism. Written texts are continually being re-performed, offering continuities to human behavior over time', in his *The Implications of Literacy: Written Language and Models of Interpretation in the Eleventh and Twelfth Centuries* (Princeton, NJ, 1983), pp. 13ff. The dispute over the rules of administration is the proper setting for this oral memory of 'prescriptions' and remedies.

4 Guamán Poma's proposal might have been inspired by the practices of the early Christians as well as doctrinary writings on the Indies not of Renaissance origin. It could be related to the hyperbolic formulations of the *arbitristas*, very much in vogue in seventeenth-century Spain, whose memoires offered radical cures for every evil. They were taken seriously by a number of those in authority, including the Conde-Duque de Olivares, although they earned the satirical attacks of Quevedo and Cervantes. In America they often had a complex and even crazy inspiration. Examined closely, every historian or chronicler of the Indies had his *arbitrista* side, even when he was engaged in juridical discourse. In this strategy almost everything remains to be done. Guamán Poma has the imposing presence of an eloquent *arbitrista*: he even imagines himself called by His Majesty as a truthful and well-informed chronicler, and writes a chapter in which 'His Majesty Asks Questions' (which allows him to propose prompt solutions). As happens in juridical discourse, which is often glossed, here it is the discourse of evangelization that is glossed: Guamán uses the format of catechumen's questions and priest's answers, but changes the roles, and the

king now appears as the novice who is going to be enlightened. Another source of the author's collective proposal could be native agriculture and its festivals, which includes communal meals in their many rituals of sowing, cultivation and harvesting. On the role of the *arbitrista*, see Fred Bronner, 'Peruvian Arbitristas under Viceroy Chinchón, 1629–1639', in *Studies in Hispanic History and Literature*, xxvi (1974), pp. 34–78, and Jean Vilar Berrogaín, *Literatura y economía: la figura satírica del arbitrista en el Siglo de Oro* (Madrid, 1973).

5 It is symptomatic of Guamán Poma's strategy that in the chapter dedicated to the Conquest (pp. 341ff) he begins with an unnatural acting of eating. First, because he constructs an emblem of the Conquest on the basis of a sort of ironic legend: the Spaniards, he says, eat gold. He gives an explanation and also draws the Inca Guaina Capac giving seeds of gold on plate to a Spaniard who he asks in Quechua: 'Cay coritacho micunqui?' ('Do you eat this gold?'). To which the other replies: 'We eat this gold.' Guamán is alluding to a typical *arbitrista* gesture: in order to describe the wealth of the Incas, Pedro de Candia, one of Pizarro's companions, speaks of people dressed in gold and silver, roads paved with gold and silver, etc.; but this hyperbole, which becomes widespread in Spain, merely confirms his greed. The Conquest, by the same token, is represented as unnatural: greed is another moment of the world turned upside down, in which people are capable of 'eating gold'. It is also interesting that the emblematic dialogue in this drawing is bilingual, and is thus the space of a translation. The explanation is in Quechua: the misunderstanding is allegorical because it is ratified as true, that is, the Spanish declaration confirms the Quechua interpretation. In addition, it is one of those fables that reverse the question of who the real barbarians are, a motif that is repeated by the chroniclers in different anecdotes. If emblems are symbolic accounts that refer to a condensed explanation, this is the first ironic emblem, that is, an allegory that refers to a larger condemnation.

6 M. Bakhtin, *Rabelais and his World* (Cambridge, 1968). The celebratory character of the immanence that Bakhtin sees in the feast presupposes its anti-institutional and de-centring level. Guamán Poma seems to emphasize the capacity of native culture to weave together a scene that calls on Christian charity whilst also alluding to legislation about poverty and its instrumental will.

7 Other readings by Guamán Poma about cultural practice propose a strategy of resistance. Sara Castro-Klarén puts Guamán Poma's proposals into the context of other rebel movements and Andean texts of reassertion in her essay 'Discourse and Transformation of the Gods in the Andes: From Taki Onqoy to Rasu Ñiti' in *El retorno de las huacas: estudios y documentos sobre el Taki Onqoy, Siglo XVI* (Lima, 1990), pp. 407–23.

8 David Brading, in his fundamental *The First America: The Spanish Monarchy, Creole patriots and The Liberal State, 1492–1867* (Cambridge, 1991), establishes the set of choices that define Guamán Poma's cultural peculiarity and that of a large number of the new *letrados* of Indian origin in the colonial world. He writes: 'Condemnation of the Conquest does not constitute a rejection of the Spanish regime. Just like the members of the college of Santa Cruz de Tlatelolco who helped Sahagún to establish the Mexican Indian version of the Conquest, Guamán Poma also tried to paint this event as a traslatio imperii which was freely accepted' (p. 175). Further on, he says: 'The comparison of the Mayan prophetic books with the New Chronicle reveals both Guamán Poma's originality and the underlying similarity of their cultural projects. In both cases, there was an insistence on the basic continuity of native history, considering the Conquest as a traumatic phenomenon, but one, which took place on the surface, and although the integrity of native society was threatened it was nevertheless maintained' (p. 186).

9 Rolena Adorno has given an acute analysis of the temporal functions of the account

in the Chronicle, and based on Uspensky's idea of the imperfect preterite introduces the notion of the 'present in the past', observing that in the story of the Coyas there is something that is also valid in this memory taken from the sowing calendar: 'The verbs of inner action, like thinking or speaking – to the extent that this latter represents an action formulated inside and perceived from the outside – constitute the key to this "presentification" . . . in which the Here – and not the Now – is the dominant category' (*Cronista y principe: la obra de don Felipe Guamán Poma de Ayala*, Lima, 1989, pp. 137ff).

10 In addition to his periodic naivety, Guamán Poma also displays courage and determination. His very name is an allegory of Andean knowledge: the *huamán* (falcon) corresponds to the upper world, whilst the *Poma* (puma, American lion) corresponds to the lower. The patronymic 'de Ayala' declares his belonging to the new language and to the new lineage. His name already announces the consciousness of his task, so that his nomadism is the mark of his occupation as *letrado*: he has lost his lands, and gives his wandering the shape of an 'inspection' in the name of his Letter to the King (as Juan Ossio calls the *Chronicle*) in which his condemnation of colonial violence and degradation is woven into a project of utopian and communal reorganization based not on an Incan model but an ethnic, regional one. Two concrete sources give a context to this project so as to make it not simply archaic: its adhesion to the laws of Toledo and its clear descent from Las Casas. Reform and reorganization also have a Franciscan perspective, a conviction that the Christian religion is for the poor, and that the Indians being 'the poor of Jesus Christ' are a Christian advent, a revelation that was prophesied and is a prophecy of new times, of justice redeemed. None of which prevents the chronicler's critical intelligence breaking through with ironic and satirical remarks about the social comedy.

11 Given Guamán Poma appears as a character, a narrator produced in crisis, it is hardly surprising that people have doubted his existence, or at least his authorship of the Chronicle, much to the horror of the academic community. In a period of overvaluation of the global and apparent dismissal of differences (although the global has always produced forms of the regional, by reaction or contrast, but also through the logic of diversification of the market) various ideologues on the one hand and opportunists on the other have tried to disqualify the regional enterprises of authors as important as José María Arguedas and forms of life as legitimate as the Andean, in the name of compulsory and authoritarian modernization. Doubting Guamán's authorship ends up seeming more of a novelistic speculation than the product of serious methodological doubt. In a linguistic, historical and critical analysis, Adorno outlines, evaluates and refutes this line of argument in her article: 'Critera of Verification: The Manuscript Miccinelli of Naples and the Chronicles of the Conquest of Peru', *Revista Antropológica*, xvi/16 (1998), pp. 369–94.

12 Raquel Chang-Rodríguez has compared the rhetorical strategies of three chroniclers of native origin Titu Cusi Yupanqui, author of *Relación de la conquista del Perú* (1570); Joan de Santacruz Pachacuti, author of *Relación de antigüedades deste Reyno del* (1613); and Guamán Poma de Ayala in her monograph *La apropiación del signo* (Tempe, AZ, 1988).

13 Bartolomé de las Casas, *Tratados*, ed. Lewis Hanke and Manuel Jiménez Fernández (Mexico City, 1965), vol. II, p. 643.

14 Miguel de Giginta, *Tratado de remedio de pobres*, ed. Féliz Santolaria Sierra (Barcelona, 2000). He once mentions Peru: 'Of the West Indias I have heard it said that in the time of the Incas in Peru there was no poor man who suffered need' (p. 185). In his excellent introduction Santolaria Sierra places the treatise by the canon of Elna in the context of European history and its tradition of social reform.

15 Massimo Montanari, *El hambre y la abundancia* (Barcelona, 1993). Montanari shows

how the transplanting of new American foodstuffs was slow and patchy, and only in
the eighteenth century were they cultivated extensively.

four Translating: *The Transatlantic Subject*

1 The historian Raúl Porras Barrenechea compiled several of these testimonies in his
Los cronistas del Perú, 1523–1650 (Lima, 1962). Porras sees the testimonies of Xerez and
Sancho as 'official' and therefore 'necessarily adapted to the political requirements of
the expedition and the defence of its actions'. By contrast, he sees the version offered
by Cristóbal de Menas as 'the account of a witness who is detached from the enterprise and free to give his impartial opinion on the matter' and he concludes that de
Mena is 'the freshest and most spontaneous of them all, the one who is most faithful
to the events at Cajamarca and the feelings they evoked'. The perspective of such an
important historian is interesting for the study of the Peruvian chronicles first of all,
because it reveals a hierarchy of historical values: to the value of truth (impartiality)
is added that of testimony (emotion). Both factors are deduced, however, not from
the account or from the discourse, but from the personal quality of the subject in
question. Secondly, it is a question of the context of the character of interpretation.
Porras pursues an impossible synthesis, that of classical objectivity with novelistic
enthusiasm. On the other hand, no less revealingly, Porras condemns Inca Garcilaso
for his interpretation of the events at Cajamarca. His eclecticism therefore leads him
to lose sight of the Andean part of the account. Antonio Cornejo Polar gives an judi-
cious balance sheet of the Spanish and Andean versions in his 'The Beginnings of
Heterogeneity in Andean Literature: voice and letter in the "dialogue" of Cajamarca',
Revista de Crítica Literaria Latinoamericana, xvii/33 (1990), pp. 155–207. Sabine G.
MacCormack does the same in 'Atahualpa and the Book', *Dispositio*, xiv/36–8 (1989),
pp. 141–68. See also the analysis by Patricia Seed, 'Failing to Marvel: Atahualpa's
Encounter with the Word', *Latin American Research Review*, xxvi/1 (1991), pp. 7–32.

2 Cristóbal de Mena, *La Conquista del Perú llamada la Nueva Castilla. La cual tierra
por divina voluntad fue maravillísima conquistada en la felicísima ventura del
Emperador y Rey nuestro señor; y por la prudencia y el esfuerzo del muy magnífico y
valeroso caballero el Capitán Francisco Pizarro Gobernador y Adelantado de la Nueva
Castilla, y de su hermano Hernando Pizarro, y de sus animosos capitanes y fieles y
esforzados compañeros que con él se hallaron* (Seville, 1534). In addition to Porras's
volume it is included in *Los Cronistas de la Conquista*, ed. Horacio H. Urteaga (París,
1938), vol. ii. The first document of the Encounter already declares in its title the
principal actors of the historic event. It also reveals the function of the letter and
the place of the *letrado*.

3 Francisco de Xerex, *Verdadera relación de la conquista del Perú* (1534). Porras includes
it in his compilation. There is a modern edition put together by Concepción Bravo
(Madrid, 1985).

4 Pedro Cieza de León, *Crónica del Perú*, third part, ed. Francesca Cantú (Lima, 1987).
Cieza is one of the most formal and lucid chroniclers, thanks to his humanist education and his common sense. He is obsessed, it has to be said, by the presence of the
Devil in the Indies, but his account displays curiosity and attention. The third part
of his famous Chronicle was only discovered in the 1980s.

5 Francisco López de Gómara, *Historia general de las Indias* (1552; Madrid, 1947). Other
chroniclers who rehearse the history of the Encounter are Francisco de Jerez, Augustín
de Zárate and Pedro Pizarro.

6 Martín de Murúa, *Historia general del Perú y descendencia de los Incas* (1590), ed.
Constantino Bayle (Madrid, 1946). There is another edition from Manuel Ballesteros

Gaibrois (Madrid, 1962).

7 Felipe Guamán Poma de Ayala, *El primer nueva corónica y buen gobierno*, ed. John Murra and Rolena Adorno, trans. Jorge Urioste, 3 vols (Mexico City, 1980).

8 Inca Garcilaso de la Vega, *Historia General del Perú: Segunda parte de los Comentarios Reales de los Incas*, ed. Angel Rosenblat (Buenos Aires, 1944). Another chronicler who also notes that translation was a determinant was Juan de Betanzos in his *Suma y narración de los Incas*, written about 1551 but not published until 1880. His knowledge of Quechua and the Inca world brought him close to the perspectives of Garcilaso and Guamán. He writes: 'Fray Vicente de Valverde came to him and brought with him an interpreter and what Fray Vicente said to the Inca I have heard that the interpreter did not know how to declare to the Inca because what the lords who were there and by the Inca's side said that what the tongue said to the Inca was that the Father took out a book and opened it and the tongue said that that father was the son of the Sun and that the Sun had sent him to him to tell him not to fight and to give obedience to the captain who was also the son of the Sun and that this was in the book and that was what the picture said and the Inca asked for the book and took it in his hands and opened it and as he saw the lines of the writing he said: this speaks and this says that you are the son of the Sun I am also the son of the Sun . . . that he also came from where the Sun was and saying this he threw the book away', ed. María del Carmen Martín Rubio (Madrid, 1987), p. 277.

9 MacCormack puts it like this: 'According to Guamán Poma, on the other hand, the silence of the book was a product not of the Inca's ignorance, but of the Spaniards' failure to communicate in an appropriate fashion' (p. 702). What is revealing is the paradigm of communication that Guamán Poma takes up in the dialogue between the agents within his project of restoration. Whilst in a gesture that is characteristic of his rather Petrarchan philological tastes, Inca Garcilaso claims to have found the text of Valverde's discourse amongst the 'torn papers' of the Jesuit historian Blas Valera.

10 María Antonia Garcés Arellano in her article 'La conquista de la palabra: el mito de los Ayar en Garcilaso Inca de la Vega', *Thesaurus*, XLVII/2 (May–August 1992), pp. 293–312, thinks that Garcilaso's interest in Italian historiography and Renaissance rhetoric stem from the Andean cult of the word. In his Commentaries the Inca stresses the properness and refinement of Cuzco speakers and time and again defends the status and difference of his native Quechua. According to Max Hernández, Garcilaso contests the events of Cajamarca, projecting himself into them: this projection is also achieved in his translation, given that the idea of Neo-Platonic love allows him to recover both paternal and maternal 'imagos'. See his suggestive analysis *Memoria del bien perdido: conflicto, identidad y nostalgia en el Inca Garcilaso de la Vega* (Lima, 1993).

11 *La traduzion del Indio de los tres Diálogos de Amor de León Hebrero, hecha del Italiano en Español por Garcilaso Inca de la Vega, natural de la gran ciudad del Cuzco, cabeca de los reynos y provincias del Pirú* (1590). In *Obras completas del Inca Garcilaso de la Vega*, ed. Carmelo Sáenz de Santa María (Madrid, 1965), vol. I, Garcilaso declares that 'excellence, discretion, wit and wisdom' are the virtues of the author of this work: virtues that connote the Christian gentleman of Erasmian teaching as well as the Petrarchan ethos.

12 Roland Greene, '"This Praxis is continuous": Love and Empire in 1590', *Journal of Hispanic Philology*, XVI/2 (Winter 1992), pp. 237–52. See his *Conquests: Petrarchan Experience and the Colonial American* (Chicago, 1999).

13 Pizarro's expedition had two translators Felipillo and Martinillo, later known as Don Martín. The nicknames indicate that they were both very young when they arrived in Cajamarca, and although it is not certain which of the two served as interpreter to Valverde in his dialogue with the Inca, it is probable that it was Felipillo. Lockhart has investigated their origins and notes that Martín was from Chincha and was therefore

Quechua and of noble origin, while Felipillo was from Piura, and therefore from the
north and of common stock. Thus one of them is given the title 'don' while the other
earns Atahualpa's complaints, the Inca being doubly offended because Felipillo
claimed one of his wives and was of low birth. It is unsurprising that the translators
were rivals and enemies. Felipillo was labelled as conspirator and traitor by several
chroniclers, and after many intrigues, marches and countermarches was finally executed for being a follower of Almagro, Pizarro's former ally and subsequently rival.
Don Martín had always been a follower of Pizarro and gained honour and riches in
Lima as an 'interpreter general' and *encomendero*: but he had the same fate as the
Pizarros and on his fall his goods were forfeited and he was sent back to Seville as a
prisoner, where he subsequently died. James Lockhart describes the interpreters in his
The Men of Cajamarca (Austin, TX, 1972), pp. 448–53. In one sense they were victims
of their position as intermediaries, lacking their own place in society, caught up
between factions and having divided loyalties. From Garcilaso's perspective, they
revealed that translation as a service contested the powers that be with the power
of the word.

14 Luis Millones has investigated the elaboration of messianic elements in modern
Andean culture, and has suggested various historical scenarios of the native mentality.
See his fundamental work *Historia y poder en los Andes centrales* (Madrid, 1987),
as well as his *Actores de altura: ensayos sobre el teatro popular andino* (Lima, 1992).
Raquel Chang-Rodriguez's article 'Cultural Resistance in the Andes and its Depiction
in Atau Wallpaj P´uchukakuyninpa or Tragedy of Atahualpa´s Death', in Francisco
Javier Cevallos et al., eds, *Coded Encounters: Writing, Gender and Ethnicity in Colonial
Latin America* (Amherst, MA, 1994), pp. 115–34, should also be consulted.

15 See Juan Ossio, ed., *Ideología mesiánica del mundo andino* (Lima, 1973); R. Tom
Zuidema, *Reyes y guerreros: ensayos de cultura andina* (Lima, 1989); Sabine
MacCormack, *Religion in the Andes: Vision and Imagination in Early Colonial Peru*
(Princeton, NJ, 1991).

16 *Tragedia del fin de Atawallpa / Atau Wallpaj p´uchukakuyninpa wankan*, Spanish
version ed. Jesús Lara (Buenos Aires, 1989).

17 In a final scene when the Inca bids farewell to his kin, he leaves them his gold and
diamond insignia as souvenir and talisman. The fragmentation of his belongings as
well as his body thus acquires the value of a legacy, shared amongst his kin, relations
and servants, and preserved as memory.

18 The future, the Inca states, will consist of rebellion against the invaders and their
expulsion. The memory of Atahualpa will be the nation's consciousness, lost now
but later to be recovered.

19 *La conquista de los españoles* (Tucumán, 1955). Text put together by Ena Dargan,
translated and published by Hernando Balmori, of the Universidad de Tucumán,
Argentina.

20 The play twice makes use of *afusilado*, which is a Quechua-influenced version of the
Spanish term *fusilado* (shot).

five Drawing: *The Wonders of the Caribbean*

1 Bernadette Bucher in his text of structural anthropology *Icon and Conquest: A
Structural Analysis of the Illustrations of de Bry´s Great Voyages* (Chicago, 1981), originally published in French in 1977. suggests that the representation of the Caribbean
replays the history of the Fall. Her thesis is based on a series of engravings by de Bry,
a Huguenot who made use of different chronicles and histories of the New World in
order to engrave, between 1590 and 1634, his monumental version of a world that was

doubly barbaric, first because of Spanish violence, and secondly by dint of native customs. The scenes of cannibalism, monstrosity and cruelty are, interestingly, represented by subjects who are more European than Indian: his Brazilian, Caribbean and North American Indians are barely distinguished from one another and all having a much stronger resemblance to their classical models. All of which makes de Bry's work less a document about the Indies and more an allegory of the Protestant European vision, which presents the Spanish Conquest as an apotheosis of savagery and an intimation of apocalypse.

2 The Tovar Manuscript has been edited by Jacques Lafaye in a careful bilingual edition in French and Spanish, with an introductory study by Lafaye, based on the text kept in the John Carter Brown Library at Brown University. What are especially interesting are the commentaries on the drawings, transcribed in the volume. J. Lafaye, ed., *Manuscrit Tovar: origines et croyances des indiens du Mexique* (Graz, 1972).

3 On Guamán Poma de Ayala's drawings, see Abraham Padilla Bendezú, *Huamán Poma, El indio cronista dibujante* (Mexico City, 1979). Also Rolena Adorno, 'On Pictorial Language and the Typology of Culture in a New World Chronicle', *Semiotica*, XXXVI/1–2 (1981), pp. 51–106, and Mercedes López Baralt, 'La Contrarreforma y el arte de Guamán Poma: notas sobre una política de la comunicación visual', *Histórica*, III/1 (1979), pp. 81–95.

4 *Histoire Naturelle des Indes: The Drake Manuscript in The Pierpont Morgan Library*, ed. Charles E. Pierce, Jr, Patrick O'Brian and Verlyn Klinkenborg, trans. Ruth S. Kraemer (New York, 1996), facsimile edition of 199 images. The manuscript was given to the Morgan Library in 1983, and although it has been available to researchers, the study of it is in its early stages. Although De Bry's fantasy-filled pathos has merited the greater part of experts' attention, surely because of the larger dimension of its vision of Enlightened Conquest, the drawings made by the anonymous artist who sailed with Drake's clandestine fleet have more value as ethnology. They are also peculiarly valuable as a Caribbean imaginary: they are testimony and at the same time typology. The immediacy of the native present, however, is achieved at the cost of communication: the Indian lacks a voice and becomes an interlocutor only when he has to receive a severe lesson in religious matters concerning the devil. On the construction of the other as savage, see Michel de Certeau's suggestive work, 'Ethnography, Orality or the Space of the Other: Léry', in his *The Writing of History* (New York, 1995). De Certeau returns to the debate about the representation of the other, again discussing the *Histoire d´un voyage fait en la terre du Brésil* (1578) by Jean de Léry in the chapter devoted to 'Montaigne´s "Of Cannibals": The Savage "I"', in his *Heterologies, Discourse on the Other* (Minneapolis, MN, 1985), pp. 67–79.

5 Gregorio García, *Origen de los indios de el Nuevo Mundo e Indias Occidentales*, ed. Franklin Pease (Mexico City, 1981), p. 63.

6 John Sugden in *Sir Francis Drake* (New York, 1990) gives an exact account of his expeditions around the Caribbean islands and coasts, pp. 44–77.

7 The facsimile edition of the *Sumario* was published in Madrid (1978) with an introductory note by Juan Pérez de Tudela, who also wrote the prologue to *Historia general y natural de las Indias*, 2 vols (Madrid, 1959). An accessible edition of the *Sumario* is that edited by José Miranda (Mexico City, 1950). Antonello Gerbi dedicated his monumental treatise *La Naturaleza de las Indias Nuevas: de Cristóbal Colón a Gonzalo Fernández de Oviedo*, trans. Antonio Alatorre (Mexico City, 1978), to the American life and work of the chronicler, with a great wealth of sources and comparative reading. He even displays a certain digressive empathy with the bric-a-brac style of Oviedo's 'varied reading'. Gerbi is right on the central issue: the notion of an extravagant nature, which Oviedo eloquently and joyously describes, on the basis of his own experience. This forces Oviedo to see the difference that attaches to American objects and customs,

even if the comparative model continues to be Spanish and the unity is composed as a divine good. In fact this articulation of difference will turn Oviedo into a subject constructed through empathy with the new, to the point that his discourse and even his understanding of the New World will shift from description to interpretation, from account to story, from natural history to personal history. Oviedo is one of the subjects produced by the discourse of abundance, in which he novelizes himself as an actor replete with the testimony of a developing, perhaps even limitless character. Gerbi underlines the sensory perspective of the chronicler's American knowledge: 'What a beautiful thing the world is', Oviedo declares.

8 José de Acosta, *Historia natural y moral de las Indias*, ed. Edmundo O'Gorman (Mexico City, 1962).

9 Chapter XIX of the sixth book of the *General History* (which the chronicler entitles 'The Book of Deposits') is devoted to the gaze in the New World; it is titled 'Of a Notable Novelty in Perspective, Contrary to The View Taught to Us by Most Parts of the World'. He states that in Venezuela, in the province of Paraguana, 'from a distance, things appear to be much bigger than they are . . . It is a marvelous matter that I will relate. A man coming along the road, if perhaps another is coming in the opposite direction, as soon as he can make him out, as he begins to appear, he seems to the one who is looking to be as tall as the mast of a ship. And it is true that the thing multiplies . . . And so it grows and seems bigger, in the plains, it is said. And this is so in the morning and at midday, and at whatever time of the day. And however often the thing is seen from a distance, it always appears much taller, and however much closer it seems smaller' (178–9). Immediately, in characteristic fashion, Oviedo cites credible witnesses (colonial authorities) who swear that they have experienced this optical phenomenon. Which allows him to conclude with a measurement: whilst the thing 'remains the same size' it is 'twenty times smaller or bigger when it appeared to them at a distance'. Oviedo might have inaugurated 'magical realism' in Latin American narrative, sowing the first seed of a paradoxical representation of nature (in process of becoming) in his early reports from the Venezuelan province. At the very least, Oviedo's report is almost novelistic: it tells us about perception, or rather the range of what appears and not what is in reality the case. Appearance becomes another way of being, in the face of which literal being is always less grand, or at least smaller. The manipulation of semantic tension is typical of Oviedo: 'twenty times bigger, or smaller'. From less to more, language increases the power of the look.

10 On the Devil in America, see Guy Rozat, *América, imperio del demonio: cuentos y recuentos* (Mexico City, 1995), which is based on the treatise by Andrés Pérez de Ribas in *Historia de los Triumphos de Nuestra Santa Fe entre gentes las más bárbaras y fieras del nuevo orbe* (Madrid, 1645). Father Acosta devotes several chapters of his *History* to proving that native idolatry is the product of the Devil. Oviedo notes that there are various names for the Devil: the Indians of Nicaragua call him *teot*, but also call Christians *teotes*, like the Indians of Cueva who call the Devil and the Spaniards *tuyra*. The notion of demon in native languages is not always univocal: in Quechua, for example, *supay* means devil, but it could be good or bad. Bartolomé de las Casas bitterly condemns Oviedo in his *History of the Indies*. He writes: 'it is true that he raised false testimony against those of these islands and of many of the Indies, branding them with being beasts and having committed great sins, because he never opened his mouth when dealing with the Indians other than to speak ill of them, and these aspersions have flown nearly all over the world, after he so brazenly published his false history, the world giving him credit which he did not deserve for the many great falsehoods he spoke of these people . . . Since if Oviedo's history had borne on its title page how the author had been a conquistador, robber and murderer of Indians, and that he had thrown their people in the mines in which they perished, and was thus

their cruel foe, as will be said and he himself confesses to it, at least amongst prudent and sensible Christians his history would have little authority and credit'(Book III, chap. xxiii, p. 518, ed. Agustín Millares Carlo [Mexico City, 1981], vol. II). This judgement is prompted by Oviedo's obsession with native 'sodomy' but also by the policy confrontation between the two, De las Casas proposing his peaceful utopia and Oviedo a pragmatic conquest. In addition, see chapters IV and V of the Ninth Book, where Oviedo gives a sarcastic account of the failure of Las Casas's social experiment (II, 197–201).

11 In Chapter i of Book VII he describes the ways that the Indians prepared their seed beds and went about sowing on the basis of classical models (Virgil, Pliny, Theophrastus) to show that the Indians 'keep to the rules'. This refers to the cultivation of maize, cassava and *ajes*, even if these last two, as tubercles, require other methods less consonant with classical models.

12 'He then recounts at the beginning that one Spaniard sent another a dozen *hutías* so that they would not rot in the heat. The Indian who was carrying them, took a rest on the roadside and fell asleep, and took a long time to get to where he was going: hence he was hungry and took a fancy to the *hutías,* and so as not to continue in temptation, he ate three of them. The letter he returned with said that he had had with him nine *hutías* and the time of the day on which they arrived: the Master upbraided the Indian. He denied it, to the letter as they say: but as he realized that it was the letter talking, he confessed the truth. He learned his lesson and spread it abroad amongst his people that letters could speak, and they should be wary of them. For lack of paper and ink they wrote on Guiabara or copey leaves with awls and pins. They also made cards out of the same copey, which it cost a lot to shuffle', Francisco López de Gómara, *Historia general de las Indias y Vida de Hernán Cortés,* ed Jorge Gurria Lacroix (Caracas, 1979), p. 54. Pedro Mártir had recounted the same fable in a lighter vein: 'It is a funny thing what the islanders make of our leaves: the good men amongst them think that leaves talk to our will. An islander was sent from the principal city of Santo Domingo to a friend of the sender, who was far away in the interior of the colony, with some roast *hutías* (which we already said were rabbits). On the way, perhaps from hunger or perhaps out of gluttony, the messenger ate three of the *hutías* (they are no bigger than rats). On a leaf the friend said how many he had received and the master said to the servant: "Ha, so where is your loyalty? So greedy that you ate the *hutías* that I entrusted to you!" Trembling, the poor and astonished servant confessed to his misdeed, but asked his master how he had known: "Look, the leaf that you brought is telling me': and it told him the very time he arrived there and the time he left"' (translation from 1892 reproduced in the edition by Luis Arocena, Third Decade, book VIII, chap. iv, p. 278). The leaf here is from the copei tree, which, says Mártir, was written on like paper. In the *Summary,* Oviedo notes that 'before I forget to tell the consternation they [letters] cause, I will say that when some Christian writes by some Indian to some other person who is elsewhere or far away from where the letter is being written, they are full of admiration because they see that the letter yonder says what the Christian who sent it wants it to say, and they carry it with every respect or are wary of it, since it seems to them that it will also be able to tell what happens on the road to the person carrying it, and often some of the least clever amongst them think it has a soul' (p. 132). In his *History* he indicates that the *hutías* are 'like a rabbit, but somewhat smaller' although he implies that he has never eaten them (II, p. 29). In his *History* (II, p. 303) Las Casas explains that *hutías* 'that are like rabbits' formed part of the first foodstuffs that were exchanged with the natives by Columbus. So in distinction to Garcilaso's melons, which the Indians of his fable had never tasted because they were newly arrived fruit of Spanish origin, the *hutías* were native animals well known to Gómara. His punishment, it could be said,

is a lesson about the goods that have been lost under the new property regime. Writing is part of the Law, it accuses and punishes as an instrument of power. In *The Barbarous Island*, a subtle comedy of shipwrecks and entanglements by Miguel Sánchez (1587–1598?), in which King Normando is blown by a storm on to an island of barbarians, the motif of the letter is more one of intrigue and recognition; ed. Hugo A. Rennert (Philadelphia, 1896); see Stefano Arata, *Miguel Sánchez 'il divino' e la nasita della 'comedia nueva'* (Salamanca, 1987). In his play *The New World* (1619), Lope de Vega uses oranges the first time that the Indian Auté is betrayed by the letter, and olives the second time, when Auté hides the letter inside a tree. If the first time he is pardoned, on the second occasion, despite the humour of the scene, punishment is forthcoming. This gesture of hiding the letter evokes Inca Garcilaso's history: his Indians hide the letter behind a stone so as to eat the melons in peace. If Cervantes had read Inca Garcilaso, or at least the translation he made of León Hebreo's *Dialogues of Love*, then Lope had read the *Royal Commentaries* (1609).

13 José María Ridao, *Contra la historia* (Barcelona, 2000). The central critique that the author mounts against canonical Spanish historiography concerns anachronism – his term for what others have called 'presentism' – that is the imposition on the past of contemporary worldviews and conceptualizations. In this sense, Ridao acknowledges the need to rework generic and ideologized constructions that have mechanically normalized phenomena such as the conquest and colonization of America, seeing them solely in terms of victims and oppressors, imperial and colonial agents, domination and resistance. It is more sensible to cast doubt on the idea of 'spiritual conquest' as well as on the idea of a native mentality steeped in messianism. Admixtures and interminglings are more interesting than these simple oppositions: acculturation, harmonious *mestizaje* and linguistic unity do not occur as such but as unequal and conflictual processes.

14 The processes through which native cultures accommodated and negotiated colonial domination are a complex and uneven strategy of reappropriation, recoding and hybridization which unfold in language and symbolic practices. This heterotopia does not follow the utilitarian and causal logic of the colonial economy, not even in the field of conversion. Rather the natives place the new objects and concepts in unexpected codes, following their own system of processing and interpretation. In this context there is the important work of Louise M. Burkhardt on what she calls 'the nativization of Christianity', based on Nahua translations of religious texts. See her *The Slippery Earth: Nahua-Christian Moral Dialogue in Sixteenth-Century México* (Tucson, AZ, 1989); also see J. Jorge Klor de Alva, 'Spiritual Conflict and Accommodation in New Spain: Toward a Typology of Aztec Responses to Christianity', in *The Inca and Aztec States, 1400–1800*, ed. George Collier et al. (New York, 1982). The work of Serge Gruzinski on the historical analysis of the process of *mestizaje* is stimulating as is the fieldwork on the popular forms of historical interpretation done by Luis Millones in Peru. For the formation of Creole national thought, the works of David Brading are fundamental, giving an insight into the flexibility and richness of this *mestizo* formation, which cannot be reduced to a mechanical and deterministic logic, where all native culture ends up in its national, Creole version.

15 The studies on the presence of the New World in Golden Age Spanish are notoriously guilty of statistical crudity: they are limited to listing the occasions when America appeared as subject matter in canonical texts and the reasons it did so. On this meagre basis there has developed the idea that the Discovery and colonization had little impact on the Spanish literary imagination. This perspective discounts the Chronicle of the Indies, which is as much Spanish as American, but it also ignores the most important interactions, such as the development of an everyday, down to earth prose, popular carnivalesque forms, the figurations of abundance and scarcity, the discourses

of religion and exceptionality, and finally the exploration of the accounts of the crisis in the peninsula in the seventeenth century. One can understand that Emilio Orozco Díaz in his 'On the Concept of the Still Life in the Baroque', *Temas del Barroco* (Granada, 1947), was unable to find in those canvases a single fruit from the Indies, but it is less easy to understand how a study on the Spanish Baroque published today could omit the pull of American experience on such art. By dint of unimaginative specialization and conventional readings of subject matter, academic criticism has lost sight of the procedural richness of cultural objects by only looking at them from one side of the Atlantic. Clearly, if these objects and texts are seen in terms of transatlantic interactions then they appear in a new light. An inspired advance along these lines emerges in the work of Diana de Armas Wilson, 'The Matter of America, Cervantes Romances Inca Garcilaso de la Vega', in *Cultural Authority in Golden Age Spain*, ed. Marina S. Brownlee and Hans Ulrich Gumbrecht (Baltimore, 1995), pp. 234–59. De Armas brings a rich analytical perspective to bear by reconsidering Cervantes as producing a riposte to Inca Garcilaso in the famous parodic beginning of Persiles. De Armas has developed her transatlantic readings in *Cervantes, the Novel and the New World* (Oxford, 2000). This chapter takes place on a certain Barbarous Isle and can be read through an ironic mediation: the comedy *The Barbarous Isle* by Miguel Sánchez, called, with some exaggeration, 'the Divine'. The legend of a letter that astonishes the natives in the comedy is a metaphor of its own fate in writing: between barbarism and reading, this role is a performance, a motif, an object recovered as the mediating testimony that moves from the oral to the written, from barbarism to humanism, and in the no man's land of the Island has the force of a new beginning, which even manages to suspend extant hierarchies. The blank parchment of the Island is overwritten by the comedy of perpetual recognition, the nostalgia of the Subject summed up by the knowledge of humanism and its promise of the polis. Perhaps because of this, rewriting the Islands of writing of his times, Cervantes suggests his own Barbarous Isle as the 'primal scene' where the Other subject in reality devours European discourse itself.

six Representing: *The Language of National Formation*

1 In the last few years a number of works on nineteenth-century Spanish American cultural and literary history have appeared, whose detailed documentation is fundamental for a better understanding of the genealogy of the texts in question, as well as the processes and theories elaborated at different times and in different regions. Such works will enable us to transcend those predetermined interpretations, global evaluations and teleological prejudices, which simplify the texts. We now have to articulate new connections and give new accounts at a Latin American level, which move beyond the limited cartography of national states. The other task is to ascertain whether it is indeed true that the most nationalist countries turned out to be the most modern, and what order of nationalism is involved.

2 Simón Rodríguez, in *Sociedades americanas* (Lima, 1842). This is probably one of his most programmatic pamphlets, inspired by Fourier's teachings. However, he reveals the originality of American reformist thought. He writes: 'The new nations of America would like to imitate France, but they lack what is the most important thing, which is the Subject'. This Subject is, in its didactic exposition, the person who is sick, that is the Political Regimes. He rejects both the French and North American models: 'Where can we go to find models? Spanish America is original, one of a kind, and its institutions and government must also be ORIGINAL, as must be the means of founding them. Either we invent or we go wrong.' He concludes with a Proposed Law 'on

two matters for the future: Colonization and Popular Education'. In one of his Considerations he says: 'Fourth Consideration: the American countryside is in large part unpopulated and the few inhabitants that it does have are packed in great disorder round the churches waiting for what providence has not promised them, poverty-stricken in the midst of abundance, and with no hope of occupying their imaginary property for many centuries for lack of direction. What makes the Solitude horrific is their incapacity to make it habitable so as to live in it, and Industry is a companion that arouses courage in the most timid of men.' This pamphlet is included in the collection of his essays *Inventamos o morimos*, ed. Dardo Cúneo (Caracas, 1979), pp. 117–84.

3 Sor Juana Inés de la Cruz, 'Aplaude lo mismo que la fama en la sabiduría sin par de la señora Doña María de Guadalupe Alencastre, la única maravilla de nuestros siglos'. The lady, Duquesa de Aveiro, was an aristocrat of Portuguese ancestry, a poet and scholar, famous for her works of charity. She was related to the Condesa de Paredes, the wife of the Viceroy of Mexico, a friend and protectress of Sor Juana, famous for having been praised by Sor Juana as the beautiful Lysis of her poems. A great part of Sor Juana's poetry has this strategy of praise and appeal, which yields its admiration and protests with the formulae of service, but which implies a subtle and intense rhetoric of petition. Its persuasion, however, is not only directed towards the subject being persuaded but also implicates the speaker, the poet herself: this is a portrait of the patron with a self-portrait of the poet in the background. Was Sor Juana seeking protection from a more powerful lady who could have rescued her from her censors? Was she perhaps thinking that the poet nuns of Portugal by whom she was amused in *Enigmas* (1695) were a possible way out from her difficulties? It could well have been another display of American appropriation of the grand tradition of rhetoric, here constructing its return voyage. Antonio Alatorre has edited *Enigmas* with an fudamental introduction (Mexico City, 1994).

4 Cintio Vitier, *Temas martianos* (Havana, 1982), p. 17.

5 José Lezama Lima, *Antología de la poesía cubana* (Havana, 1965), vol. II.

6 An interesting interpretation of Bello's *Ode* is found in Mary Louis Pratt's *Imperial Eyes: Travel Writing and Transculturation* (London, 1992), pp. 144ff.

7 Doris Sommer, *Foundational Fictions: The National Romances of Latin America* (Berkeley, CA, 1991), pp. 204ff.

8 Valeri Borisovich Zemskov, 'Proceso y coincidencia de la formación étnica y nacional de la cultura latinoamericana del siglo XIX', in *Contextos: literatura y sociedad latino-americanas del siglo XIX*, ed. Evelyn Picon Garfield and Iván A. Schulman (Urbana, IL, 1991), pp. 66–72.

9 Francisco Sosa, *Escritores y poetas sudamericanos* (Mexico City, 1890).

10 Josefina Ludmer, *El género gauchesco: un tratado sobre la patria* (Buenos Aires, 1988), p. 232.

11 Miguel Antonio Caro, *Páginas de crítica* (Madrid, 1919), p. 399.

12 On Juan de Arona, see my book *Crítica de la identidad: la pregunta por el Perú en su literatura* (Lima, 1988), pp. 46–61.

13 Caro, *Páginas de crítica*, p. 134.

14 Francisco Gavidia, 'Diccionario del idioma "Salvador"', in *Obras* (San Salvador, 1913).

seven Judging: *The Paternal Desert*

1 Juan Rulfo, *Toda la obra*, ed. Claude Fell (Nanterre, 1992).

2 Louis Althusser, 'Ideology and Ideological State Apparatuses (Notes towards an Investigation)', in *Mapping Ideology*, ed. Slavoj Zizek (London, 1994), pp. 100–40.

3 This melancholic perspective subordinates the subject to the real, revealing the feeble power of decision the former has with respect to that real. It could be argued that this perspective goes back to colonial experience, given the dependent character of the peasants in relation to their *cacique* Pedro Páramo. In reality, these characters submit themselves to their *cacique* with all the innocence of the victim. Their subjection to an authoritarian system can also be understood as ideological, in this case, fantasmatic: submission occupies their subjectivity, de-substantivized as they are by the will and arbitrariness of pre-modern power.

4 This is another theme central to the discourse of lack: subjects acquire a differential value according to their use value or exchange value. The over-valuation of subjects and objects in abundance, in the relation that represents them as of mutual origin, creates a situation, where, ironically, there is no agreed value for exchange. By contrast, in scarcity subjects almost entirely lack value, and are disposable and redundant. The momentary value they possess is determined by power, which uses and discards them. Or rather, that value is arbitrary and subject to the accumulation of power.

5 The subject of abundance becomes the poor man, the native represented in the landscape of his extravagant natural world. Faced with the paradox of the colonial world, another one is generated, the paradoxical identity of the subject of scarcity. This would be the helpless or vulnerable human being. Both by his origin without foundation, his present without function, and his baseless future, this orphaned subject has the quality of a victim, first of the ideological system that has constructed his subjectivity, then of the socio-economic regime when his social relation confirms his subaltern condition, and finally, of language itself, which confirms the whole programme of domination and finds in this subject the agent of its reproduction. He is neither citizen nor peasant: he is the product of feudal power. Thus, he comes to embody the negativity of the system, the residual character of the dominant discourse.

eight Interpreting: *The Authority of Reading*

1 The history of reading lacks a chapter on reading and tears. This would be the history of sentimental reading, and would be at the centre of the composition of melodrama with its strategy of replacing suspense by tears. But it also touches on the rhetoric of the confession, when tears are the most convincing authority, because they say more than words, as in the famous poem by Sor Juana Inés de la Cruz, where the reproaches of the beloved are answered by revealing the heart undone by tears. That is to say, the naked truth as rhetorical trophy. Tearful confession, furthermore, makes the victim the guilty party, the high point of the strategy of the confessional subject. Desdemona replies to Othello's story with sighs and piety. Tears dissolve reading into a symmetrically novelistic 'history of life'.

2 The idea comes from Bataille. Julia Kristeva develops it in *Powers of Horror: An Essay on Abjection* (New York, 1982).

3 Antonio Benítez Rojo offers a mythical reading of the fable in 'Eréndira, o la Bella Durmiente de García Márquez', in *Cuadernos Hispanoamericanos*, 448 (October 1987), pp. 31–48.

4 Carlos Rincón in his stimulating book *La no simultaneidad de lo simultáneo, Postmodernidad, globalización y culturas en América Latina* (Bogotá, 1995) underlines the metafictional character of the narrative in García Márquez. On reading and the fable in *Cien años de soledad*, see my *Gabriel García Márquez and the Powers of Fiction* (Austin, TX, 1988). From the extensive bibliography on the author the texts that are

important from our perspective are those of Michael Bell, *Gabriel Garcia Márquez* (London, 1993); Gene Bell-Villada, *García Márquez: The Man and his Work* (Chapel Hill, NC, 1990); Peter Earle, ed., *García Márquez* (Madrid, 1981); Martha Canfield, *Gabriel García Márquez* (Bogotá, 1991); George R. McMurray, *Critical Essays on Gabriel Garcia Marquez* (Boston, MA, 1987). About the method of reading/writing, which assumes a distinctively different mode of operation with each novel, there remains much to be said. A good example of this is documented in the article by Eduardo Posada-Carbó, 'Fiction and History: The *bananeras* and Gabriel García Márquez's *One Hundred Years of Solitude*', *Journal of Latin American Studies*, xxx (Cambridge, 1998), pp. 395–414.

Conclusion

1   In Gravelot and Cochin's book one reads the following: 'ABONDANCE, Divinité allé-gorique, représentée par les iconologistes fous les traits d'une nymphe couronée de fleurs. D'une main elle porte un faisceau d'épis de toutes sortes de grains, & de l'autre la corne d'Amalthée remplie des fruits que rápand l'Abondance. On la couronne de fleurs, parce que ce sont elles qui l'annocent. La charrue designa les travaux a qui nous la devons; c'est-a-dire l'agriculture, fource des vrais richesses. Le caducée, embleme du comerce, est encore un des pricipaux attributs de l'Abondance' (vol. I, fig. 3). On the allegory AMERIQUE, one reads: 'On sait que cette partie du monde, la plus étendue de toutes, étoit cependant ignorée des anciens, & qu'elle ne fu découverte par Christophe Colomb qu'en 1598 [*sic*]; entreprise continuée cinq ans apres par Améric Vespuce, qui ravit au premier la gloire de lui donner son nom. L'Amérique est représentée par une femme ayant le teint olivatre, coëffée & en partie vetue de plumes; ajustement particulier aux peuples de ce continent. L'arc & les fleches sont les armes lesquels, non-seulement les hommes, mais encore les femmes, vont combarte leurs ennemis. La tete séparée du tronc & percée d'une fleche qui se voit au bas du tableau, sert a exprimer l'inhumanité des anciens habitants de cette partie de l'univers. Le caumet, c'est'a'dire la pipe place a coté, est chez ces peuples le signe heureux de la paix; c'est pour qu'on y a attaché les ailes du caducée de Mercure, symbole connu de la paix. La peche & la chasse, dont ces peuples se nourrissent & sont leur principale occupation, est designée par les deux enfans, charg'es l'un de oisson & l'autre de gibier. Le caïman, sorte de cocodrile, & l'arbre nommé bananier, contribuent a caracteriser le nouveau monde, qui, en doublant les richesses de l'ancien, ne l'a pas rendu plus heureux' (vol. I, fig. 21).

Acknowledgements

The year I spent at Cambridge University as Simón Bolívar Professor of Latin Americana Studies (1995–6) enabled me to begin the research for this book and its transatlantic scope. I thank my colleagues at the Centre for Latin American Studies, especially David Brading and David Lehmann. I benefited from the sustained dialogue with the members of Emmanuel College where I was a fellow, including Steve Boldy and Peter Burke. I have shared many of these topics with William Rowe in our periodic colloquia at the Institute of Latin American Studies in the University of London.

At the Institute for Cultural Criticism, directed by Nelly Richard in the Universidad Arcis, Santiago de Chile, and at the 'Julio Cortázar Chair' in the Universidad de Guadalajara, Mexico, directed by Raúl Padilla, I was able to develop some of these questions on Latin American hermeneutics.

A Salomon Faculty Research Fellowship from the Graduate School of Brown University made the research for the book possible. I must make special mention of the splendid Benson Latin American Collection, in the University of Texas at Austin; at Brown, the exquisite John Carter Brown Library has been a source of inspiration with its notable community of scholars. The Morgan Library in New York, the Houghton Library in Harvard University, the Biblioteca Nacional de Madrid and the Archivo de Indias in Sevilla have been helpful throughout these years. The title-page from Francisco de Xerex, *Verdadera relación de la conquista del Perú*, which also appears in Mena's *La conquista del Perú*, is reproduced (page 85) by courtesy of the John Carter Brown Library at Brown University, Rhode Island. The illustrations on pages 95 and 97 are reproduced from Felipe Guamán Poma de Ayala's manuscript *El primer nueva corónica y buen gobierno* (1615) in the Kongelige Bibliotek, Copenhagen (Gl. kgl. S. 2232), pages 390 and 451.

This work on the cultural formation of transatlantic writing in the New World is part of a larger debate on representation (abundance), exchange (translations) and negotiation (reappropriation, hybridism). A post-colonial mapping of these 'geotextualities' looks to advance a practice of difference and a politics of renew interpretations.

Index